I0141141

Life

— The Spiritual Essence

*An Engineer's Insights into the
Integrated Nature of Divinity*

DEEPAK PARASHAR

The book (and related research) compiled over a twelve-year period celebrates the interconnectedness of our existence. It represents the personal journey and opinions of the author, by way of an engineer's travelogue on the integrated nature of divinity. He examines the energetic convergence of nature, people, science, spirituality, and religions while traversing thirty-eight countries, duly supported by a cadre of related experts. All the ideas, concepts and opinions are offered for educational purposes only with sensitivity and respect in the hope that it will help others make their lives extraordinary.

License to use background cover picture of the Aurora Borealis obtained from BPENNY.

This book is not meant to treat any health conditions, physical or otherwise, for which the reader should seek professional medical advice. The author and publisher disclaim any liability, loss, or damage caused or alleged to be caused directly or indirectly from the use, application, and interpretation of this book.

Copyright © 2024 by Deepak Parashar

Integrated Divinity Publications LLC, Clifton Park, New York

This book, *Life—The Spiritual Essence*, contains copyrighted material, trademarks, and other proprietary information. It is not permitted to publish, transmit, participate in the transfer or sale of, create derivative works of, or in any way exploit, in whole or in part, any material. No part of this document may be altered in any form whatsoever, electronic or mechanical including photocopying, recording, or by an information storage or retrieval system without express written, dated, and signed permission from the author.

Library of Congress Control Number: 2023916326
ISBN: 979-8-9889518-0-3, *print edition*
      979-8-9889518-1-0, *black & white print edition*
      979-8-9889518-2-7, *digital edition*

Deepak's research on the complex interactions of nature, people, faith, energy and spirituality spanned thirty-eight countries over a twelve-year period. His insights provide an overall appreciation into the principles of creation, sustenance and dissolution comprising universal balance in our collective existence.

Life—The Spiritual Essence can be carried as a resource, given its encyclopedic nature. Deepak's myriad journeys test the integrated philosophical principles of divinity from the viewpoint of an engineer, leading into the spiritual essence of life. I was particularly fascinated by the structured methodology with which this multifaceted book traces the underlying commonality of leadership in multiple professions, including the armed forces, space, industry, sports and the arts, back to original scriptures of the world's great religions and spirituality.

These values incorporated into our daily lives assure us of extraordinary self-esteem to pursue excellence and to be the best in all our endeavors, both personal and professional, despite the odds.

—Lt. **COLONEL JAMES H. HARVEY III,** Tuskegee Airmen,
332nd Fighter Group (US Army/Air Force)
Recipient of the Congressional Gold Medal,
and World War II/ Korean War Veteran

It gave me immense pleasure after coming to know the book *Life—The Spiritual Essence.* Deepak Parashar has brought out the true essence of life and its purpose through the comparative study of many major religions in the world today. Apart from this, his exposure to many saints and saintly personalities have opened in him a new, deeper and greater as well as subtler insights which he has graciously shared in his book.

The author has brilliantly brought about the fact that the true purpose of life is spiritual unfoldment and eventually entering into the state of total self-realization or Nirvana. The reader will get a chance to peep into subtler thoughts of religion which will steadily lead him to the greater understanding of the purpose of life.

I congratulate Deepak for his sincere and hard efforts in collating the spiritual and religious thoughts across the globe and presenting them to the readers.

This book speaks loudly without any doubt what the title says.

—**SWAMI CHIDRUPANANDA**
Chinmaya Mission, Noida, India

Deepak recounts a several year personal journey in *Life—The Spiritual Essence*, both physical and spiritual, to examine principal precepts of the world's great religions. He finds commonalities in how each faith tradition grapples with timeless questions, of free will vs. destiny, the manifestation of the deity in nature, and the search for divinity in both nature and in human activity: "All accept that this world is not our permanent home, there is suffering, bondage here; so the search is on to find solutions for eternal joy devoid of fear."

Students of the American experience will recognize these issues in the writing of Jonathan Edwards, on predestination; the founding fathers (particularly Franklin and Jefferson), on Deism; the Transcendentalist thinking of Emerson and Thoreau. Parashar's illuminating journey takes him geographically far beyond the borders of the United States, but the inquiry he makes fits directly into preeminent strains of American intellectual and theological inquiry.

—SUSAN P. SCHOELWER, PhD
Robert H Smith Senior Curator,
George Washington's Mount Vernon, VA, USA

I was amazed at how Deepak's enthralling philosophical journey over a quarter of the planet by way of intense, situational analysis made simple through the lens of his professional expertise relates to key principles of corporate social responsibility.

Through illustrative tables and diagrams, pictures and in-depth spiritual and methodical religious analyses, *Life—The Spiritual Essence* blazes a path for each one of us to utilize our unique skillsets through integrity, grit and strategic vision to become opinion leaders reinforcing the interconnected nature of our global community while appreciating our natural environment. Including the holistic practices summarized in the daily "Six Trigger Points", the book creates a common platform to grow from, and examines how a series of miracles take place when inspired teams come together to focus on philanthropic and professional efforts globally.

I congratulate Deepak on his twelve-year research to extend so far beyond his professional reach as a veteran of the energy industry to create a diverse, inclusive network to put together this scintillating book for the benefit of all.

—KISHORE JAYARAMAN, Officer of the Order of the British Empire (OBE)
President of Rolls-Royce, India and South Asia

CONTENTS

March 2019. With His Holiness Tenzin Gyatso, the 14th Dalai Lama of Tibet, Dharamshala, India. I was so fortunate to take my father (center) and son (left) to receive his blessings.

A chance meeting on a business trip in May 2009 sparked my research on the energetic convergence of science and spirituality, fifteen religions, nature, people and places over a twelve-year period. Juxtaposed against my travels across thirty-eight countries, this revealed scintillating conclusions about the integrated nature of divinity and the spiritual essence of life.

September 2021. With Lt. Colonel James H. Harvey III, 332nd Fighter Group, Tuskegee Airmen (Red Tails), VA, USA.

As an engineer and a mathematician, trying to work out the scientific probability of this meeting was most interesting. Just two weeks prior, I had taken out a famous quote of another legendary Tuskegee airman from the book since I could find him to obtain permission. And I then ran smack into Colonel Harvey who graciously allowed me to use his mantra for my book!

Two of my colleagues and I spent the evening with 98-year-old Colonel Harvey, along with his family and others. This great "Warrior-Monk" recounted his experiences at the famed WWII airbase and his incredible 126 Korean missions. His message to us—*was to always strive to be the best despite the odds.*

CHOICE REFLECTIONS

Guru, picture taken c. 1945, Jalandhar, Punjab, India.

I met him when I was a young lad many years later, and he gave me a mantra that I use daily. He barely spoke, and when he did— it was in Sanskrit, one of the original languages derived from the subtle laws of creation of our pulsating universe.

It is said that the face reflects our inner being—note his focus! And I fondly recall how he smiled, ever so slightly, when I asked if he had seen God.

Tornado Alley, USA, 2018. We tracked this supercell (rotating thunderstorm capable of producing tornadoes) for six hours. The base varied anywhere from the width of a mile to two miles wide. A thought arose while watching these great storms—how insignificant we are compared to Mother Nature, yet how complex we make our lives.

PREFACE

Three seemingly unrelated events within a six-month period materially changed my life. I received *chance* blessings from His Holiness Tenzin Gyatso, the Fourteenth Dalai Lama of Tibet, met a US Marines Vietnam veteran with healing powers (he calls it light energy), and picked up a commentary by Swami Chinmayanada on Hinduism's revered scripture the "Bhagavad Gita."

I am an electrical engineer with an MBA in marketing and over twenty-five years of experience building energy-efficient power plants globally. Being of a curious disposition, this six-month period grew into a transformational twelve-year journey covering thirty-eight countries. I researched the links between science and spirituality, philosophy, fifteen religions, nature, people, and places. In essence, I explored *how the substratum of energy interconnects all aspects of existence, both material and subtle, under the auspices of divinity.* Reinforced by a cadre of leaders from diverse professions, clergy, religious educators, and holistic experts who synchronously surfaced to help, I embarked on this experiential pilgrimage, continuously bridging over 25,000 pages of research into practice through my global travels.

The cumulative results include a syncretic, strategic, holistic (mind-body-spirit) system for daily improvement, a structural analysis of five major religions, and a pictorially depicted spiritual travelogue (including visits to historic locations) which dares to explore divinity across twenty-two diverse themes. Further insights include the derivative spiritual principles of leadership in multiple professions, the relative confluence of science and spirituality, and the interconnectedness of our existence.

The results iteratively led to integrating all these elements of nature, science (including metaphysics), faith, and holistic practices into a harmonious energetic convergence to bring forth the underlying commonality of people, the integrated nature of divinity and the spiritual essence of life. I noted the astonishing concurrence of views that this world is not our permanent home, there is suffering and bondage here; and the search was on to find solutions through multiple avenues for eternal joy devoid of fear.

As mentioned, diverse interactions with people, places, and nature ensued as part of this global research. I was so fortunate to interact with over a hundred accomplished individuals from myriad professions, including NASA shuttle astronaut Dr. Story Musgrave, President of India Dr. A.P.J. Abdul Kalam, and special prosecutor of the Nuremberg war trials Benjamin Ferencz. I also collaborated with religious establishments, culminating in a second round of blessings from His Holiness the Dalai Lama in 2019.

Some of my experiences with nature included witnessing the mystical northern lights (sub-Arctic Circle) and the great storms of Tornado Alley (USA), admiring grey whales off the Baja California Mexican coastline, and filming Mount Everest located on the border of Nepal and Tibet (autonomous region of China). I visited historical sites like the Egyptian and Mayan pyramids to research ancient religions, and traveled to WWII concentration camps (Auschwitz-Birkenau, Dachau) and the beaches of Normandy (venue to WWII Allied landings) to understand the extremities of the human condition.

And documented herein after much trial and error over a period of more than seven years is a common thread of specific lessons learned for initial mental housecleaning, notwithstanding beliefs as a means to simple, holistic living. These are translated into a one-page visual, subliminal, strategic "Six Trigger Points" to improve one's daily quality of life. One example is: *"Try to turn every act into an inner meditation for yourself."* You will note a step change in your attitude and actions. The six trigger points represent a structured, pre-engineered approach to our basic nature split up into quadrants to effect analysis and subliminal improvement as a first step. And as you begin to *develop a daily rhythm*, you will note subtle, positive changes in your character (month to month), given that you will find plenty of low-hanging fruit to work with. The speed of change is contingent upon the level of concerted effort. I had the great honor of meeting Lt. Colonel James H. Harvey III of the Tuskegee Airmen, who said that his mantra for success was to *always strive to be the best despite the odds.* Colonel Harvey went on to state in his inimitable fashion that *consequently, there were "no problems" given that he diligently worked through extreme situations instead of harboring fear, and that he never worried about what he could not control.* It's entirely up to you to accept ups and downs as part of your remarkable journey!

As you change, the world changes itself. As you further center yourself via concentration, meditation and other techniques, your actions progressively get into synchronicity as the thrilling mission to perfect your life takes over. True courage is facing up to what you are afraid to do; so make fear your friend, show up for that meeting you most wish to avoid. Understand the immense power lying dormant in all of us to organize and create a tremendous quality of life for ourselves, and most importantly for others. And try to envision the sheer, continued, unbridled joy of life, like listening to your favorite music. Is this the same kind of instinctive joy our ancient sages felt given their *fearless, blazing* existence in perfect synchronicity with cosmic laws and the rhythms of nature, thanks to their control over energy via intuition mastered through the highest stage of meditation?

With folded hands, I Bow to You: *Welcome, Vítej, Mrehba, Fùnyìhng, Namaste, Bienvenido, Selamat Datang, Wilkommen . . . !*

ACKNOWLEDGMENTS

To my parents Indira and Vijay, and Lalit for his incredible guidance on the strategic vision for the book. My sincere thanks to Ajay and Professor Jatinder Sharma for their continued encouragement, also a special thanks to Shaila for her extraordinary book design for the front and back covers.

To the establishment of His Holiness, the Dalai Lama of Tibet, Swami Chidrupananda, the late Benjamin Ferencz, Dr. Story Musgrave, Colonel James H. Harvey III, Dr. Arun Shourie, Maja Daruwala, Joe the Aurora Hunter, Dr. Bheema Bhat, Kishore Jayaraman, Dr. Susan P. Schoelwer, and Lauren Landress of the Self-Realization Fellowship for their incredible support.

To Daniel, John, Jorge, Herschel, Haider and Jamie for their vision and research in critically developing the Five-Religion Structural Analysis.

To Hani, Archie, Bhadresh, Stanley, Amar, Ramid, Sumedh, John, Keith, Nitu, Rashid, Deepak, Georg, Michelle, Sioned and Ali Reza, all situated in different parts of the globe who provided great encouragement over the 12-year period.

To all my friends the world over at General Electric Company for their encouragement to put this book together.

To Shantanu Ray Chaudhuri for his advice and incredible attention to detail. And a special mention for the late Linda DeMasi, who was ably supported by Jeff, Cathy and Meradith in assimilating this book in record fashion.

To Anthony for keeping me critically focused from a legal perspective.

To my newfound friends Valerie and Charlie, Kymberly, and all my nature-loving friends including Mike, Kelly, Adrianne, Jeanne, Rook, Bill, Chris, Gwen, Lorianne and others who have become an integral part of my life.

To my family, their support transformed my casual observations and notes into a book with a vision to help others, and to aid and inspire our youth to pursue excellence in all their endeavors.

INTRODUCTION

"It doesn't take much to see that the problems of three
little people don't amount to a hill of beans in this crazy
world. Someday you'll understand that."

Humphrey Bogart ("Bogey") to Ingrid Bergman,
in *Casablanca*, 1942[1]

"Only when we see the total logic of things, can we
really come to feel the insignificance of our individual
ego in all our achievements in our successes."

Swami Chinmayananda,
The Holy Geeta: Commentary[2]

Similar? Let us try another which every golfer will *instinctively* understand.
Some days we can do no wrong, almost as if an unseen hand is guiding the ball
to the pin. What is this miraculous hand in play? Analyze it, chances are you
slept well the night before and came out to play with a mindset devoid of any
fear about your overall golf score. A certain detachment, almost as if you are a
disinterested observer (witness) comes into effect, leading to intense focus on
each stroke with superb mind–body coordination. Indeed, you have briefly
tapped into your higher Self by living in the moment.

And there it is. We tend to ignore some of the main themes of intrinsic
spirituality in our daily lives, perhaps due to their inherent simplicity. The unsaid
call of man to take on the great battle between right and wrong within himself,
while in parallel meeting life's challenges with grit and cheerful dynamism.

---

[1] Permission granted by Warner Bros. Entertainment Inc.

[2] *The Holy Geeta: Commentary by Swami Chinmayananda*, Central Chinmaya Mission Trust,
Mumbai.

Creation, sustenance and dissolution taking place concurrently, all is contingent upon the view we choose to approach it from.

My sincere hope is that the four tables (A, B-1, B-2 and C)—which expound the principles of energy, nature, faith, and holistic methods into practical examples to bring forth the integrated nature of divinity—are used as a stepping-stone in one's search to become that spiritual billionaire. With daily emphasis on Table A, "The Six Trigger Points," to get one started. I humbly offer that most of the sub elements listed within each of these triggers are universal, spiritual, and not religion specific, given that they focus on the subliminal essence of what makes the human mind tick.

And only when we realize just how small a speck we are in the universe, does nature and life truly divulge its pearls of wisdom! A crushing burden is relieved once we consciously decide to toss our ego out of the window, and our path of genuine holistic improvement begins with profound service to humanity following involuntarily.

Ultimately, the ancient writings by our sages can be used as a daily tool to literally yank yourself inside out and ask, "Do I like what I see?" One can only marvel at their strategic vision—while written over thousands of years, they intimately and unfailingly describe the traits of people I know today (friends and family) and their likely future behavior! As we progressively gain an entirely new set of values and a sense of discrimination, our fears and weaknesses begin to fail in their grip over us. The path opens up for all of us to examine ourselves deeply and truthfully. We come to feel that raw inner power lurking beneath our ego, reinforced by a growing sense of wondrous comfort and ecstasy!

Strive to make your life extraordinary. Recall Mahatma Gandhi's quote: "Live like you will die tomorrow, learn like you will live forever, find a goal and you will find the means."[3]

Paramahansa Yogananda once said, "Walking away under the guise of renunciation or non-attachment is the easy path. . . . It shows more spiritual fiber to live a godly life in the jungle of civilization . . . because you are doing good."[4]

---

[3] Permission granted by Navajivan Trust, Ahmedabad, India.
[4] From *Awake: The Life of Yogananda*, copyright © 2015, Self-Realization Fellowship, Los Angeles, Calif. All rights reserved.

Introduction to Tables A, B-1, B-2 and C on Spirituality

Table A deals with initial steps to mental housecleaning, namely the "Six Trigger Points." These are holistic in nature with universal applicability. We must face the truth—try inwards for starters—bridging the gap between our ego and the highest Self at the core of our being. These daily triggers reviewed five minutes first thing every morning gets you started, the process of re-engineering within, by progressively working through six broad segments of the mind. Learn also to develop a rhythm of analyzing how you fared against each of the points the previous day. You will easily note that a significant portion of your daily activities are somehow encompassed in the permutations and combinations of these six points. Note also that detailed explanations behind each of these points are provided in this section.

Table B-1 summarizes the process of Involution and Evolution of life seen primarily through Hinduism. It examines the origins and steps of creation, then the reverse cycle commencing from universal mental housecleaning (Table A) to the progressive steps of concentration and meditation towards self-realization by working through multiple levels of transcendental experience of *samadhi*. Again, detailed explanations are provided in this section.

Table B-2 constitutes a summary analysis on the key structural tenets of five religions: Hinduism, Christianity, Islam, Buddhism and Judaism which constitute more than 80 percent of world religions. Why this structural analysis? The answer is simple. Having researched Hinduism for around seven years to understand its principles on how the universe operates (Table B-1), my sheer curiosity on other beliefs and on how people the world over lead their lives got the better of me!

Table C represents the overall system of spirituality seen through the recurrent life cycle model entailing the birth-death-rebirth cycle. Accordingly, Table A (mental housecleaning), Table B-1 (Hinduism), Table B-2 (five-religion analysis) plus ancillary research into other religions, nature, holistic practices and global spirituality all constitute subsets to Table C. Put another way, Table C takes all these deconstructed individual moving parts (like a car owner's manual) to make it work as a whole to bring forth the interconnectedness of our existence, with juxtaposition of these taught principles onto practical life experiences in the global Spiritual Travelogue in Section 2. This composite energy model ultimately examines the relative confluence of spirituality and science (including metaphysics), while cumulatively reinforcing a simple universal message for holistic improvement. I did contemplate putting together the alternate single life cycle model, but it would have delayed this book by more than a year, perhaps to be completed as a future endeavor!

The universe exists for us to grow, the aim being to excel as human beings at all times. Religion or spirituality are not a matter of convenience. Spending an hour in a religious establishment and then reverting to our basic flaws for the rest of the day is not concerted effort. The world ultimately works in harmony and perfect balance, and we instinctively sense that we should help others. To master these actions means we should first strive to perfect ourselves by overcoming our desires; they may exist and yet be rendered harmless through concerted control. Once we truly look beyond ourselves, this ultimately leads to impartial and universal love for all.

At this stage, it is necessary to advise the readers to read with patience, given over 25,000 pages of research are compressed herein. Find your rhythm early and follow the flow of information to ensure best understanding. I strongly recommend printing all the tables for ready reference for seamless step-by-step analysis through related explanations. And when you need a break *to let thoughts simmer*, flip over to the Spiritual Travelogue (pictorial) in Section 2 for a lighter pause!

A critical point to note is the genesis of religious research, insights, and related terminology. The initial six to seven years were spent on Hinduism, expanding into Christianity, Islam, Buddhism, Judaism, and miscellaneous ancient religions. While every effort was made to highlight original terms by way of parenthesis, italics, or quotation marks, along with an explanation in English to enable smooth information flow, please see two further clarifications:

- In the analyses for Tables A and C, you will note some dual terms—for example, purity (sattwa), traits (gunas), etc. Unless otherwise indicated, these terms originate from Hinduism.
- For the Table B-2 analysis, we came across a wide array of terminology in the five religions, including variations within each belief. Consequently, the team collating these exhaustive insights had to make assumptions with respect to transcription, transliteration and romanization, including the use of diacritics, with English as the common platform to work from. While it is respectfully acknowledged that the resident power of terminology (for example, mantras) can only be fully realized in the original (intended) script, the said assumptions had to be made to bring about the interconnectedness of our existence through the integrated research and insights.

References to gender in this book are used only as expression of speech for convenience to embellish points.

Universal, Basic Mental Housecleaning— The Six Trigger Points

The six trigger points took several years to develop, and are to be practiced daily in order to progressively seek that highest knowledge in the Self or God. These are inherently spiritual, universal for all. And ultimately, your conscious choices (if purified) become instinct leading into intuition. Those who try this self-sustaining energy tool will find that positive change is difficult, almost impossible at times. It takes concerted effort, grit and continued introspection daily to make these conscious choices deep-seated, operational on an involuntary basis. Laughter is involuntary, just like anger!

One can spend an entire lifetime in these efforts. Imagine your mind being akin to a rubber ball—squeeze it one way, it pops out another way! Have you ever seen how some ex-smokers suddenly put on weight? It takes a larger strategy to contain excesses. Here is a hilarious story of a relative who tried the six trigger points. She said, "For a week I was walking on water doing everything right. And then I fell off the cliff, all my old negativities resurfaced!"

Good intent is never enough. One can only consistently maintain selfless acts from a higher state of being, hence aim high! Commence by understanding that your mind and body are your temple of heaven, and should only contain good energy. Just as you keep that little prayer room in your home spotless, you need to keep that living temple of heaven cleaner; it will help you to begin to understand that awe-inspiring, dormant power within. And to transcend our inner tension and pain, one must first acknowledge them and let go instead of protecting against. And it is critical to get your immediate environment conducive to spiritual growth. We all fall into easy traps where one just gets lazy,

TABLE A

Universal, Basic Mental Housecleaning—The Six Trigger Points

1. Rise above the Traits
a. Three basic traits drive our thought process at any moment: purity, passion and dullness. Which one governs is key.
b. Unchecked negative traits turn chronic with hugely adverse impacts. Greatest mistakes are usually made by the most intelligent.
c. Good and bad comes from the same source within us. Understand why and how to offset the bad and grow by dynamic actions.
d. Transcend via purity and actions from the heart. Devote your life energy in pursuit of excellence and service to others.

2. Work into Worship
a. Work "in the moment," without ego, past fears and attachment for future results. Try to turn every act into an inner meditation, you will commence on the path to reach the highest "witness" within.
b. Conserve your energy for strategic efforts, control your emotions, delay your reactions to enable equanimous responses for everyone's benefit. Give it your absolute best daily, live outside comfort zone.
c. Confront your fears daily, they will progressively dissipate. Ultimately, fear is always about the future, eliminate it by focusing on the present.

The Six Trigger Points
1. Rise above the Traits
2. Work into Worship
3. Dynamic Quietude
4. Cosmic Power within Self
5. Eye of Wisdom
6. Progressive Fearlessness

3. Dynamic Quietude
a. With action, knowledge and renunciation comes austerity of mind, body and speech—"silence in action."
b. Introspection clears the mind, enables concentration and meditation.
c. Use wisdom, economy in speech to ensure permanent benefits for all. Be humble and benignly humorous. Note overenthusiasm brings exhaustion.

4. Cosmic Power within Self
a. Try to sense the interconnectedness, the "oneness of all" at a higher level. This helps preclude animosity and jealousy. Positive thoughts, speaking well of others are key to boosting your energy levels.
b. Nature's laws are irrevocable, to get into synchronicity is key.
c. Prayers, chanting and mantras enable inflow of healing cosmic energy.

6. Progressive Fearlessness
a. With knowledge (1–5 above) comes progressive fearlessness.
b. With ego subdued comes that subtle quality to pursue goals with unwavering determination and spiritually elevate.
c. Stay centered, dare to dream and take strategic risks—your best will consistently emerge.
d. Be intensely aware of your surroundings, strive to preserve that element of control in all your activities commensurate with the great knowledge acquired.

5. Eye of Wisdom
a. Continue to analyze what makes you tick to best understand the keys to making changes within yourself.
b. The vision of the man of perfection is being spiritual, cheerful and a dynamic force to contend with always.
c. Always keep the larger perspective, try to view all situations through the "eyes of spirit"—grace, compassion, forgiveness and honesty.
d. We are a soul with a body, not the other way around.

It's all about making conscious choices—tap that dormant temple of heaven within; introspect intensely, act, and a dynamic process of spiritual elevation commences.

and develops involuntary commitment to resistance to change. And acknowledge and remember successes, however minuscule; they are all part of the larger interactive equation. And remember that each person who comes into your life is there for a reason, to teach you something.

Over the years, I found five daily benefits of the six trigger points, in no particular order: (a) it promulgated easy self-analysis on a timely basis daily, which in turn effected consistent, subliminal improvement; (b) I was able to explain away just about all the events of the previous day via the multiple permutations and combinations of the six triggers; (c) applying concerted strategy, as an example, focusing on combining Points 2a and 3c "*Try to turn every act into an inner meditation*" in tandem with "*Be humble and benignly humorous*" resulted in an immediate step response; (d) achieving a high percentage of the six triggers daily inevitably led to a much higher quality of life, given that I was able to seek selfless solutions; and finally (e) working through the six triggers for five minutes daily re-centered my mind each morning.

Set your strategy first thing each morning to win daily. The great learning and joy begin in the journey itself. And in the process, these daily trigger points make your life effective and spiritual. When the mind is peaceful, all the right actions are taken. Offset stress through concerted action. After more than seven years of daily effort I have personally noted material changes within myself. Better still, others have attested to these positive changes. For example, I used to express much anger often witnessed after a golf stroke. Now I just laugh for the most part. Where did all that anger go? And what a great statement to make: "*I can proudly state that I truly have lost my temper for the most part!*"

Trigger 1: Rise above your Mental Traits

Purity, Passion and Dullness

We possess three basic traits called purity (*sattwa*), passion (*rajas*) and dullness (*tamas*) in varying combinations depending on our level of spirituality. Note that the terms in parentheses are from Hinduism. Pure (*sattwic*) people typically display a deep desire for knowledge, as opposed to seeking material gains. Passionate (*rajasic*) people are typically described by restlessness, material passion, constructive action, energy to remove obstacles and physical courage.

Negative *(tamasic)* people are typically described by laziness and ignorance, however this trait also aids in necessary rest and being grounded.

In the highly evolved, realized soul, all three traits are progressively transcended with the path out through purity *(sattwa)*. For the rest, all three traits are in play at any given moment, with one prevailing. The question is which way is that passionate *(rajasic)* energy pointed, towards purity or dullness.

Our desires are borne of an instinctive need for happiness. Our continued repressions promulgate these desires leading to recurring mistakes, given we tend to repeat our thoughts *(vasanas)*. This recurrence exacerbates our confusion, patterns get set early on in life leading to chronic problems if not timely checked. This can overshadow our great qualities, and even a single such negative chronic trait will perhaps drag down your whole life and also others around you with it. Miscalculations continue unabated, often masked by displays of morality in the name of achieving social status.

Sages of old worked out that such desire-driven pursuits yield only trouble. The ego in all its variance produces permutations and combinations of thoughts akin to several subset minds, all controlled by the central mind. Look deeper at your object of desire in all its apparent attractiveness and you will progressively begin to see its transitory nature. Without renouncing attachments and its by-products, spiritual progress is impaired, and yet we continue despite the laws of diminishing utility in play.

In most cases of self-control, willpower alone will not prevail, and there must be a process of concerted and progressive elimination of desires. Deliberately discipline the mind initially through (a) active avoidance of sensual stimuli, and (b) focusing on a higher ideal to work to (for example God, principle, guru) until we can get a grip on our impulses. And to run away from desires yet mentally indulge in them constitutes suppression, not control, often with disastrous results. Think of inspired activity to offset improper impulses. Take for example the sacrifices parents make for their children, readily transcending their own needs without a second thought.

Note also that while dullness *(tamas)* is the primary cause for distractions, we should not get despondent; indeed, there are times we may be growing the most during dark moods, provided we recognize they are some of the great learning experiences. Conversely, spiritual growth will have its share of challenges including variant moods, ecstatic delusions and some discouragement. You may also experience criticism from others along the way as your energies change. This is quite normal: keep your head down, maintain an indifference borne of growing self-confidence and stay the determined course! And a key point, learn to admit that we are often responsible for negative situations, and be humble to say sorry. Start small, and you will note a step change in your overall outlook. And the inability to do so will directly or indirectly, invariably result in fraying even long-term relationships. Try your best to not speak ill of others, issues notwithstanding, it lowers your energetic vibrations. This does not mean that one should refrain from speaking the truth when the occasion calls for it, but one should do it in the most positive light without ill feelings. Never be judgmental, be cognizant and respectful that each is in their own stage of spiritual growth. And given that the body is an extension of our mind, staying positive energetically aids in combating sickness. Note hospitals hire people to visit patients to keep their spirits uplifted.

Working through Fear, Desire and Anger

Let us consider the relationship between fear, desire and anger. When we desire something, with it comes the anxiety and fear of losing it and the resultant anger. We also become impatient towards others thereby creating an environment of negativity, which numbs our senses and makes us insensitive to their plight. Imagine an entire lifetime spent in such manner—what a waste of untapped potential. Be constantly vigilant for that inner tension culminating in explosive anger. Consistent recurrence of this means you have much work to do. And when you learn to manage and control desire, you involuntarily and subliminally overcome the other two.

Consequently, our struggle requires perseverance and discipline to achieve a very difficult task. The mind of an evolved person is calm, and by determined effort of will and discrimination we can overcome sudden waves of lust or greed. Temperance is the key, let it prevail. Try at least to contain the damage via introspection and related inactivity. And even these early, small successes will bring a sense of freedom, cheerfulness and peace.

Many are well versed in theory but lack the drive to make the leap into pure action. Most people end up taking the scenic route. They think they can do it but in practice never take up that necessary responsibility to evolve. Perhaps this is the primary reason why only a select few pass through the gates into becoming great realized masters, whereas the rest are left behind discussing it.

Our body, mind, intellect and ego are continually challenged by pairs of opposites that affect our equanimity. For example, heat and cold are felt by the body, pleasure and pain by the mind, honor and dishonor by the intellect, and affection and jealousy by the ego. These opposites are all subsets of a term called "cosmic delusion" responsible for our confusion. Terms synonymous with it include "maya" in Hinduism, "yin and yang" in Far Eastern religions, etc. Incidentally, Hinduism also refers to "maya" as creative powers playing a key role in the creation of the universe. Hence there is some confusion around this terminology. Both delusion and creation of the universe are discussed later while explaining Tables B-1, B-2 and C.

Be an Opinion Leader through the Path of Purity

He who develops in the path of selfless, detached activities gains poise, temperance and a sense of discrimination in all situations. By minimizing engagement in gratification of our desires, we discover untapped reserves of energy for higher activities. Never live your life as a helpless victim! And the greatest mistakes are usually committed by the most intelligent, utilizing that same dynamic energy source within our being. On the bright side, the reverse is equally true. These same people have the greatest propensity for positive change and can become great opinion makers and leaders in society if they can motivate themselves to change.

Pursue what you were born to do, not just what you were born into. Think of what motivates you to enthusiastically commence your day when you wake up. This partially helps explain our basic nature in our current existence. Some believe we have certain God-given talents to grow with; yet others believe these are a carryover from past lives. Either way, it works. Ever hear of child prodigies? And while life throws all sorts of challenges and variance during our unique individual journeys, we must persevere to develop our instinctive traits, be comfortable in who we are instead of trying to emulate others, thereby introducing a high chance of failure. And how about putting our skills to helping others? One of the coolest stories I came across in my research was about the legendary Muay Thai champion Buakaw Banchamek driving a taxi in his native Thailand asking and encouraging people about achieving their dreams in life. What a novel approach to helping, now there goes an opinion leader! And fortunate indeed are those who find their calling. We often come across great stories of people overcoming severe odds to reach out and help others. For example, many war veterans dedicated their lives to global humanity by becoming preachers, professors, intellectuals, great leaders in politics and industry.

Introspect deeply, challenge and question yourself daily. Men with the least desires have the greatest advantage of achieving true knowledge. And spirituality focuses on eliminating the sin, not blaming the sinner. We must face ourselves continually in a non-judgmental manner to overcome our pain.

Ever heard the expression "Don't laugh or cry too much"? The true spiritual meaning of this is that happiness dependent upon variant moods of the three traits (*gunas*) can only be transitory, given even pleasure is ultimately a form of attachment, with inherent craving and fear of its loss. And given that our minds have a tendency to repeat thoughts, consequent channeling of these hidden desires into our senses and bodies causes a continued cycle of attachment, with the negative aspects leaving us exhausted and confused. Consequently, transcend by way of purity (*sattwa*) to ultimately rise above all three traits (*gunas*). The first sign of becoming spiritual is innate joy and equanimity, and your real test comes in the midst of society, not in isolation. It is critical to know how your mind works. Develop your technique to allow change with perfect detachment. Become almost a disinterested witness to the play of the three traits, and as you elevate, purity (*sattwa*) flourishes while the other two traits get permanently reduced.

And when you start operating without agitation, efforts become efficient leading to the best results in all aspects and situations, be it professional or social. Once this mental discipline is gained, the mission of self-perfection becomes a thrilling passion. Also understand that we never really control actions of others in the first place, so give it your best effort and let go!

Before we move on, a quick word on miracles. Just know that what we deem as a miracle is in fact only a byproduct of growing spirituality. Too much emphasis is placed on this; indeed if one diligently tries to better oneself, the rest takes care of itself. And as a minimum, making a concerted effort to not self-destruct, come what may, drastically increases our chances of success.

Trigger 2: Work into Worship, be that magnificent Warrior-Monk in Action!

To ensure continued spiritual growth, mental purification efforts in your daily activities is the key. Work without any expectation of results, understand there is dignity in labor. With dedicated effort comes an innate confidence in your worth. Always be cognizant that rejection is not personal, rather it is a tremendous opportunity to develop grit. And try to control your emotions at all times, thereby maintaining equanimity in both success and perceived failure. In all my travels, I found that controlling emotions was a near-universal challenge for most. One must intensely cogitate and work out an individual strategy to offset this. I try to delay my reactions during stressful situations, thereby creating space for all to react in the most positive manner. And if you are able to achieve this, you will realize the trivial and transitory nature of daily stresses and strains, given they do not matter after some time.

Be mentally agile and intimately aware of your strategic vision during execution, set hard to achieve goals; it makes *normal living* a piece of cake. As a great singer once said, it was not about being competitive but rather just exceeding his own expectations. And being intensely energetic in both mental and physical activities to the extent you can *precludes* that all-powerful mental fatigue impacting people of all ages. It is said that we use a small percentage of our mind; thoughts are a powerful force (like muscles) and with concerted increased effort emerges brilliance. Ever come across that "Eureka" moment after intense effort?

The combination of our fears given past impressions and present desires, coupled with a stumbling effort in our chosen endeavor preclude us from blazing a path towards true transcendence. Perhaps this in part explains the life cycle of men, their rise and fall with subsequent comeback in many cases. Initially, dedicated activity without pressure for results leads to brilliant activity; then pressure to preserve leads to fear and lack of concentration leading to fall. And then those who understand this make a return much more seasoned and experienced.

Types of Yoga: Devotional, Action, Intellectual Reasoning and Combination

For those who practice devotion, note there are many facets, and efforts should be best adapted to suit one's nature. In Hinduism there are four main paths to perfection. We see similar analogy in other religions and beliefs also.

- *Devotional or Bhakti Yoga:* Expressed through ritual prayer including devotional songs and repeating mantras, the process is called *japa* (*dhikr* in Islam, prayer by ten males over the age of thirteen in Judaism is called *minyan*), often aided by use of rosary beads. Practiced with great effort either in seclusion or in groups to create that wonderful, ecstatic relationship with God, it appears the most followed path across religions.
- *Selfless action or Karma Yoga:* The path of action is best suited for the energetic types delving fully, immersing themselves, mind, body and soul, to perfect their craft, dedicated towards a religious entity personal or impersonal (guru, deity, God) or equivalent spiritual principle.
- *Intellectual analysis or Jnana Yoga:* The path of deep, rational study is best suited for the studious, analytical types who end up believing after progressive discrimination on the extent of available facts.
- *Meditation or Raja Yoga:* This is a combination of the aforementioned paths, best suited for the highly adaptive types believing in both strong mental and physical capabilities. This is sometimes referred to as Ashtanga Yoga, and it stresses on the multiple occult centers (chakras) within our being as an integral vehicle to our mind–body spiritual transcendence through meditation while reinforcing both mental and physical perfection. These chakras are discussed often later in different parts of this analysis.

One of the simplest rules we all ignore is that an exhausted person can never practice devotion efficiently. The average good sleep cycle appears to be six to eight hours/day for most. However, spiritually advanced people require less, given their mastery of techniques to recharge the body, for example, through the chakras. And while opinions are offered on the best body position (left side, right side, etc.), it is best to sleep with your head pointing east to avoid adverse impacts of the earth's north-south magnetic forces which can lead to disabilities (hemorrhages, strokes). As a minimum, do not point north in the northern hemisphere or south if residing in the southern locales. And given that the average person only accesses limited energy, they should learn to use it strategically. This also applies to speech; we scarcely realize how much energy we drain through such activity. Ask professional singers after a concert or TV personalities after a live studio session.

Yoga, diet, exercise, and calm regulated breathing are key to ensuring selfless activities with a vibrant, decisive mind. Diet is a studied science, ancient sages (rishis) worked out the best foods to aid spiritual growth. As you will find later in this study, the body is literally developed and sustained by the mind as a result of our strengths and weaknesses percolating progressively through our consciousness. These traits manifest into daily habits which in turn result in our physical condition, fit or otherwise. We get so used to poor habits that by sheer habit we reject positive change, and inertia settles. The body then turns around and eats us through viruses! It is therefore suggested that one should give oneself the privilege of being able to indulge by exception, and by not eating after a certain time at night because indigestion due to late eating produces toxins. And as a rule, one should try and eat half of what one was planning to, so that one may *feel so different, vibrant*. Effective fasting is a natural cleansing method, a superb form of austerity.

And while meditation is dealt in detail later in the text, for now we need to understand that our bodies constitute cells with vibrational energies working in unison, which when disturbed lead to imbalance and diseases. Higher activities and meditation help restore natural healthy rhythm by resonating with the chakra system thereby releasing a marvelous flow of subtle energies which raise our vibrations leading to a state of blissful joy. Effectively, meditation allows for our nervous system to settle and cause appropriate release of tension to enhance the transcendent experience.

One style of yoga practice is pranayama, the breathing technique. Given breathing changes with moods, this helps settle the mental chaos and thus focuses on dedicated activity. And meditation is a means to an all-concerted process of assimilating knowledge by withdrawing, initially through concentration, our senses of reception away from desires of the mind, then yanking the mind into the higher intelligence to focus upon our highest goals.

In pursuing the multiple paths aforementioned, one develops equanimity, discrimination and superb efficiency. As long as you have done your best, never despair if you do not succeed at first. Conversely guard against vanity if you do. The only true reward is knowing that we did our best, and the result will come. And what about enjoying material gains as a result of our labor? Many discussions have taken place on this engaging subject. The answer will surface naturally and instinctively. We become progressively detached from the benefits of resultant fruits of our labor as we spiritually transcend.

Law of Karma

Let us introduce a key concept, the law of action and reaction or Karma, initially through Hinduism and how it equates to destiny; with expanded analyses across the multiple religions following later in Tables B-1, B-2 (Item 1), C, etc. Let us take it in steps. First, since every action has a reaction, this results in impacts (destiny) both positive and negative via astrological influences in our current or future existence. Second, our ego (and body) represents our cumulative Karmic balance born and thrust into our surroundings manifesting as desires, fears and positive traits, and it is only at this human level that we fully connect with our true nature to achieve liberation. Third, Hinduism mentions certain predetermined Cosmic Governance cyclical time periods (each cycle covering billions of years) with guiding energies imposed upon us that influence our thinking patterns (see Table B-2, Item 12.1 and C analyses). Fourth, add our current choices (free will) into the mix; and spiritual progress is cumulatively regulated by how we deal with our present desires and impacts of our past Karma via astrological influences (detached positive, negative radiations) affecting our being in our current environment. Hence, our immediate moment of existence constitutes *destiny, with free will to make future choices.* The catch is that pending material change, our patterns of behavior (free will) are largely predictable given inertia of the mind, intellect and ego thereby boxing us into the cycle of attachment.

According to Hinduism, the overall process takes countless life cycles through the multiple stages of involution and evolution (see Table B-1) commencing from the inanimate to cells to plants to animals to humans, by progressively elevating from instinct to intellect to the highest levels of intuition. Note also that many religions accept the Karmic impacts of astrological influences due to free will translated into positive and negative energies, notwithstanding belief in single versus multiple life cycles. For example, Judaism believes that each of the constellations corresponding to the twelve months of the year has a different energy, also recorded in the Talmud (written version of oral civil and ceremonial law) by sages in conformity with ancient Greek thought. Conversely, while Islam strongly refutes astrological influences as being a central tenet to core teachings, there is an expression, *Qamar dar Aqrab* which refers to the moon residing in Scorpio for 2–3 days per month, generally considered as an unfavorable time for marriages, commencing journeys, etc.

You have no doubt heard the expression "right time, right place and luck." Per Hinduism, these are subsets of Karma from previous life merging with current diligent actions borne of undivided focus to achieve one's goals in the present. Act in the moment utilizing the best tools you have to work with, and the results will come, now or in the future.

I must conclude this discussion on Trigger 2 with some marvelous experiences and vibrant principles on Leadership:

Captain of an American 777-200 Flight—Heathrow to JFK, January 2008

I was coming from a brief transit stop in London after an exhausting work stint in Doha (Qatar), where the temperature used to be around 130°F or 54°C. I was dozing as we were taxiing for take-off at Heathrow. Suddenly I heard much clapping and hooting, and as I looked out I saw a fire brigade hosing down the jumbo.

On enquiry the air hostess told me it was the captain's final flight, *he was retiring*; and it was a flying tradition to hose down the jet. She also mentioned this captain was simply a great guy, regarded as one of the finest in American Airlines.

After a perfect take-off amidst much cheering over the roar of the engines, I offered to take a picture of this lady and three children who were taking pictures of each other. I later found out they were the captain's family. An hour away from JFK, he came on the air and quoted text from Henry Thoreau and George Washington in a deep calm voice, again to much cheer. Even before meeting this man, you had a subliminal impression formed . . . *must be simply a great guy, humble to the core, a true family man; and a great achiever borne of a life of discipline and devotion to work.* As we looped over the New York City shoreline, we came in on reasonably high winds. I was half musing "hope he does not get too emotional while landing," but the captain achieved a *precision landing* to much collective joy. We then did a full circle around the JFK perimeter, and as we came in towards the gate we saw the JFK firefighters waiting to hose down the jet.

And there he was, as we exited. A tall and distinguished man, standing at the gate shaking hands with all, smiling hugely, tears running down his face. People were openly crying, clapping this great guy on the shoulder, giving him their contact information.

Now how is that for an *everyday warrior-monk*? And talk about synchronicity of events for all of us who were so fortunate to be there to witness this beautiful event, and meet this lovely man as it all unfolded.

Meeting Mr. Arora

I met him at the JW Marriott, Mumbai, indeed one of the great hotels worldwide; down in the gymnasium, a pilgrimage place indeed for those who love to work out. A seventy-five-year-old with a physique that would make a twenty-five-year-old envious, he came up to say hello and told me a little bit of his life. He mentioned he had been with the Indian Army where he had seen action, took early retirement, and came to Mumbai to start a business. It was his little piece of advice that has my ears ringing to this day, "Deepak, make sure you go that extra distance every day. Let no day pass without this extra little effort, never give up."

His statement spoke volumes. Live outside your comfort zone. Try it and you will see your energy levels change; a sense of exhilaration comes into effect. Life is challenging at each step; everyone goes through ups and downs. The best boxers possess tested chins, our true nature comes out in times of challenges. And actions taken devoid of attachment and fear for the outcome release the mind. Our focus then changes from desire (latent fear)–based to desireless activities, leading to detachment and elevation.

Flamenco Dance

Visit establishments like "Corral de la Morería" and "Cardamomo" in Madrid, reputed amongst the finest in Spain for this art form. Dating back to the 1700s, Flamenco is believed to have iterative Indo-Aryan roots from Rajasthan, India, where gypsies migrated westward from cities like Jaisalmer and Barmer. The passionate singing, clapping and guitar combined with a unique dance is a philosophical experience—their art, agility and display of subtle strength within limited spaces personify so many spiritual principles cited herein. Artists hone their natural skills from a tender age, powered by their intense concentration ("Work into Worship") to give us a peek into the incredible power of the human spirit. I noted many guests in tears during these heart-warming experiences.

The Armed Forces

I spent a great deal of time during my travels analyzing how the defense forces of a country translate spiritual and religious principles into *leading from the front.* Indeed it is a customary practice for industry to leverage from these disciplined, magnificent men and women for training their corporate leaders. Cumulatively, I visited the beaches of Normandy, France (WWII D-Day Landings), read voraciously on World War II, Vietnam and Korean conflicts, examined the winning mindset of premier special forces globally, and researched some of the greatest leaders of the twentieth century. Indeed, I had the great honor of connecting with Ms. Maja Daruwala, daughter of Field Marshal Sam Manekshaw of the Indian Army whose distinguished military career spanned four decades in five major wars including WWII (Burma campaign). Ms. Daruwala guided me into some scintillating insights on this legendary man of action (Karma Yogi):

My own sense of the ingredients of my father's mantra for leadership is to inspire confidence and trust from those who look to you for leadership. The contents for inspiring confidence and trust are: loyalty to the mandate, being no one's man except that of good conscience and the law, recognizing you have the 'chair' but treating others equally and with fairness, being accessible, balance, understanding others' difficulties without making either too much or too little of it, keeping to honorable ways of acting. Standing true in the face of challenge. I suppose your integrity must shine through for others to see.

There are many articles and programs easily accessible to understand his principles of leading from the front. I found most fascinating his inimitable humor—a comment he made about being *kicked by a mule* after regaining consciousness from injury during the 1942 Burma campaign, when nine bullets from his lungs, liver, kidneys and most of his intestines were later removed.

Leading from the front is best achieved by striving to live beyond your comfort zone to excel at what you do, blossoming into a growing self-confidence; truly great work is borne of the highest self-esteem and integrity. You must learn to make fear your friend, thereby leading to its involuntary control as a self-propelling mechanism. And while inward equanimity must be maintained at all times, perceived anger is an effective tool utilized by leaders to varying degrees irrespective in government, public administration, corporate, defense services to achieve desired team results. And one of the great compliments that a leader can receive is when his staff or team approach him without fear of reprisals and complete transparency to resolve an execution issue; in fact this presents a great opportunity for the leader to offset their stress, particularly in extreme professions by collectively focusing them in the moment, thereby never losing control. This is coupled with that certain sense of humor that comes with facing adversity borne of the task at hand.

A well-organized team inevitably leads to success, inculcates camaraderie, trust and looking out for each other. Read about veterans the world over stating how facing adversity was all about *looking out for the guy next to you*. Accept what is happening to you, instead of lamenting *how this could* happen to a person like yourself. Interactively start to work your way out from there with that seemingly effortless, relaxed demeanor that comes with high competence whilst maintaining an element of control in all your actions. Converting fear correctly helps adjust very quickly to work efficiently, enables timely focus and laser-controlled action while staying calm. Aggression is good, but control is the key, work the problem unto its last second—note how great achievements arise out of time-sensitive projects given that the mind focuses on creative solutions within the allocated window. Most impressive is how many in the special forces have stated that dying is just *part of the job* they took on, and they are just going to keep coming at you with concerted focus until the very last second. And before we move on, pause for a moment to understand how powerful this last statement is, and how one truly captures the actions of a Karma Yogi by living in the moment while leading from the front. Most impressive also is how training programs in the armed forces are to first break everyone down to a common platform, then build them back up as one team with a vision to serve for the greater good of all. Indeed superior quality systems in corporates the world over try to achieve the same for efficient practices. Any deviation from quality equates to a loss of profits!

I visited Arlington Cemetery near Washington DC to witness the Changing of the Guard, and watched the ceremonial 'Taps' bugle being played to venerate the beloved who gave their lives in defense of their country. Even a cursory glance at the intensely slow, measured march of these Old Guard soldiers (the Sentinel) not only demonstrated the stringent training to achieve such timely dedication, somber respect and commitment to their cause, but also the vision of such military institutions globally to blaze such a path to be followed borne of thousands of years of experience and lessons learned.

I also had the great fortune to visit a "shrine," the beaches of Normandy, France, where D-Day took place on June 6, 1944 when the Allies re-entered France in the greatest amphibious landing of the twentieth century. An estimated 10,000 soldiers either perished, went missing or were wounded that first day on those beaches. There is a quarter mile of beach head at Omaha, and as you walk through the American Memorial, you begin to understand the fate these soldiers were dealt—the words came to my mind *"they had no chance."* I later attended a business leadership session at West Point, United States Military Academy, and asked our instructor, a formidable Marine colonel with FBI experience: "How does a general live with his strategic decisions knowing the inevitable?" His answer was incredibly direct, simple: "*We send the officers in with the troops.*" Indeed, General Norman Cota and General Theodore Roosevelt III (son of President Franklin D. Roosevelt) were on those beaches amongst many others, *leading from the front.*

I have also had the great honor of meeting many veterans from several campaigns including WWII, Vietnam, Korea and others. Working to a higher ideal, "love for country," many later went on to enhance the lives of others through the lens of their extreme experiences by becoming refined educators, statesmen and leaders in their vocation. And the visit to Normandy remains as one of the great, momentous days of my life.

Gene Kranz, Flight Director for the Gemini and Apollo Programs Including the Apollo 11 Moon Landing and the Apollo 13 Missions

After the oxygen accident that killed three astronauts at Mission Control during ground tests, I read about how this legendary flight director materially changed the way NASA operated by using two simple keywords, effectively translating to tenacity and skill. He promulgated that accepting mistakes and failure for the said loss of life because of not having caught the tragic defects (in design, build, or test) was the first step towards advancement, and that taking personal ownership and collective accountability to achieve the highest levels of competence was the way forward to perfection. He emphasized that this methodology was the price of admission to the ranks of Mission Control. Indeed, one of the engineers later related during an interview how this critically changed the way the teams collectively worked and took responsibility henceforth.

Music

And last but not least, as mentioned in the discussion on traits/gunas earlier, we must persevere to find ourselves—*pursue actions we were born to do, not just what we were born into.* Be the absolute best with what you have. Let's discuss the music legend Kishore Kumar. People from most Hindi, Urdu and Bengali speaking countries will perhaps agree that in any field of art and entertainment, Kishore Kumar, along with Lata Mangeshkar, Asha Bhosle, Mehdi Hassan and Mohammed Rafi easily fare amongst the top entertainers of the twentieth century. What was so remarkable about Kishore was the rate of ascension of his voice to a weapon of unbridled power, polish and repertoire that continues to mesmerize generations since, and that too with minimal training. Singers of today by their own admission do not come close notwithstanding lessons learned, technology and natural evolution in music. I tracked his voice during various points of his career, it is a lesson in life in its own right. How his voice took on a haunting quality after the demise of his second wife (the actress Madhubala), his rise to the top in early 1970s culminating in utter polish and perfect energetic timing until his demise in 1987. I suspect that Kishore's acts of eccentricity were the perfect guise ("hiding in plain sight") for dedicated research on other types of music (jazz, reggae, soul, etc.) which perfected his technique and repertoire. Of particular note is the use of concentrated energy bursts to create the perfect rhythm and echo effect; it sometimes even appeared as if he was doing a 360-degree revolution around a lyric!

He executed "in the moment," his rare visual recordings demonstrate how he broke up singing into little sections, and it always appeared that he had *all the time in the world* to complete perfect pronunciation for every lyric. With full concentration on one piece at a time reinforced by that millisecond slower, latent power in play. He also made fear his friend to overcome severe stage fright, and it has been voiced how one ultimately would be drawn to his voice in any duet. Truly a man of action and far ahead of his time, he was reportedly very close to nature. This man in some unique way keenly understood key concepts of the Bhagvadgita. The Sanskrit word "mantra" ('man' means mind or thought, 'tra' means free) literally means 'instrument to free the mind of thought.' Just as Sanskrit is used to recite mantras where vibrations borne of perfect pronunciation create positive material effects (note parallels in great speeches the world over), so did Kishore and other greats instinctively understand the explosive power of words and links into Aum, the universal energy sound representing the subtle laws of creation, thereby mesmerizing generations with their unique interpretation and presentation. Aum is discussed in detail later in this commentary, for now assume that all creation, sounds, vibrations, etc., are linked and represented by Aum.

I saw several concerts of his, in fact even saw a joint Kishore–Mohammed Rafi Nite, truly an evening from the gods. And speaking of the latter, Rafi's humility was legendary. He spoke very little, always looking down in respect. When praised, his customary response was *"it is the grace of Allah."* He also practiced for hours daily in silence, akin to meditation! Note that mental practice of reciting mantras (japa) is considered higher than vocal japa, given it requires more concentration. Try to practice for a major presentation in perfect silence and you will see how difficult it is!

Ancient scriptures state that rhythm in music is associated with human movements, for example, the double beat of walking. A legendary music director who was once hospitalized was gazing at his heart monitor and remarked that if one creates music centered around one's heartbeat, the results will always be successful!

Try it, analyze the operating walking beats of people at airports, you will come to understand so much about the human condition and our collective fascination with rhythmic movements. A formalized example today constitutes models doing ramp walks the world over.

Trigger 3: Dynamic Quietude

Be Impersonal and Healing in Wisdom

With renunciation, action and knowledge comes a sense of fulfilment, dynamic quietude (*silence in action*). Men of great wisdom conserve their energy, often utilizing economy in speech while performing action with deadly efficiency. I have personally seen this in luminaries such as Satyajit Ray, Oscar-winning film director, Pandit Shiv Kumar Sharma, maestro of the musical hammered dulcimer stringed instrument santoor. There is divine, focused action in seeming inaction when the mind slows down its incessant chatter. I once attended a concert of Ustad Zakir Hussain, considered the foremost expert on the twin-drum Indian instrument called the "tabla," his intense focus represented pure yoga of action in utmost silence while creating wonderous vibrations borne of the heavens.

One must learn to introspect deeply on one's daily actions, vices, habits; this helps to clear the mind, progressively enabling the road to concentration and meditation. A true philosopher is a scientist in disguise! One who perseveres daily to distance himself from desires and does not engage hence becoming a witness to them while involuntarily increasing his reach into the higher Self/being. Holistic living and a disciplined routine integrate a person. It is critical to create a system that works for you, be it reading scriptures, practicing rituals, or simply being the best person you can be. A word of caution on hyperactivity: examples such as religious over-chanting, utter self-denial, incessant speech—all lead to emotional ecstasy, hysteria and exhaustion.

Practice speaking quietly and sincerely for the benefit of others, for permanence. Be impersonal and healing in wisdom, note how sages create an atmosphere of serene joy and peace all around thanks to their inherent divinity. And as mentioned earlier, it is sometimes necessary to show anger but do not mean it. *Not easy in practice!* Same goes for unnecessary movement of limbs. Laughter is tremendous if used in a benign context, not nervous giggling to offset tension. And if you wake up chuckling, it is Nature's way of telling you that you are doing something right! Conversely, if you find yourself exploding in rage, that is inner tension that needs pause and concerted action to resolve—you have much work to do.

Trigger 4: Cosmic Power within Self

Interconnectedness and the Natural Laws of the Universe

Do you ever get the feeling that the world somehow manages to operate in perfect balance, that our individual actions constitute a certain contribution within a larger, interrelated scheme? Spirituality talks about the "*oneness of the universe,*" everyone has a precise place in an overall plan, with factors such as DNA, genetics, etc., to get us appropriately positioned for continued efforts and future cycles. Take the time to study the lives of politicians, actors, generals and singers, analyze what made them who they are, and look at your own life path. Would the reverse roles have worked? It may just occur to you that while seemingly unrelated, we are all working in perfect synchronicity for a higher cause that transcends us all. Creation, sustenance and dissolution in perfect concurrent play—understanding this implicit law of the universe is key.

Nature (like all else) is also a subset of this universal consciousness, its laws operating in their own rhythm. Normal distribution curves, probability theory, law of diminishing utility, etc., are all subsets of this. *It's just the way it is.* Take even the simplest of examples, try defying nature by maintaining late nights for a month and see how you fare. Note the tired look of friends who do this routine for a living! Or why do only a small percentage of humans achieve realization? Try visualizing a normal distribution curve (a bell curve) on man's basic nature, you will find extreme purity (*sattwa*) and extreme dullness (*tamas*) at extreme ends of the curve, whereas the majority constitute varying combinations in the large rounded peak area. And as a key lesson that I picked up, given that we are all interconnected, learn to cheer for the success of others! Centering the mind on a simple, powerful thought such as this will step-change your outlook by precluding jealousy and animosity whilst promoting humility and respect towards all beings. Even your viewpoint towards your perceived enemies will begin to change as you view all beings as a global family. How can you maintain enmity for someone whom you consider as one of your own? Try it, you will begin to discover a unity in the world notwithstanding your variant experiences.

The concept of oneness commences at the minutest of levels. Look at NASA astronaut Dr. Edgar Mitchell (Apollo 14) describing his experience on the way back from the moon:[1]

> *The biggest joy was on the way home. in my cockpit window every two minutes—the Earth, the Moon, the Sun, and a whole 360-degree panorama of the heavens. And that was a powerful, overwhelming experience. And suddenly I realized that the molecules of my body, and the molecules of the spacecraft, the molecules in the body of my partners, were prototyped and manufactured in some ancient generation of stars. And that was an overwhelming sense of oneness, of connectedness. It wasn't them and us, it was—that's me, that's all of it, it's one thing. And it was accompanied by an ecstasy, a sense of "oh my god, wow, yes," an insight, an epiphany.*

---

[1] *In the Shadow of the Moon* (2007), film directed by David Sington and produced by Duncan Copp.

NOTE: The confluence of matter at its basic level (molecules, electrons, etc.) with energy and spirituality has been the subject of much study including quantum physics. Discussed later in this commentary.

Prayers, Mantras, Aum and the Rhythms of Nature

Prayers, chanting and mantras help us get into synchronicity with the rhythms of nature, and enable inflow of healing energies. Note how group chanting creates positive vibrations in a church or a temple. Techniques vary amongst religions (see Table B-2, Item 5 for detailed explanations). For example, Christianity does not use mantras as understood in other traditions, but repeated prayer may work as a mantra. In Judaism, certain aids are utilized to communicate with God, for example, cumulative effort by a group speaking certain words, prayers, the seventy names of God reportedly aiding immediate connectivity with the divine realm.

Buddhism and Hinduism have many mantras, the most utilized is "Aum" regarded as one of the highest vibrations known to man. This universal energy sound originated in scriptures and represents the created universe including nature and life in all its myriad forms. Similarly, "Aum Tat Sat" is also chanted to transcend. "Tat" means the eternal goal, "Sat" is existence (see further explanation in Table B-2, Item 3.1). Cumulatively, they represent our overall reality. Aum (like all mantras) must be recited with focus. This mantra can be traced through the annals of history, representing God via this basic, all-enveloping sound. "A" is the root, first sound, produced without touching any part of the tongue or roof of the mouth; "U" stems from the very root to the end of the sounding area of the mouth; "M" represents the last sound produced by our closed lips.

Hence, Aum represents the complete sound promulgation encapsulating the experience of the pulsating universe, audible or otherwise (thoughts, emotions). Chanting Aum gets one into synchronicity with the subtle laws of creation, thereby enabling inflow of healing energies. Additional details are included in Tables B-1, B-2 (Item 5) and C commentary.

Pursuant to deep effort and meditation, we naturally come to understand these rhythms of nature and laws of creation. We progressively reach into our resident divinity and begin operating involuntarily out of the higher chakras (Table B-2, Item 8 lists multiple beliefs) to perfect synchronicity of actions in perfect tune with these unsaid laws. Utilizing the highest wisdom or *dharma* (discussed later) applicable to any particular set of circumstances, we largely preclude mistakes henceforth. Note that all these concepts were deeply studied by our ancient saints and sages who honed their knowledge to the point of even examining the effects of the Sun, the Moon and stars over life and nature.

You have perhaps deduced by now that right time, right place and luck are in fact a subset of the above. Continue to refine your abilities to enable sound judgement, be a master of your craft with no reason for stress, and consider nature's laws as irrevocable, best obeyed. As an example, our purity trait (*sattwa*) is primarily dominant in the early morning hours (4–6 a.m.). Note how this time is naturally benevolent towards noble activities of meditation, introspection, body relaxation activities and creativity across all cultures, thanks to predominance of pure cosmic energies reinforced by ether. This is said to be the time of the creator, and the flow of divine energies translates into the subconscious mind being the most conducive to advancement with ease at such time. Go outside your home and you will find that nature welcomes you, makes you literally feel the freshness and joyous calm in the air. Note the rejoicing songs of our wonderful birds! Our passion trait (*rajas*) then dominates until 4 p.m., with dullness trait (*tamas*) governing for the remaining period. The recommendation down the ages is to get into synchronicity with these timings and watch the natural resultant effects of self-purification by increasing our purity (*sattwa*) while reducing the other two traits/gunas!

Positive thoughts uplift; speaking well of others is key to boosting your own energy levels. Conversely criticizing others lowers your vibrations; you will only invite further negative energies. The key point to note however is that speaking the truth with sincerity is fully acceptable. As for cheerful acceptance from the Lord, this is only possible when your basic physical and mental faculties are largely intact. I visited Dachau and Auschwitz-Birkenau concentration camps. You come away knowing that it is not possible for the common man to withstand torture. Akin to the heat of battle, these poor souls were operating out of survival instinct from the lowest of the chakras or occult centers within us. At best you can approach it with great premeditation and strategy that many such complexities can only be explained through a tremendous understanding of the Karmic law of justice (see Spiritual Travelogue #16 for details of these visits). Pain unwanted in our great school of learning ultimately reminds us that wisdom is gained through understanding the endless cycle of creation, sustenance and dissolution (threefold nature of God) constituting overall universal balance.

Trigger 5: Eye of Wisdom

We are a Soul with a Body, not the Reverse

We are a soul with a body, and not the other way around. Endeavor to be the best possible person you could be, make your life spiritual, extraordinary. Take advantage of being so fortunate in the human condition!

A man of perfection is spiritual, cheerful and a dynamic force to contend with. Armed with a wonderfully trained mind and a larger perspective, viewing all situations through the "Eyes of Spirit"—with grace, temperance, compassion, forgiveness and honesty. And higher the goal or platform one operates from, greater the self-control! An offshoot of equanimity is to be armed with higher predictive knowledge. Anticipate how people will act, and adjust accordingly in the most positive manner. True leaders share the pain of others while subliminally guiding them into higher spiritual pastures. And one who literally watches the play of the three traits (*gunas*) within himself with dynamic quietude gains the "Eye of Wisdom," also called intuition. This is discussed in detail later.

An interesting side effect is the ability to become a witness to intense activity all around you despite being fully immersed in it, where one seemingly revels in nonchalant indifference despite the engagement. What is truly happening is that when you work without fear of gains, your best, even true genius emerges as you reach into your higher Self (the witness). Watch out for this *extraordinary* feeling, it signals a sign of tremendous spiritual growth.

Something to be keenly watchful and aware of is that the energy of one impacts others and vice versa. Take the energies of a husband–wife team. When one's energies work against the other, a myriad of outcomes can take place including cowardice and codependence. Cowardice is the failure to face oneself, and we become cowards both individually and as a team. Codependence is the resultant inertia in our way of life with no motivation to change for the better. The following also needs to be stated very carefully: We should not deviate too much from our path to help others and may even end up completely derailing our own spiritual growth. While we fervently want to help others, best results are derived from giving detached advice.

Wife of a Firefighter

I must relate this experience with respect to the statement above on our innate instinct within all of us to feel the pain of others. I was on a Virgin Airlines flight (Heathrow–JFK) two months after 9/11, and met the wife and her three-year-old daughter of one of the firefighters who perished in Tower 1. Also amongst us were some London-based firefighters heading for a memorial service in New York City. The Virgin crew had opened up the bar, we were all milling around in the upper deck of the jumbo, and this remarkable lady was relating her final interaction with her husband: "He had called to say he was going in and later as I saw the first Twin come down, my first reaction was that he could not run that fast." All of us were visibly upset, and then she did a remarkable thing. Seeing my discomfiture, she reached out to console me and patted me on the shoulder. I will never forget this kind gesture, and while not knowing anything about the background of this wonderful lady, in that instant she personified some of the glorious traits aforementioned.

Read this marvelous quote by Swami Chinmayananda,[2] so uniquely applicable to all our lives.

A mere spiritual consideration should not be the last word in the evaluation of all material situations. Every challenge should be estimated from the spiritual stand-point, as well as from the intellectual stand-point of reason, from the emotional level of ethics and morality, and from the physical level of tradition and custom. If all these considerations, without any contradiction, indicate a solitary truth, then that is surely the Divine Path that one should, at all costs, pursue.

---

[2] *The Holy Geeta: Commentary by Swami Chinmayananda*, Central Chinmaya Mission Trust, Mumbai.

Daily Improvement Tips

Continue to analyze what makes you tick to best understand the keys to making changes within yourself. Here are some simple tips to help create a system that helps you in your normal day to achieve stellar results:

- Exercise. Many do not have a natural inclination, so how to make it work? One of the greatest lessons an experienced salesman taught me was this. Note that this guy could sell anything, but he truly sweated bullets when asked to do the mundane task of putting the purchase order to paper! He said: "Deepak, most brands are competitive, it's the hidden benefits of the product that you should learn to promote." What he was really saying was to let the overall system work for you, and to use all available means to sell. So try this: If your system can take it, set up your home office on the second floor or similar unobtrusive challenge; understand just how many calories you will burn without giving it a second thought. Or if you have to exercise, cogitate on an issue or venture while exercising, and time will fly!
- Have a quick response to negative feelings. An energy healer advised me to try saying "I hereby shed all my negative energies," and have a timely pause from activity to get recentered. Another cool technique from a Swami which made me chuckle, was to face old hanging regrets as they surfaced by detachedly ballooning them away into the sky. And gather your thoughts over time. If you develop sympathy for the animal world, your urge to eat meat will naturally diminish without continually fighting it. Herein lies the difference between repression and natural progression. And the same goes for indulgence. Cogitate on your walkaway point, then execute with dignity. Slow down your action to a crawl and become a total witness, you will learn to conquer fear and control your urge at will as you involuntarily begin to look through (and not at) your object of desire which withers away! The point being, if you do not lend wheels to it, it has no impact. And the less the intake, the less you need!
- Do you hate your job, and find Monday mornings are hard to get going? Face the problem head on, exercise first thing Monday to the extent you can. You will note a step change in your energies and vibrancy.
- It is critical to know our sleep patterns. Many of us are light or disturbed sleepers, and the pressures of work and travel can severely hamper energies.

Accordingly, try and adjust your routine to catch light naps when you can. There is nothing worse than going into a workday feeling like a deer in headlight. A super technique which I stumbled into through sheer introspection was to tell myself at the end of each day that I had done my best that day (you will know if you truly did), and that the result would take care of itself. And an alternative technique was to balloon my thoughts away as mentioned above. Either way, I found I was sleeping like a baby notwithstanding the pressures!

- Whether you are a believer in God or not, do not be shy of asking for help! A Swami advised that help is usually available if asked for, be it from God or through the rhythms of the universe, and comes to us in many ways. It may be advice through friends and family, meeting a random stranger, watching a TV program, or simply through a new thought emergent in the mind. What is important is to maintain an awareness, humility and a gratefulness at all times, pending which you may be bypassing help that emerges by courtesy of strangers, friends and foes alike, and even out of the blue through an impersonal medium.

- Meditation to offset daily struggles. While we can only minimally influence the larger outcome given we may not be developed enough, at a higher level meditation calms the mind, which in turn will change your attitude and attract resultant energies (note explanation on synchronicity in Table C later). A natural honesty utterly devoid of fear shines through, resulting in right actions. This in turn helps you influence group dynamics to naturally evolve to a higher level. For example, note the marvelous energies of the Pope or the Dalai Lama. Would you ever consider using vulgar language in front of them? And last but not the least, pick a phrase or word that vibrates with you and is easy to remember during stressful situations. I chose "centered," which implies that I maintain an equanimity at all times.

Trigger 6: Progressive Fearlessness

Stay Centered, Dare to Dream

With progressive knowledge comes an innate confidence, fearlessness and grit to strive towards your goals while minimizing indulgence. Obstacles now only elevate one's courage and dynamism to overcome them with humility, knowledge and efficiency. Stay centered, dare to dream and take strategic risks, and your best will consistently emerge. Be intimately aware of your surroundings, strive to preserve that element of control in all your activities commensurate with your great knowledge acquired through dedicated activities.

Scriptures advise us that while our niche in life is generally carved out based on our Karma, our overall contribution is relatively minimal compared to the larger hand of nature. We combine things, sometimes bringing out the marvels of technology and nature in step fashion with perfect synchronicity. For example, study how programs for yellow fever and malaria control coincided with construction of the famous locks at the Panama Canal! And yet we are discovering things that always existed.

As one gets more detached from one's senses, one begins to see divinity in every experience, meeting both joys and sorrows in such fashion. One's trained mind now provides one that unique skill of knowing when and how to withdraw from negative influences. Training the mind is critical given its powerful nature. Change comes with time through the links of our Karma even though it may feel instantaneous. Our sense organs faithfully and instinctively follow our desires and fears, given that years of conditioned impressions of what is attractive are imprinted on our minds and taken for granted. The suggested technique is to focus by looking through the object of desire, and you will begin to understand its temporary nature. Look at the personification of Lord Shiva with eyes half closed, seeing the outer world through inner vision, later exemplified by saints and sages the world over.

A Conversation with Ben Ferencz, WWII Nuremberg Special Trials Prosecutor

I must conclude this discussion on the six trigger points by mentioning the extraordinary life of Benjamin Ferencz, the Hungarian born, then twenty-seven-year-old Chief Prosecutor at the Special Nuremberg Trials (WWII) in 1947–1948. His career ultimately spanning seven decades, Mr. Ferencz maintained a 15-hour-a-day work schedule at the age of 100! His untiring efforts materially influenced the creation of the International Criminal Court (ICC) of the UN at the Hague in 1998. Mr. Ferencz was later bestowed (amongst many honors) with the Harvard Law School Medal of Freedom which pleased him the most given it was earlier awarded to Nelson Mandela whom he much admired.

I was stunned at how he personified a multitude of the six trigger points mentioned above, which led to my reaching out to him. Note the chain of events in his life. From his childhood experiences in Hell's Kitchen (New York) was born a deep desire to stop crime, blossoming into a resolute lifelong vision to establish an international rule of law to protect the rights of people the world over. This was followed by a series of timely job "rejections" including one from the US paratroopers (WWII)—they said he would go up, not down given his tiny stature. His relentless pursuit to serve his country despite all these setbacks—as the saying goes, it takes courage to not get discouraged—eventually saw him stumbling into the legal field. His innate ability to live in the moment to take on all experiences coupled with a fearlessness to speak the truth regardless of the situation. That is how he was able to harness his emotions while gathering data at concentration camps, with sharp focus on key details to build a rock-solid prosecution case. Combined with his strategic vision, he could also sense the impending historic importance of the war trials towards international justice and the rule of law. His sobering view that war ultimately makes mass murderers out of decent people guided him unerringly into a life of legal jurisprudence for the next fifty years.

And this great Karma Yogi donated generously all his life. Note also how he maintained a true work–life balance, spending premium time individually with his children, asking his family every evening what they had done *that day* for humanity. And how about his marvelous relationship with his wife for seventy-four years and their combined energies in play, how she understood and encouraged him to take on a two-year assignment with a classical comment that *knowing him, he would complete it in one year.*

I had the great honor of a lengthy discussion with Mr. Ferencz, indeed a life-changing event—easily amongst the most integrated luminaries I have met in all my travels. What will always stay with me from this discussion are:

- His compassion—he visited Dr. Otto Ohlendorf (the Einsatzgruppen head who was executed) because he felt sympathetic to the fact that this was a family man with five children. This after Mr. Ferencz witnessed so much as he went through multiple camps while they were being liberated.

- His incredible ability to live in the moment, the hallmark of the detached Karma Yogi. Mr. Ferencz described how he was able to shut off his emotions and stay centered. He was fully cognizant that he was indeed a one-man-army and the responsibility *was his* to collect timely evidence, once it was reasonably safe to enter the camps.
- How he harnessed such a marvelous relationship with his wife over the said period. He mentioned they never once shared a moment of anger. When I asked how this was possible, with his inimitable humor which I had sensed within the first two minutes of the discussion, he stated they probably each realized early on it was best to say "yes dear" to each other!
- His sheer courage—he said he had never felt fear, be it when he had landed at Omaha Beach, engaged in the Battle of the Bulge, crossing the Maginot Line, or going through multiple concentration camps collecting evidence.
- The humility of this great soul—I had been trying to reach him, and he called a nobody like me!

I asked if he had ever felt there was a higher guiding hand positioning him through his series of early job rejections into a life of law. Mr. Ferencz stated that his wife had mentioned this thought, while he in turn had asked God why all of this had happened to him. My response to him was, "Sir, after 25,000 pages of spiritual research, I can give you the answer. Nature played its unseen hand with perfect synchronicity to place you under a precise set of circumstances given only you could handle the extreme nature of events for the timeless benefit of humanity."

The parting message of this great soul to me was to continue his work for the benefit of all humanity. What an honor, and rarely does one come across such an expert on the extremities of the human condition. As it turned out, I visited Auschwitz-Birkenau precisely a month later (January 2020) to pay my respects, and the thought came to mind "Deepak, if you prepare your mind-body-soul to save one tiny life henceforth, now there is a mission."

Last but not the least, I was most impressed by his sense of "witness," that detached overview (see Trigger 5) that I have noted in accomplished people of great wisdom the world over during my travels.

Involution and Evolution of Life in Hinduism

Introduction to Table B-1: Key Concepts of Involution/Evolution

Have you ever come out of a deep thought and said, "Where did the time go?" Well, you are on to something. The objective is to develop that intense concentration leading to meditation and transcendent spiritual growth—from gross to subtle, from instinct to the intellectual to the meditative—by developing "intuition" or primed spiritual guidance to the soul.

Synonymous with theories such as the big bang where scientists advise us that our bodies are comprised of matter originating from stars and supernovas, Hinduism professes the oneness of nature starting with God ("Ishwara") or pure undifferentiated consciousness—the Brahman—progressively working through a process of creation of life called Involution (left-hand side of Table B-1). During my global research and travels, I was continually being asked what exactly "pure undifferentiated consciousness" or "pure consciousness" meant in Hinduism; and it was only after researching other religions that I realized the need for clarification. So let me explain notwithstanding the expanded details later, because redundancy is critical here to effect best understanding. I suggest you *slow down* over the next few pages, until beginning of Step 4, pause timely to absorb, make notes as you go along and reread as necessary.

Let us first commence with three Abrahamic religions: Christianity, Islam and Judaism. All believe that God created the universe which evolved along with its trials and tribulations ending in resurrection, messianic redemption and end judgement, leading to finality by way of heaven, hell and the Promised Land. It is a primary belief (some variation) in one earthly life, followed by a purgatory (debated) to achieve eventual purification and timeless, blissful existence. But Hinduism believes that the universe cyclically patterns in and out of a divine, subtle, unmanifested, infinite consciousness called Brahman comprising the divine spirit (Purusha, male) and the material, creative powers (Prakriti or three-fold gunas, feminine) of God. Initial interaction of these two arms created differentiation and imbalance, causing vibrations (energies) and commencing the creation of the universe from the macro to the micro level, synonymous with scientific theories such as the big bang.

Pursuant to myriad permutations and combinations of creation, the universe appeared progressively in both subtle and gross forms (including combinations) within Brahman. The material powers or threefold gunas like purity (*sattwa*), passion (*rajas*) and dullness (*tamas*) manifested themselves in this resultant creation as both qualities and energies. Examples include qualities of the human mind (recall Table A, Trigger 1), and energies creating subtle and gross forms (like the subtle intellect, the gross physical body, etc.) in the animate and the inanimate.

Let us now introduce a key, new energy called *prana* that supports the above process of creation called Involution. "Universal prana" is that initial, macro-level, subtle substratum energy that is released pursuant to interaction of the two arms of Brahman, and the said energy not only structures and supports but also pervades all vibrational creation in multiple ways. Prana is subservient to God's divine spirit (Purusha) and obeys the rules of Involution but has no consciousness as in tangible life forms. Coming down to manifestation of prana at the micro-level creation, a simplistic analogy would be that it is like fuel for a car, or electricity for a machine without which neither can function. Prana is less spiritual than the divine source emanating out of Brahman but highly spiritual when compared to material atoms.

Prana is therefore a subtle energy force supporting all creation including life. It manifests in the human body in multiple ways including the five specific pranas to drive one's specific Karmic evolution, thereby displaying memory and intelligence. Think of prana obeying the soul and then carrying out the orders on the body. Given that the mind (subset of the soul) literally fabricates the body as its extension, if you were Karmically destined to be a 6'4" rugged personality, prana takes these orders and runs with it to support and organize your body structure from birth through your stages of growth to adulthood.

Hence linking the three-fold energies (gunas) and *prana*, the gunas create while prana supports and structures this creation in the inanimate and animate. Note that all the three gunas are always present in each object. The question that arises is which one prevails. Each object hence ends up with a dominant purity (sattwic), passion (rajasic) or dullness (tamasic) condition faithfully supported by this subservient prana. For example, when the mind is driven by purity, sattwa trait (guna) governs and the resident prana duly supports the mind and body to become pure, flexible, receptive, uplifting. In the inanimate, look at the pure (sattwic) beauty of a rainbow or sunlight where prana will be adaptive and flexible as opposed to the dullness (tamasic) nature of a piece of mud where prana will be heavy and slow-moving to effect related condition. Indeed, mastering control over your prana through specialized breathing techniques (pranayama) will lead to the admiration of envious, aspiring yogis the world over! More to come on prana in the subsequent text.

And the entire universe (vibrational) comprising these aforementioned subtle and gross energies is represented by the resonant sound/mantra called Aum. This realization was worked out by ancient sages. Meditating on Aum links us automatically to the rhythms of nature, with resultant perfected synchronicity of action leading into involuntary transcendence as we progressively get closer to the divine source. Later in the text we shall introduce Tables B-2, Item 9 and C to illustrate that the universe constitutes (commencing at subatomic levels) tiered levels of light energy in ascending order of purity guided by this celestial intelligence, with heaven as the highest with its own divine light. Indeed, many religions the world over exemplify in our daily lives the confluence of divinity with light energies.

The manifested universe, after a predesignated time period or condition where the three-fold energies (gunas) achieve relative balance, then cycles back into the unmanifest condition of the Brahman which retains all the divine knowledge for commencing the next round of creation (see Tables B-2, Item 12.1 and C analyses and insights). Note that these continued cycles individually constitute billions of years. Put another way, the cycle of creation, sustenance and dissolution of the universe goes on cyclically through these periods of time. And Hinduism believes in cyclical life (rebirth) to achieve redemption from our confusion, attachments and cosmic delusion based on our Karmic path. It may be noted that hell is considered a temporary place synonymous with purgatory in other beliefs.

Meditation enables Evolution (right-hand side of Table B-1), precisely the reverse process to Involution. Beginning at the superficial levels of life that we experience, it goes inward, seeking answers until the highest levels possible within manifested Brahman are realized through the stages of preliminary mental housecleaning, concentration, and the progressive levels of meditation to transcendental super conscious experience, "Nirvikalpa Samadhi." This is the highest level achievable on the earth plane, and only then the realized soul comes back here at will (primarily to help others) while continuing its further purification journey through the highest subtle and the causal plane. This will be discussed further under Table C.

One other clarification: Brahman is often confused with being in the unmanifest condition only. But this is true only when the created universe has cycled back into the subtle absolute divine state of pure consciousness. When the universe does exist, Brahman constitutes both the unmanifest (undifferentiated) and the manifest (differentiated, universe/cosmos).

Now let us first go through Table B-1 to initially understand this overview and then follow steps 1 to 8 and related explanations: Involution commencing from pure undifferentiated consciousness working its way (left-hand side of table) down through cosmic ego progressively to individual ego (life) via a combination of gross and subtle elements. Then Evolution comes up on the right-hand side via mental housecleaning, concentration and then meditation through to the superconscious transcendental experience, that is Nirvikalpa Samadhi and beyond.

TABLE B-1

Involution and Evolution of Life in Hinduism

Brahman is twofold: the unmanifest (pure consciousness) and the manifest (cosmos/universe).
Brahman's two creative energies: spiritual (God, Purusha) and material (driving, Prakriti) combine to form Life.

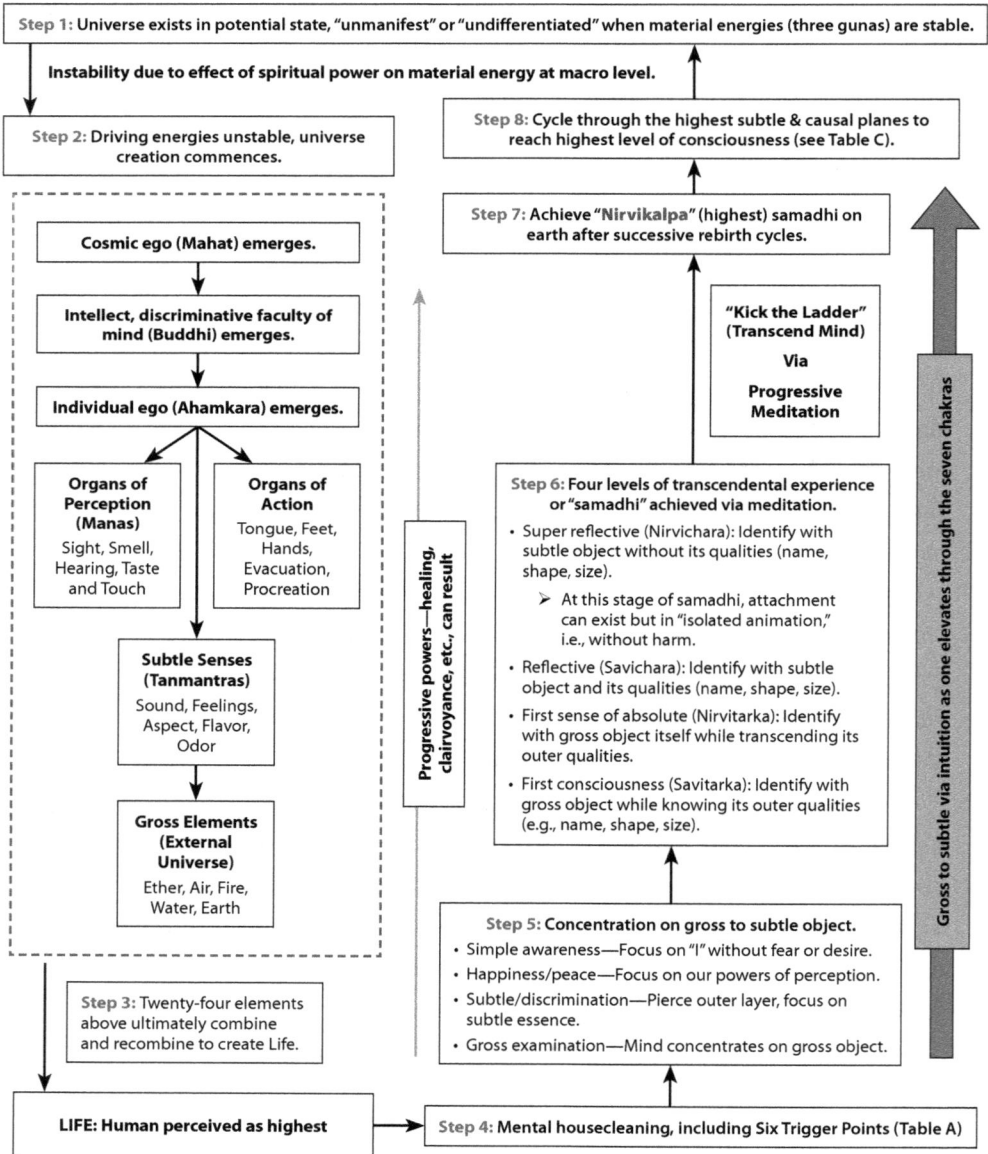

Step 1: Universe exists in potential state, "unmanifest" or "undifferentiated" when material energies (three gunas) are stable.

Instability due to effect of spiritual power on material energy at macro level.

Step 2: Driving energies unstable, universe creation commences.

Step 8: Cycle through the highest subtle & causal planes to reach highest level of consciousness (see Table C).

Step 7: Achieve "**Nirvikalpa**" (highest) samadhi on earth after successive rebirth cycles.

Cosmic ego (Mahat) emerges.

Intellect, discriminative faculty of mind (Buddhi) emerges.

Individual ego (Ahamkara) emerges.

"Kick the Ladder" (Transcend Mind)

Via

Progressive Meditation

Organs of Perception (Manas)	**Organs of Action**
Sight, Smell, Hearing, Taste and Touch	Tongue, Feet, Hands, Evacuation, Procreation

Subtle Senses (Tanmantras)

Sound, Feelings, Aspect, Flavor, Odor

Gross Elements (External Universe)

Ether, Air, Fire, Water, Earth

Progressive powers—healing, clairvoyance, etc., can result

Step 6: Four levels of transcendental experience or "samadhi" achieved via meditation.

- Super reflective (Nirvichara): Identify with subtle object without its qualities (name, shape, size).
  - ➤ At this stage of samadhi, attachment can exist but in "isolated animation," i.e., without harm.
- Reflective (Savichara): Identify with subtle object and its qualities (name, shape, size).
- First sense of absolute (Nirvitarka): Identify with gross object itself while transcending its outer qualities.
- First consciousness (Savitarka): Identify with gross object while knowing its outer qualities (e.g., name, shape, size).

Step 3: Twenty-four elements above ultimately combine and recombine to create Life.

Step 5: Concentration on gross to subtle object.
- Simple awareness—Focus on "I" without fear or desire.
- Happiness/peace—Focus on our powers of perception.
- Subtle/discrimination—Pierce outer layer, focus on subtle essence.
- Gross examination—Mind concentrates on gross object.

Gross to subtle via intuition as one elevates through the seven chakras

LIFE: Human perceived as highest

Step 4: Mental housecleaning, including Six Trigger Points (Table A)

Explanations on Table B-1: Key Concepts of Involution/Evolution

Steps 1 to 3: Universe Creation Leading to Life

Creation is Involution emanating from undifferentiated to differentiated consciousness—macro to micro, cosmic mind to matter and life. And as mentioned, pure undifferentiated consciousness or Brahman is the ultimate, impersonal divine reality from which creation cyclically patterns in and out over certain time periods. Brahman is twofold: the unmanifest condition (pure consciousness) and the manifest (cosmos/universe). And seen from our point of view within creation, God and Brahman are ultimately synonymous. Commencing from intellectual study, our mission is to realize this intuitively, leading us into the meditative experience.

Brahman has twofold, macro-level energies that combine to progressively create the universe leading into life: spiritual (God or Purusha or Ishwara) and material (three forces/gunas or Prakriti or maya). It is important to understand that maya here refers to its powers of creation, as we have mentioned its delusive power earlier. Both are further discussed in Tables B-2, Item 7.1 and C.

Spiritual and Material Energies

Spiritual energies of God are self-explanatory. As for Material energies, these are the three elemental forces (gunas) that act as the driving power for creation: purity (sattwa), passion (rajas) and dullness (tamas). These are fundamental energies working cooperatively to entail creation. Sattwa can be thought of as the vision to be created, tamas acts like a counterbalance behaving as the obstacle, while rajas is the force that removes the obstacle to create this vision. These threefold energies manifest in both gross (physical matter) and subtle forms and, as mentioned earlier, also constitute our three basic mental qualities (purity, passion, dullness) or basic nature seen in all beings. It may be noted that one trait/guna dominates, be it in subtle or gross form of creation.

It is critical to understand that all matter and beings comprise these three basic forces or qualities in varying degrees, the presence of the soul being what differentiates life from matter. We should keep this in mind for our later discussion on interchangeability of objects, powers (psychic, occult) and cycles of cosmic governance (universe cycling in and out of Brahman). For now, suffice it to say that these three qualities/forces are elemental to all creation, inanimate or otherwise.

Simply put, when these three forces (gunas) are undisturbed and in perfect balance, we have pure undifferentiated consciousness and the universe exists in a potential state (unmanifest). Note that the word *consciousness* is often used by yoga practitioners and spiritualists alike. And when these three forces are in imbalance, creation/recreation of the universe occurs (manifest) through multiple permutations and combinations. It may also be noted that these two states are referred to as higher (undifferentiated) and lower (differentiated) Prakriti respectively. You will also come across related terms like Maha-Prakriti, Para-Prakriti and Apara-Prakriti in other literature to define these highest (undifferentiated) to the manifested pure and impure states respectively, both subtle and gross in decreasing order of divinity (purity). An additional point to note is that Prakriti is also used in Hindu philosophy to represent the prime material powers or energies (gunas) of the universe themselves leading to such creation.

So what causes imbalance. A simple example: just as the soul infuses life into a human body, at a macro level the initial interaction of spiritual energy (Purusha) and material powers (Prakriti/the threefold gunas) creates imbalance with these three forces/gunas—pure, illuminative (sattwa), creative, dynamic (rajas) and dense, inactive (tamas) leading to consequent permutations and combinations promoting Involution (left-hand side of Table B-1). The material rajas energy is pulled in opposite directions by these opposing sattwa and tamas energies, and ultimately the stronger prevails, pulling creation in that direction. It may be noted that Prakriti is considered to be feminine, symbolic with creative energy, whereas Purusha is masculine energy constituting the Self giving life to that which is primal and created.

At the human level, it is the calculated imbalance of these fundamental forces promulgating continued change and evolution that controls our life cycle from the birth of a baby to its evolution as an adult driven by Karmic forces and our free will, leading to related purity of our mind. Similarly, this is the process of creation, sustenance and dissolution of a seed to a flower or a full-grown tree and of its eventual return to Mother Nature. This will be explained further while discussing prana, the subtle energy force.

Here comes a delightful twist. Given that pure undifferentiated conscious-ness/the Brahman is universal, its essence is captured in "the Self" or "atman" (also referred to as Purusha), which is the innermost reality of any being (human or other) in its purest form, the highest witness within us. Hence, in all living beings the experiencer is ultimately the same Self or Purusha but due to ignorance (ego) we do not realize this.

Continuing on, the progressive stages of Involution, thanks to the imbalance of the three forces/gunas leading to initial creation (lower Prakriti) from the macro to the micro levels, are as follows:

- Cosmic ego/"mahat" or first stage of initial differentiation,
- Discriminative mind faculty/"buddhi" comes next and initial identification and segregation of external factors including reactions take place,
- Next comes our well-known ego/"ahamkara"—which claims ownership of these initial inputs.

From the ego sense emerge three streams of creation:

- Our five subtle Senses/"tanmantras"—the inner essence of sound, feelings (touch), aspect (form), flavor (taste) and odor. These subtle elements then combine/recombine to produce five gross elements (external universe) in progressive order: space (ether), air, fire, water and earth.
- The reception faculty/"manas"—five perception powers: hearing, sight, smell, taste and touch.
- Five action organs: tongue, feet, hands, evacuation and procreation.

Let us look at an example of creation linkage within the ego sense, that is, from subtle senses to gross elements to reception facility to organs of action. Take ether. This gross element emerges from its unmanifested form (inner essence) of sound which is the primal space from which vibration emerges long before it translates to tangible sound in the ear (our reception facility), ultimately leading to tongue (voice) as the designated organ of action. Consequently, when loss of ether takes place within our bodies, we note downstream difficulties with speech and hearing.

However, marginal offsets may occur. For example, if one is born deaf, other senses are strengthened. Two additional points may be noted: (1) there is no swapping around of duties; for example, the eyes cannot hear, the ears cannot see, and (2) the tongue is both an organ of reception (taste) and of action (voice).

Coming back to creation, ultimately the permutations and combinations of the twenty-four elements aforementioned combine and recombine to create nature and life as we know them. As mentioned earlier, "universal prana" is released to support and structure the aforementioned vibrational creation when the spiritual and material forces of Purusha and Prakriti (gunas) interact, manifesting as specific creation in both inanimate and animate objects. Prana in human beings manifests in multiple ways as a subset of our subtle body (mind), permeating and sustaining all aspects of our existence as individual beings and materially driving our Karmic development through our multiple life stages starting from birth. Examples include directional or upward prana (breathing in), location-based or chakras, and the fivefold specific pranas for specific actions (digestion, excretion, etc.) to sustain life. One may survive with a malfunctioning organ, but when specific prana ultimately leaves, life ceases to exist. More about this follows in discussions on Table C later in the text.

Hence, macro-level (universal) prana comes as the subtle, highly spiritual yet subservient, link to the highest spiritual realm (Purusha), structuring and sustaining all forms of material creation (Prakriti), and it is resident in every atom and all forms (animate, inanimate) of the universe. It is cumulatively an expression of vibrational energy represented by Aum.

Step 4: Mental Housecleaning (Six Trigger Points in Table A)

This has been discussed at length (Table A), hence only brief comments are provided here. Given that the universe exists for us to evolve and become liberated, we stand united notwithstanding our beliefs in cyclical life patterns or otherwise. Higher knowledge within us shines through once impurities from the mind are eliminated. However, this is often precluded because we continually repeat the same mistakes and fruitless experiences driven by our false impressions. We must know that no good effort is in vain, and truth lies in every trivial experience leading us towards wider spiritual knowledge.

Let us also briefly mention impartial love, something our great sages were able to accomplish. The realized soul shifts his outlook from the "I" to a "We" that transcends the immediate domain (example family) given that he sees the integrated, interconnected nature of all. Hence they are able to naturally project that certain sense of detachment, and are sometimes being misconstrued as indifferent. Most of us however are unable to achieve the same. Let us examine a normal husband–wife relationship. Our love for the other is possessive, hence emotional, and we identify the marvelous qualities as specific to our spouse, thus establishing them as individual—compounded further by how our ego reacts to them. The realized being on the other hand sees these qualities as common to all!

And as our awareness grows and we understand our own struggles to spiritually evolve, we begin to also see the challenges others are facing—the Self struggling to come out. We must stay in our determined course to transcend and know that there will be ups and downs, and, on the lighter side, we may even have to hear comments from others about how we have changed in a manner they do not understand! Moderation and self-control are key, and we must avoid extreme austerity to the point of self-punishment. Also, have we ever wondered why we are so good at helping others but cannot admit our own flaws? It is critical to introspect on where we are spiritually—the "real me" versus the "perfect me," the ego versus the Self. We should realize that one's spiritual journey commences from the former to grow in incremental steps to preclude disappointment. While we sense our inherent divinity, we must admit that our ego leads us down the vicious cycle of continued flaws. Mistakes duly acknowledged propel growth, and we should analyze them intensely as a great learning tool. Indeed they are all borne out of an innate desire for happiness, albeit misguided. And we should remain intensely cognizant that others are also similarly searching!

Steps 5 and 6: Concentration, Meditation and Transcendent Levels ("Samadhi")

We have now gone past initial preparation and are entering the stages of concentration and meditation which can only be through commitment and relentless dedication. Agitations of the mind are silenced by focusing it towards the superconscious experience.

Concentration is the preliminary path. Whilst many techniques have been developed, in general there are four stages leading us from the gross (outer) into the subtle (inner) experiences:

- *Gross Examination:* The mind analyzes all outer aspects, both positive and negative, of the object of study (for example, physical body of person), including a holistic 360-degree view, until perfect focus is achieved on the outer characteristics.
- *Subtle/Discrimination:* The mind now gets past the outer layer and focuses on the subtle, inner characteristics elemental to the object itself. Our sense of awareness begins to accelerate as it transcends or looks through the mind and its limitations and ignorance.
- *Happiness and Peace:* Herein commence our steps to true realization. We concentrate upon our underlying powers of perception, gain bliss by sampling and understanding these inherent abilities of the mind which are beyond the analytical and cognitive.
- *Simple Awareness:* We begin to achieve identity with the object of study itself. By now we have gained that introspective, divine vision, having achieved control over the mind in all its fluctuations (both good and bad). We now look directly at the mind and ego as the object of concentration itself, and begin to understand the true meaning of self-awareness without fear or desire. We are now at the foothills of meditation, with the ability to focus on consciousness itself, with true non-attachment, the latter being integral to achieving realization.

As concentration is within the bounds of lower creation (differentiated Prakriti), it is subject to the lure of misuse for selfish gains. Spirituality professes that to thoroughly understand the inner structure and nature of an object is to gain power over the same. We can develop extraordinary abilities including performing healings, telepathy, past life regressions, etc. Purity of our intent is key when utilizing these newfound powers to preclude the possibility of staying trapped in the vicious cycle of desires. We hear many stories of fallen angels and earthly spirits who still have to work out their Karma, given that their enticing powers lead them astray for personal gains and thus keeping them trapped within the lower realms of nature.

Speaking of earthly spirits, an extension of this overall belief inevitably leads us to a discussion on ghosts. The theory about their existence in an interim state due to unfulfilled Karma is widely prevalent, and even considered an extension of purgatory. Common naming include (but are not limited to) restless spirit, wraith and poltergeist in Christianity; *ruaḥ tezazit* and *dybbuk* in Judaism; hungry ghosts and *yakshas* (nature spirit) in Buddhism; *bhoot, vetalas* and *pishachas* in Hinduism; *jinns, ghouls, ruh* and *nafs* in Islam—the list is endless.

Living amongst us in both geographical and dimensional zones, they are generally cast in a more negative light, doubtless because of their challenging circumstances. These include possessions of spiritually vulnerable humans, residing near graves, haunting houses due to strong resident (unresolved) attractive energies, causing diseases, possessing great knowledge to promote illusion and delusion. However, on the flip side they are known to be benign, even helpful spirits aiding us in our journey. And the stronger their subtle Karmic signature (strength), the more likely one can experience them aided by one's own level of awareness.

Reasons for their presence may be attributed to a variety of causes including untimely passing before completing predesignated number of breaths due to accidental or other reasons resulting in unresolved issues, strong Karmic affinity to their circumstances, or simply the failure of their loved ones to assure smooth passing via proper funerals. Belief in ghosts is prevalent since the time of ancient civilizations and original religions. For example, Jesus had to convince his disciples that he was not a ghost, the Hebrew Bible makes references to ghosts, the Egyptians in their Book of the Dead mention funerary practices, the writings of the Greek philosopher Homer (*Iliad* and *Odyssey*) refer to them. Also supernatural experiences and dream sequences within the "Realm of Dominion" or *Al-Malakut* between the material and the spiritual realms in Islamic belief contain encounters with jinns, etc.

Appearance is indelibly linked to subtle body material (soul)—translucent, analogous to one's breath in cold climes. An interesting side note, the Bible depicts the first man Adam as being made from the dust of the earth and breath of God. Note also that extreme representation of ghosts as powerful demonic entities is heavily weighted with the gates of hell subservient to the devil (see Table B-2, Item 7). A great deal of effort is expended by ghost chasers and by scientific experimenters yielding readings of electromagnetic variations and flickering light energies; spirit mediums (including seance, Ouija boards) and the much debated exorcists have also turned their efforts to contact and work with them into a semi-professional vocation.

Indeed, many religions pay homage and pray for the well-being of ghosts. Practices also extend to ancestral and noble spirits. Examples include the Buddhist and Taoist Hungry Ghost festival, Qingming Festival and Double Ninth Festival, Ghost Dance (native American) and shamanic practices to invite, interact with and venerate these souls. Christianity celebrates All Souls Day paying respects to the departed including saints, Christian martyrs and the all-faithful. Religious practices and funeral rites fervently aided by members of religious orders the world over are utilized to bring peace to newly departed souls to preclude the possibility of creating eternal suffering for them. Such practices vary globally ranging from parades, cremation and scattering of ashes (Hinduism) in holy waters to progressive elimination of all attachments (physical and mental) between the departed and the loved ones, to the process of consecrated burial (Christianity), sky burial in Tibetan Buddhism, water-related burials in many countries, etc. Personal possessions are often buried with the cleansed body duly clothed in colors associated with knowledge and purity to aid the soul in his journey, including extended prayer practices to preclude any lingering specific prana energies.

Coming back to concentration and the derivative powers that may result, it is imperative that we treat these as a by-product of progressive enlightenment and do not get attached to them for personal gains. Regarding the time needed to achieve this highest rung of concentration, while it is said that it can take a lifetime or many lifetimes (depending upon one's belief) for most, this is contingent upon your level of spirituality. Ancient scriptures prescribe some interesting techniques to master concentration. I was particularly fascinated by one method where one focuses on the persona of a god, a prophet or a sage like Jesus Christ, Lord Krishna, Lord Buddha, Lord Rama, Prophet Muhammad, Sage Shankaracharya, Swami Chinmayananda, the Dalai Lama, Ramana Maharshi. Try to imagine how would it change you having their outlook on life.

Next comes meditation leading into the higher levels of transcendental experience or samadhi. Achieving the highest levels of concentration brings the ability to focus on consciousness itself. Meditation is uninterrupted concentration in action—the fluctuations of the mind progressively ceasing leading to the achievement of complete identity with the object of focus. Meditation commences with the gross qualities, then with the subtle, and ultimately transcends and merges impersonally with pure consciousness itself. These are called progressive transcendental states or samadhi.

Table B-1 shows five levels of transcendental experience or samadhi within our realm (the earth plane): Savitarka, Nirvitarka, Savichara, Nirvichara (these also go by differing names), and the highest of all, the Nirvikalpa Samadhi. The first four Samadhis are conditional but progressive as we transcend our attachments, desires and the last vestiges of mental impressions. As a simplistic example of levels achieved, let us take meditating on the universe itself commencing from the gross to the subtle. Stages of meditation go from consciously understanding its name and gross qualities (space and time) while treating it as separate from our being to progressively merging with it with a growing understanding that the universe is conscious and contemplating itself. Next steps include transcending space and time, shape of the universe (stars, galaxies) and merging with pure energy itself on to cosmic consciousness.

Liberation is fully achievable provided one stays the course, as focus shifts from the attached to the detached. Table B-1 (Step 6) outlines the focus of the first two samadhis (Savitarka and Nirvitarka) on gross objects, moving progressively on to its subtle aspects in Savichara and Nirvichara Samadhi. Once this latter level is achieved, all our attachments have been transcended, and concerted effort is now replaced by the divine rhythms of the universe involuntarily pushing us towards Nirvikalpa Samadhi.

Step 7: Attainment of Nirvikalpa Samadhi

Given the above, let us now try and imagine what intense effort it takes to achieve this highest state of detached, impersonal union on the earth plane by way of Nirvikalpa Samadhi. We have achieved this state where attachment for a personal god translates into an impersonal love, given the realization that God is synonymous with Brahman itself. We experience endless, involuntary bliss despite all the daily distractions. We have transcended any concept of space, time and limiting condition while perceiving the primal nature of the universe.

Step 8: The Aftermath of the Highest Level of Achievement

Given this level of achievement on the earth plane, the sage now embarks on his journey between the highest subtle and the causal plane to ultimately merge into the sea of causal cosmos (see Table C later in the text). He can also, at will, travel back and forth between the earth and these higher (subtle, causal) planes to help others in need (note analogous beliefs in other religions in the following Table B-2, Item 3). And the subtlest understanding of the nature of the Brahman itself has now been achieved.

Additional Notes on Table B-1

Before we delve into two final topics with respect to Table B-1—the occult centers (chakras) and powers—it must be mentioned that there are many methodologies to achieving realization. For example, modern-day yoga practices have evolved in varying degrees from the Yoga Sutras, one of the sixfold philosophies of Hinduism developed by Sage Patanjali (circa second century BC). The sage's teachings are structured into an eightfold path constituting refraining from evil thoughts and acts (*yama*), multiple observances to promote purity (*niyama*), appropriate body posture (*asana*) to enable proper focus and meditation, control of our subtle life energy or *prana* through *pranayama*, withdrawal from sense objects (*pratyahara*), aforementioned practices of concentration (*dharana*) and meditation (*dhyana*), leading into transcendental experience (samadhi) to ultimately achieve impersonal union with pure consciousness. Consequently, yoga practitioners (yogis) the world over have inevitably come across this philosophy in varying degrees as part of structured yoga teachings (hatha yoga, ashtanga yoga, etc.) to improve oneself mentally, physically and spiritually.

Let us examine Buddhism where you will immediately note similar analogy to the aforementioned. Its philosophical principles are known as the Four Noble

Truths: nature of suffering, their origins, cessation, and the path to cessation of suffering. It promotes the noble eightfold path to achieve Nirvana or escape from suffering—taking the path of right view, speech, thought, behavior, livelihood, effort, mindfulness and concentration. Note however that Buddhism does not believe in the existence of an overall creator, God. Instead it teaches us that the universe emerges out of a primordial state of pure infinite knowledge called *sunyata* (emptiness) or *tathata* (thatness or true state of things). While these terms are used interchangeably in some sects, note that sunyata refers to the doctrine that phenomena are devoid of an immutable or determinate intrinsic nature. It is often regarded as a means of gaining an intuition of ultimate reality. Tathata is the ultimate nature of all things as expressed in phenomena but inexpressible in language. This creation is due to a chain of related events called dependent origination which are impermanent with no beginning and no end, with the cycle of life and creation eventually repeating (samsara). The goal of Buddhism is to transcend samsara by achieving nirvana via attainment of Buddhahood, which is a state free of all disturbing emotions and obstructions to knowledge.

How about more examples of achieving realization? These include, but are not limited to, deep contemplation and methodical analysis, dedicated humanity service, single-minded devotion to God, tremendous powers of concentration, practicing mantras, and complete control over desires. Indeed there are many amongst us who do not advertise their level of transcendence, nor have they even heard of words like "yogi." The point is that one must question, analyze, leave nothing to chance, and find one's own distinct rhythm!

Occult Centers (Chakras) and Powers

Many belief systems generally acknowledge seven centers of consciousness in the human body called chakras or light lotuses that channel our subtle life energy also known as prana in Hinduism, "Qi" or "chi" in Buddhism and other oriental beliefs, in ascending order of purity as follows: coccygeal, sacral, lumbar, dorsal, cervical, medullary, and the *thousand-petaled lotus of light*.

Seventh Chakra	**Crown** "Sahasrara"	Located at the top of the head; represents enlightenment, cosmic consciousness; governing element: consciousness
Sixth Chakra	**Third Eye** "Ajna"	Located at the center of the forehead; represents intuition, psychic abilities, imagination; governing element: light
Fifth Chakra	**Throat** "Vishuddha"	Located at the center of the neck; represents healing, communication; governing element: ether
Fourth Chakra	**Heart** "Anahata"	Located at the center of the chest; represents hope, love; governing element: air
Third Chakra	**Navel** "Manipura"	Located below the chest; represents energy, desire, will power; governing element: fire
Second Chakra	**Sacral** "Svadhisthana"	Located below the navel; represents emotional instincts, sexuality; governing element: water
First Chakra	**Root** "Muladhara"	Located at the base of the spine; represents survival and safety instincts; governing element: earth

What is lesser known is that there are in fact 112–114 chakras (two outside the body) arranged into these seven dimensions (the seven chakras) serving as major junction points within our cumulative psychic energetic system constituting a network of about 72,000 pathways (psychic nerves) which serve as the subtle guiding link to our physical nervous system. Known as *nadis* or "meridians," also felt in our hands and feet (the minor chakras), these pathways constitute energy flow coming from three basic channels in the spinal column: the left called *ida* which is introverted, feminine, intuitive; the right called *pingala* which is extroverted, masculine, logical; and the central channel *sushumna*. The ida and pingala control all the mental and vital processes, respectively, the stronger characteristic (masculine or feminine) prevailing upon our being and character.

This naturally leans into the logical conclusion that balancing the characteristics of the ida and pingala is key to the building of an effective and spiritual life to ultimately open up the main spiritual channel sushumna to achieve realization, attained only by a small minority. Most of us live (and die) in the ida and pingala while dealing with their effects on our personality and health, consequently leaving the central space sushumna untouched. Our subtle life energy, prana, is also called *kundalini* energy, which is compressed and coiled, sits at the base of the spine in this central space awaiting its release—in turn dependent upon our level of spirituality through concerted, aforementioned practices. Once this central sushumna channel is opened up, this leads to an all-enveloping, eternally blissful, spiritual experience as the released kundalini energy strikes the chakra centers causing progressive degrees of enlightenment. It is said that one may also inadvertently release a small vestige of this amazing power accidentally, the experience of releasing the kundalini energy transcends all other spiritual experiences known to man.

Our level of consciousness varies over our lifespan(s). When the mind, through conscious choices (free will), consistently resides in:

- the three lower chakras, one is largely involved in the material aspects of life, with likely minimal spiritual ambitions;
- the fourth, the Heart (Anahata) chakra, true initial awakening occurs, with return to the lower centers now precluded;
- the fifth, the Throat (Vishuddha) chakra, the mind becomes free of ignorance, and focus on God is all-enveloping;
- the sixth, the Third-Eye or forehead (Ajna) chakra, experiences directly the vision of God continuously, with minimal ego left;
- the seventh, the Crown (Sahasrara) chakra, transcendental experience "level(s) of samadhi" are achieved. This seventh center or the thousand-petaled lotus is the throne of infinite consciousness. The realized soul intuitively senses the creator in this state of divine consciousness; he now routinely exhibits outward habits such as sleeplessness, breathlessness, lack of heartbeat and unblinking eyes in utter meditation and divine peace.

Throughout my twelve-year research, the interconnectedness of it all has never ceased to amaze me, as I stumbled from one link into another. Take for example the original elements of creation, the chakras, body constitution, astrology and energy healing, including holistic practices and aids. Given that the subtle and gross elements of creation (Table B-1) are all interlinked, each chakra constitutes varying proportions of these creation energies with a consequent governing element and is integrally linked with all aspects of our being, both physical and spiritual. Put another way, each of the five original elements of creation (ether, air, fire, water and earth) exists in each chakra, and the variant subtle vibrational frequencies of each chakra exhibiting different colors give rise to a governing element with distinct characteristics. For example, earth element governs the Root (Muladhara) chakra, water governs Sacral (Svadhisthana), fire is for Navel (Manipura), air for Heart (Anahata), ether for Throat (Vishuddha); each affecting the body in a certain way resulting in associated body patterns and reflexes.

Hence, for those of us operating primarily from the Root (Muladhara) or first chakra with earth element governing are coined as "earthy" types who tend to exhibit strong materialistic needs, are likely to have strong body structures, and exhibit great courage, rage and passion, complete with a related aura or subtle body essence that we sense. Conversely, those who learn to consistently operate from the Throat (Vishuddha) or fifth chakra with ether as the governing element tend to be deeply spiritual, capable of great communication skills and humility, of slender build with thin bone structure. Note that each chakra exhibits both positive and negative qualities. These classifications have also led to related categorization links into astrological signs, for example Aquarius with Heart (Anahata) chakra, Leo with Navel (Manipura) chakra and so on.

Pairing of the chakras is also done with colors. As our emotions change, so do resultant colors, indicating our emotional, spiritual and physical conditioning at any given time. This in turn links into healing aids such as crystals, gemstones, etc., whose vibrational frequencies emanate colors resonating with the chakras, and whose proximity (these are routinely carried in one's clothing and/or kept at home) focuses healing energy to unblock negative energies accumulated in specific parts of the body. Note that external factors such as stress, abuse and others—all adversely impact our psychic energetic system balance in turn leading into a range of negative impacts such as disease, discomfort, mental disorders, etc., thus necessitating the need to look after ourselves in holistic fashion.

And if this is a bit of a mouthful to swallow, how about relating ancient (over 5,000 years old) diet and holistic healing practices to the above? For example, the holistic medical science of Ayurveda also categorizes the human body and our individual personalities stemming from a unique combination of the same five elements—ether, air, water, fire and earth into three physical constitutions or "doshas," namely, (1) Vata dosha with governing elements ether and air, (2) Pitta dosha with fire and water governing, and (3) Kapha dosha with water and earth governing. The aim of Ayurveda is to balance the impact of our threefold qualities of the three gunas comprising purity (sattwa), passion (rajas) and dullness (tamas) on these doshas via holistic herbs and medications to eliminate diseases by promoting ideal balance of mind, body and soul.

And along with the oft-quoted prana which is considered as the primary essence of Vata dosha (ether, air governing), given its links to breathing (pranayama) which also manifests and functions in all aspects of our being, Ayurveda additionally discusses the energies related to prana associated with rebalancing our physical bodies and subtle chakra energies. These energies are called *ojas* related to heart organ, vitality, immunity, essence of Kapha dosha; and *tejas* related to metabolism, digestion, courage, inner glow, essence of Pitta dosha. Cumulatively, the critical balance of prana, ojas and tejas work hand in hand to achieve our ideal holistic existence. Ayurveda will be discussed further later under Table C.

Powers and Self-Restraint

We have all heard of people possessing the ability to heal others, being capable of telepathy, performing regressions, including other extraordinary capabilities that people possess from a young age or suddenly develop. These abilities are in fact a natural by-product of growing spirituality, and should be treated as such only. One comes to understand that there is a lot more to the mind than just analytical and intellectual abilities, thanks to our combined efforts (process called *samyama*) in concentration, meditation (and equivalent practices) and consequent realization (samadhi) to understand the true nature of the universe.

Furthermore, Table B-1 defines that any object comprises the three forces (gunas) in varying combinations (gross, subtle); and while one dominates, this relationship varies leading to a consequent change of the object over time. Take for example the moods in the evolution of a human being. The soul retains its basic nature varied by the change in the leading trait/guna. While evolution knowledge is never lost, sometimes purity (sattwa) leads, sometimes passion (rajas), and our moods also vary governed by the phases of the day, cumulatively leading to a change in body and mind over time. Examples of evolution were clearly noted at the Galapagos Islands (Ecuador) where life adjusted based upon differing circumstances at the multiple islands, and a concerted study of this contributed to Darwin's theory of evolution by natural selection.

Consequently, it follows that any object can change into another thanks to the variant combination of the three traits/gunas. To understand the microcosmic nature of matter is to ultimately gain power over it. Sages understand this and through their tremendous powers of concentration and meditation can rearrange these subatomic energies to change one object into another, something we describe as a miracle. However, some people may temporarily experience or sense powers under the influence of alcohol and drugs, but the physical and mental downsides are permanent.

Note also the marvelous analogy with quantum mechanics, the study of minutest particles and energies such as atoms, electrons and protons, quarks and photons, etc. Through science we know they are in continuous motion with negligible to no mass or structure exhibiting varying speeds, position and color. These basic energies are common to all matter, both inanimate and living. And experiments conducted studying electrons indicate they change their patterns of movement between waves and particles, leading to some interesting conclusions that thoughts can influence the behavior of matter. Experiments on time have also yielded some fascinating results indicating that it functions in ways contrary to traditional beliefs. Results of certain experiments have led to findings that photons, which are heated packets of energy elemental to light, can travel through time (both past and future) including interaction with a previous state or coexisting in multiple locations with other photons. This opens up theories on parallel existence and parallel universes.

Coming back to spirituality, Sage Patanjali quoted some marvelous examples of these powers. For example, when focusing on every moment in time including their sequence, the sage transcends by realizing the impermanent, changing nature of the universe in all of his experiences, devoid of memory of past pain and perceived future suffering. We may find this hard to swallow, but indeed there are sages amongst us who can pierce through the dimensions of time (transitory) to perceive the true state of one's existence in totality—not the way we perceive another in present time—but through their life cycles, past present and future including as an infant, child, adult and in old age, all at once.

Time has indeed been proven through science as being relative, further discussed later in Table C. And on transcending time, there are many lesser examples in daily life. A captured soldier during the Gulf War (1991) was able to limit pain to the extent he could during torture by focusing on each individual moment in time. A recent joint interfaith discussion on religions and spirituality also discussed methods for the sick to transcend pain. These processes however require a great deal of forethought and preparatory contemplation.

Let us discuss some further examples from Sage Patanjali. When focused on the sound of a word and its meaning and effect, one obtains an understanding of all sounds produced by all life irrespective of species. It may be noted that there are many derivative examples of people communicating with animals, in particular those who live close to nature. How about past life regressions? These are executed by focusing on previous thought waves, given that all of the knowledge in this universe is retained in subtle form. And when focusing on friendliness, one develops the power of becoming a beacon of hope, love and joy to all, alleviating the stress of others. And about strength, there are many examples of sages focusing upon the incredible power of an animal, thereby acquiring the same power. Abstaining from desires also provides similar results. Many ancient martial arts are based upon gaining spiritual energy by abstaining from sexual activity, which draws upon our limited energy, to achieve synchronicity and perfected mind–body technique. On sexual activity, it may be noted that we are dealing with developed instinct, so don't try to force it, recall the known facts of fallen souls abusing their powers. Once you are developed spiritually enough, it naturally draws you away from sense and bodily desires, thus diminishing its grip over the mind. Similarly, abstaining from greed and want for possessions may even result in the opposite! Donate without expectation, and a feeling of spiritual wealth emanates and empowers you as you harness these subliminal, resident energies for the benefit of others.

Hence, as a consequence of the aforementioned, the sage or the yogi gets into synchronicity (and control) with the laws of nature in perfect mind–body harmony. And one who treats these powers as a by-product with purity and non-attachment (this being key) in mind is said to be liberated—now on the sure path to the highest realms of knowledge the universe has to offer.

Concluding Summary on Tables A and B-1

Let us now summarize and take stock of where we currently are, having worked through Tables A and B-1. It is all about conscious choices whether we want to stay in lower nature or differentiated Prakriti or let go these bonds and leap into a higher realm. We went through initial mental housecleaning and then on to multiple methodologies such as concentration and meditation to transcend the mind, progressively destroying attachment, delusion and suffering. Given our integral knowledge on the interchangeability of the three gunas and their interplay with prana, we can now control energies at will. Common feats include levitation, transmutation and teleportation, see Table B-2, Item 11 and C for further details. We then ultimately unite with our resident divinity, that essence (Self/Atman) of pure consciousness or sublime knowledge in the universe. We sense the interconnectedness of all, and that our existence in the earth plane is now voluntary, coming back at will to help others. We have now reached the highest level of achievable transcendental experience—Nirvikalpa Samadhi—on the earth plane leading a life of divinity, bliss and peace in pure meditation. The universe now presents no secrets to us, and we are well on the way to the next ascension planes (subtle, subtler, causal) discussed under Table C. What a wonderful feeling to be a sage! But before we get into the said discussion in Table C, let us pause to review a structural analysis of some of the world's major religions in Table B-2.

Structural Analysis—Hinduism, Christianity, Islam, Buddhism and Judaism

Introduction to the Key Structural Tenets for the Five-Religion Analysis

What started as an intended three pages on the structural tenets of five religions grew into a consolidated set of cool notes, through research and timely help from strangers. Men of great experience and wisdom—a rabbi, a high Buddhist practitioner, a Christian minister, a swami and an Islamic scholar who showed up just when I needed the help (talk about synchronicity of events!). For example, the Islamic scholar surfaced on the day I decided I had reached the end of my tether on Islam research; I then ran into the Buddhist practitioner and the rabbi on a flight to Chile just as I was commencing my research on Buddhism and Judaism.

I had picked these religions out of sheer curiosity, in particular Judaism, given my near-total ignorance of it. As it turns out, these five cumulatively constitute a following of more than 80 percent of global population, but the reach is wider much to my progressive amazement, given the interconnectedness of it all. Ultimately, I ran into more than a dozen religions including localized geographical offshoots via interactive research running into thousands of pages, also taking into account evolving religions such as New Age, the Baha'i Faith, etc. For example, the Baha'i Faith promotes the integrated nature and message of world religions, has no clergy, with one God who is inaccessible, creating an eternal universe without beginning or end. Given the enormous complexity of this effort, I ultimately incorporated a hybrid version of my research and relatively unedited inputs received from the experts aforementioned. The consequent text herein may be personal, constituting a wider set of beliefs, differing—or even erroneous—from the point of view of others, but that was not the point of this structural analysis. Achieving a 100 percent accurate version that all may agree upon is a bridge too far, so the intent was to attempt a bird's-eye view with references to larger trends, differences and similarities, just to let it all hang out and see what emerges. Note that the length of text in each of the boxes/categories in the following table varies depending upon the complexity and breadth of the subject matter.

The results are staggering, constituting an amalgamation of the spiritual thoughts behind these religions. All accept that this world is not our permanent home, there is suffering, bondage here; so the search is on to find solutions for eternal joy devoid of fear. Note the relative confluence on majority of the points, yet some key differences exist, for example, some religions commenced from a personality and others from a system, some believe in a single but others in multiple life cycles. But all are unified by the underlying spiritual principle of ascending through multiple levels of purity to a personal or impersonal union with a higher power or energy level. Examples of other striking commonalities (partial or otherwise) include Abraham being revered (in differing degrees) in Christianity, Islam and Judaism; the belief in nature; the reverence to light energies, the laws of action and reaction and so on. And to talk about the sheer knowledge of our sages—for example, Hinduism, from my humble viewpoint, represents an engineered study of how the universe operates including the confluence into science. Ultimately, all of our gods, prophets and sages—be it Jesus Christ, Lord Krishna, Prophet Muhammad, Gautama Buddha, Moses—all understood the universal laws of nature and creation, and all stood unified in their advice to us to go within ourselves to find answers. Even a cursory glance offers that all religions dictate a finer doctrine or way of living—call it spiritual, agnostic, atheist, religious or by any other name. Cumulatively, temples, churches, mosques, synagogues and monasteries represent the symbolic, harmonious confluence of divine energies and the created universe (gross, subtle planes) in perfect synchronicity, serving as a source of inspiration for the community, while preserving spiritual and religious traditions, interconnectedness and our communion with nature.

Our sincere hope is that Table B-2 as a reference guide effects a step change for those interested in theology to accelerate their personal journey to become a spiritual billionaire! And while someone may not have a specific belief, they can actively question, introspect, and strive to be the best possible person they can be. We avoided comparing the timing (emergence) of these doctrines, which can make for intense debates. And given the variations in terminology (example, the mantra AUM or OM) used by subgroups within each religion, and the multiple interpretations of text/original teachings through the ages, our humblest apologies to anyone who may justifiably interpret this information differently.

Enjoy!

1. Law of Karma: Free Will and Destiny

1.1 Hinduism: Law of Karma/Free Will and Destiny

It is all about action/reaction and moral responsibility. First, since every action has a reaction, this results in impacts (destiny), both positive and negative, via astrological influences in our current or future lives (births). Second, our ego (also body) represents our cumulative Karmic balance born and thrust into our surroundings, manifesting as desires, fears and positive traits; and it is only at this human level that we fully connect with our true nature to achieve liberation. Third, Hinduism mentions certain predetermined "cosmic governance" cyclical time periods (each cycle spanning billions of years) with guiding energies imposed upon us that influence our thinking patterns (see Item 12.1 below and discussion on Table C for details). Fourth, add our current choices (free will) into the mix. Spiritual progress is then cumulatively regulated by how we deal with our present desires plus the impacts of our past Karma through astrological influences or detached positive, negative radiations impacting our being in our current environment.

Hence, our immediate moment of existence constitutes destiny, with free will to make future choices.

1.2 Christianity: Law of Karma/Free Will and Destiny

"Don't be deceived. God is not mocked, for whatever a man sows, that he will also reap."[1]

The larger plan (will) of God calls upon us to persevere through the hybrid set of universe conditions including our intentional acts, some predefined events and our ultimate fate. Actions in our single allocated lifetime determine consequences in the current or the afterlife. The latter includes heaven, hell and purgatory (debated) with a chance to redeem. Predefined events may also include challenging circumstances through which we stay resolute to continue to fulfill God's will by promoting love and compassion for all beings, aided timely by the benefit of God's grace (gift, unequivocal favor not earned), given his son Jesus Christ's sacrifice on the Cross for all mankind. And while destiny is a debated subject—note concepts of double predestination, conditional election, middle knowledge and other—it is generally accepted that salvation is offered to all conditional upon their choices. Note that variations in interpretation of destiny and free will including God's prescience and consequent disposition exist across the umbrella of Abrahamic religions.

1.3 Islam: Law of Karma/Free Will and Destiny

Emphasis is on religious practices following the five pillars of Islam and the divine "Sharia" laws (see Item 2.3 below) as core acts of worship. The five pillars include: (a) "Shahada" or complete faith in Allah as the one God with Prophet Muhammad as His messenger, (b) "Salah" or prayer five times a day when the individual has to meet certain guidelines for prayer, (c) "Zakat" or giving alms to help the needy, (d) "Sawm" or encouraging fasting as inherent natural cleanser, mandatory in the month of Ramadan, and (e) "Hajj," the pilgrimage to Mecca. Note Zakat and Hajj are obligatory for able Muslims only.

Destiny (Taqdeer, Qadar) and free will are interrelated. Given Allah (all-knowing) foresees beyond the limitations of time, the Sunni view is that He recorded events in a five-step process as follows: (a) overall destiny of the universe prerecorded on a preserved tablet before creation started, this decree

---

[1] Galatians 6:7. Note: all biblical quotes are from the *World English Bible*.

being changeless, (b) decree created post-Adam determining one's fate (heaven or hell), (c) specific lifetime, (d) yearly, and finally, (e) daily decrees of an individual. A person's destiny is iteratively modified by their free will to do good or bad in their one lifetime culminating in impartial judgment, and Allah may choose to forgive (if He so wills) conditional upon one's genuine repentance. This is cumulatively all captured under the larger umbrella of Allah's divine will (Hukm) in the original preserved tablet. Note that the concept of destiny is debated among denominations (Shia, Sunni, other) ranging from the belief in people having complete control over their destiny to having none. However, all are substantially unified in the knowledge that Allah is all-knowing and all-merciful. It may also be noted that both Judaism and Christianity scriptures include the Book of Life with respect to those who are destined for everlasting redemption; with exclusion of names signifying the opposite.

1.4 Buddhism: Law of Karma/Free Will and Destiny

Karma is not just action/reaction, it is about responsibility—how your actions affect others as well as yourself. Karma of course involves intentional actions (free will) and its effects may be localized or in the future, i.e., actions in the present including thoughts that have impacts on future events including rebirths. It is not about predestination (events willed by God), as Buddhism does not believe in a creator (God), but rather that all creation is due to a chain of related events called "dependent origination" whereby evolution is conditional, interdependent (see Item 2.4 below).

Karmic action and reaction cycles were defined in the first of the "Four Noble Truths" or the nature of suffering, their origins, cessation and the path to cessation of suffering. The latter defines the strategy to be free from suffering (dukkha) as per the Middle Way or the eightfold path including 1) right view, 2) speech, 3) thought, 4) behavior, 5) livelihood, 6) effort, 7) mindfulness, and 8) concentration (meditation). The path includes the five precepts held by all Buddhists: 1) Refrain from taking life, that is, not killing any living being. And while specific dietary practices are not mandatory, many Buddhists choose to be vegetarian, 2) Refrain from taking what is not given, not stealing from anyone, but this goes beyond physical theft to include right speech, that is, no lies or gossip as these steal the reputation or good name of a person, 3) Refrain from the misuse of the senses, for example, not too much worldly pleasure or sadness or joy, 4) Refrain from wrong speech, not lying or gossiping, 5) Refrain from taking intoxicants that cloud the mind.

And while there are variations on the path to achieve salvation, diligence is critical in lieu of faith only as being sufficient to get there.

1.5 Judaism: Law of Karma/Free Will and Destiny

One possesses free will, *yetzer hatov* to do good, or *yetzer hara* to do bad. Free will is an extremely important part of the human existence, where the expression "created in the image of God" or *be'tzelem elokim*[2] refers to a human's ability to choose right or wrong. This essential "power" separates humans from angels and other emissaries of God and therefore primes humanity to live in a world full of opportunities to reap reward and punishment. Hence, free will is given to humans to choose between these two compelling forces, a human's choice to fulfill God's commandments and follow in God's ethical ways leading to reward (schar), both physically and metaphysically, and choosing not to do so resulting in punishment (onesh). A soul may hence continue to be reborn on earth (birth-death-rebirth cycle) for multiple reasons, including but not limited to completing specific goals in pursuit of perfection (and consequent liberation), or to perform assigned tasks to help others as part of God's larger plan.

For those who choose (as per free will) to transcend, kind acts follow as a natural progression of belief that God appointed the Jews to be his chosen people as an example of holiness and ethical behavior to the world. *Kedushah* constitutes emulating God with emphasis on humility, respect and community, including being *kadosh* or holy, pure, removed from the worldly involvement, fearing and loving God, following His commandments and adhering to His ways.[3]

Jews worship three times a day for Abraham in the morning, Isaac at lunch, Jacob in the evening. These forefathers were the originators of instituted prayer that keeps humans bound in time and space to God within the confines of

---

[2] Genesis 2.
[3] Deuteronomy 10:12.

physical life. Also read about "Jacob's Ladder" as the symbolic connection between God and humanity.

Acts are seen as a form of worship, i.e., faith of action in lieu of intellectual effort. Destiny and free will are also much debated. An interesting median approach put forth by the Pharisees was that destiny (good or bad fortunes) applies to one's material life whereas spiritual tendencies and related eventual fate (e.g., heaven) are subject to one's free will. And that while God may foresee all, freedom of choice to act remains unmanipulated.

2. Levels of Purity and Systems

2.1 Hinduism: Levels of Purity and System (Religion, Philosophy)

Levels of Purity: A soul cycles through three main levels of gross and subtle planes (with sub-levels) which are tiered in increasing order of divinity: (a) the first gross/subtle plane of the universe comprising inanimate and animate creation, both gross and subtle, (b) the higher subtle/subtler planes, and (c) the causal plane. The realized soul (the Self) ultimately merges into this vast sea of causal cosmos which is the highest achievable level (see discussion later in Table C). Cumulatively, these levels represent the manifested aspect of Brahman/pure consciousness. This creation is represented by gross and subtle Aum vibrations, and cycles (as per defined time periods in Item 12.1 below) in and out of unmanifest Brahman.

Defined areas of heaven and hell are encompassed within, these may be geographical and dimensional zones (for example, hell under the earth plane). The belief in multilayers segregated by varying levels of purity is generally accepted in all the religions discussed. Additionally, the concept of seven layers in heaven and hell also features prominently across these religions, with offshoot variations on the number of levels. Continuing on, hell in Hinduism is considered a temporary destination, where one is given the chance to burn off bad Karma, sort of a purgatory.

The goal is to transcend to the highest achievable plane (sea of causal bliss/cosmos) by working through successive cycles of purity, rebirth and evolution by mastering our egocentric attachments and delusions through primed spiritual instinct or intuition. Common names of heaven and hell respectively include *Swarga* or *Satyaloka* or *Brahmaloka*, and *Naraka, Patalaloka*, etc. You will also find synonymous terms associated with aforementioned layers of creation called physical, astral, mental, intellectual (buddhic), spiritual planes, etc., in increasing levels of exclusivity and purity.

System: Hinduism comprises sixfold main, broadly tolerant philosophies originating from ancient scriptures called the "Vedas" based on the direct experiences and revelations of the sages, which were eventually recorded in Sanskrit text. These systems are: *Samkhya* (oldest), *the Yoga Sutras, Nyaya, Vaisheshika, Mimamsa* and *Vedanta*. They promote concerted, interrelated paths to achieving realization through a personal or impersonal union with God. This is achieved through detached service to mankind, mastery of passions, dharma or highest applicable universal law maintaining cosmic balance, laser-focused love for God and concerted practices borne of tremendous focus (rituals, yoga). This sixfold philosophy deals with the interconnected nature of creation and metaphysics commencing from the marriage of material (Prakriti/gunas, female) and spiritual (Purusha, male) energies of God at the macro level leading to the minutest levels of creation; and recognizing the essence of pure consciousness (the Self/Atman) at the core of the individual level of life cloaked by the deluded soul. This leads to the journey of the soul (jiva) through multiple cycles of life (rebirth) and the planes to achieve progressive liberation through cleansing and separation from the three traits (gunas) of purity, passion and dullness and cosmic delusion (maya). Note that these six systems include subtier philosophies. For example, Vedanta includes the *Advaita* school (oldest) borne of the principles of the holy books *Upanishads and Brahma Sutras* (see Item 4.1 below), emphasizing the ultimate unity of the soul and the Brahman. Its text was consolidated by Sage Adi Shankracharya in AD 8th century, who is widely acknowledged and revered for substantially unifying the key principles of Hinduism. Hinduism represents the confluence of practice and theory to effect physical and mental progress to remove suffering and bring lasting bliss.

About derivative religions that emerged from Hinduism, Buddhism is included here. Sikhism is discussed later under Spiritual Travelogue #14 in Section 2. Jainism is being discussed in brief here. Jainism was established by

Lord Mahavira in the sixth century BC, although it originated much earlier given a lineage of twenty-four Jinas (conquerors). There is some debate that Jainism predates Vedic scriptures. Mahavira (c. 599–527 BC), the last of the twenty-four Jinas, was born into the warrior (Kshatriya) class in Patna, India. Jainism believes in the journey of the soul (jiva), a temporary physical body, and the law of Karma and liberation (moksha). It stresses upon proper faith, knowledge and appropriate conduct as the methodology to achieving liberation. It promotes spiritual independence, the equality of all life with particular emphasis on non-violence. And similar to Buddhism, the existence of God is questioned. It may be noted that ancient Indian philosophies that rejected the Vedas include the *Cārvāka*, *Ājīvika* and *Ajñāna* schools of thought. These non-believer philosophies are collectively referred to as *nāstika*, whereas *āstika* refers to those philosophies who believe in the traditional teachings of the Vedas.

2.2 Christianity: Levels of Purity and System (Religion, Philosophy)

Levels of Purity: Gross and subtle universe with multiple layers of heaven and hell, including a purgatory (debated). Belief in the system of judgement post-death, including but not limited to a particular judgement (immediate), interim after-life including a purgatory with a chance to redeem; leading into a certain overall period of destabilization and degradation ultimately redeemed by the Resurrection of Jesus (second coming) since his initial ascension to heaven 2,000 years ago. This also results in universal resurrection and a last or final judgement thereafter to determine the permanent status/abode of our spiritual bodies. Associated keywords: Heaven, hell, new earth or world to come. Other common names of multilayered heaven and hell include paradise, Garden of Eden, and Kingdom of Heaven; and Hades and Tartarus, respectively.

System: Christianity is a monotheistic Abrahamic religion centered around the life and teaching of Jesus Christ (Jesus of Nazareth), with the Bible (Old and New Testaments) as central governing text. Main philosophies comprise Catholicism, Protestantism, the Eastern Orthodox, and Oriental Orthodox. All believe in Christ as the Son of God, as the savior of humanity and that he died for their sins. The difference comes in interpretation of the Holy Trinity (Father,

Son and the Holy Spirit), biblical canons (authoritative scriptures), manner of worship, role of Mother Mary, church hierarchy and jurisdiction.

Additively, the guiding principles of the Roman Catholic Church include (but are not limited to) multiple doctrinal texts called creeds or statement of shared beliefs promoting a united orthodox consensus. Examples include Apostolic, Nicene, Athanasian and Chalcedonian creeds promoted by the first seven ecumenical councils while preserving the sacred tradition and apostolic ministry, including succession of church hierarchy derived from the apostles (primary disciples of Jesus). These are cumulatively interpreted authoritatively by the magisterium (college of bishops) overseen by the Pope as head of the Catholic Church. Worship is ordered by means of the Liturgy and Mass, regulated by church authorities including the Rosary, Stations of the Cross and Eucharistic adoration. It includes important rites called sacraments symbolizing the Lord's presence and inviting grace. It incorporates Baptism, Confirmation, Eucharist, Penance, Anointing of the Sick, Holy Orders and Matrimony. The Eucharist, also known as the Holy Communion and the Lord's Supper, is the most important, and considered an ordinance in some churches. At the Last Supper, Jesus gave his disciples bread and wine during the Passover meal and bade them to "do this in memory of me" while referring to the bread as "my body" and the cup of wine as "the new covenant in my blood." Hence was born the sacred act of consecrating bread and wine at church altar or Communion table, and consumed in the name of the Lord. This esoteric change is called transubstantiation, but its principles are debated amongst multiple sects. Note that the cup used by Jesus at the Last Supper is called the Holy Grail in which Joseph of Arimathea later collected the blood of Jesus at the Cross. Of interest also is the discussion (debate) on the Shroud of Turin regarding the burial cloth of Jesus.

Catholics also firmly believe that what one does in life is just as critical as believing in both God and Jesus. Consequently, they came up with a system of acts of contrition (perfect, imperfect), confession for forgiving sins, both mortal and venial; and hold that all who die in God's grace and friendship but are imperfectly purified undergo the process of purification so as to achieve the holiness necessary to enter Heaven. Note that Christianity lists both seven deadly (cardinal) sins, and seven virtues (including four cardinal of the greatest importance) for believers. Jesuits, a religious order within Catholicism, are committed to evangelism and restoration of the apostolic ministry to support the teachings of Christ, and additionally, like many sects are engaged in social service, research and education. Catholics also believe in the Holy Trinity and Mother Mary (note the popular Hail Mary prayers as part of the Rosary, with derivatives in other sects including Eastern Orthodox, etc.), the latter being venerated as a Saint.

Protestants take exceptions on certain points (five solae). They believe salvation is by faith alone, through grace alone, in Christ alone. That believers are justified, or pardoned for sin given their faith in Christ and his sacrifice for humanity to achieve salvation, rather than a combination of faith and good works. With strict emphasis on the Bible as the highest authority (sola scriptura), they take a more direct approach to God while questioning the authority of the Pope and church traditions and priesthood, as well as the role and veneration of Mother Mary despite her being held in high esteem. They also have a differing opinion on the Eucharist, and are of the limited belief that the ritual serves only to commemorate Jesus' death and resurrection (as compared to the importance in Catholicism). Additionally, baptism is for professing believers only, not infants, children; performed by temporarily submerging people under a body of water. Protestant sects include Methodist, Reformed, Lutheran, Anglican (Church of England), Baptist, Quaker, Seventh-day Adventist, Presbyterian, Congregationalist, Pentecostal, etc.

Eastern and Oriental Orthodox Churches share many beliefs and practices marvelously diversified in traditions and culture of each region, for example, Greece, Middle Eastern and Slavic countries, Russia, Africa (Egypt, Sudan, Eritrea), Armenia, India. They also share the same differences as the Protestant, additionally including the interpretation on the Holy Trinity or Filioque controversy (Eastern Orthodox only) in which the text of the Nicene Creed was altered during the sixth century, to include "and the Son." While Catholics believe that the Holy Spirit comes from both the Father and the Son, Eastern Orthodox believes that the Holy Spirit only comes from the Father and not the Son. On venial sins and purgatory, both believe that cleansing of sins can only be done in this life. View on purgatory ranges from rejection (Oriental) to interim waiting place (Eastern) pre-final judgement.

Both also believe in Mary's high divinity but differ from Catholicism on the Original Sin and Immaculate Conception to the extent that while Catholics believe she was born free of original sin from the moment of conception, the Eastern and Oriental Orthodox holds that she chose to reject sin. Note that Mary is venerated as Theotokos which is Greek for God-bearer. And Oriental Orthodox strictly rejects the Chalcedonian Creed which holds that Jesus is one person in two natures: a divine nature and a human nature. Oriental Orthodox follows the Miaphysite philosophy that Jesus is fully divine and fully human, in one physis (nature).

Along with Eastern and Oriental Orthodox, other churches falling under the umbrella of Eastern Christianity also exist which may be independent or affiliated along with their related ecclesiastical polity. Examples include Eastern Catholic, Eastern Protestant, Assyrian Church of the East (branch of Syriac Christianity), etc. In fact, the latter establishment, along with other Syriac churches, uses its own version of the Bible called the "Peshitta" including the Old Testament (translated from Biblical Hebrew) and New Testament (translated from the Greek). Other sects of Christianity include non-Trinitarian beliefs such as Jehovah's Witnesses and Mormons who are synonymous with Latter-day Saints, who see themselves as restoring early Christian beliefs and traditions including additional revelations while differing on the belief in the Holy Trinity. Rastafari, originating in Jamaica, is a hybrid religion incorporating partly traditional Christian beliefs, and partly New Age and social movement concepts. This includes belief in God (Jah) being incarnated as human (for example, Emperor Haile Selassie as the Messiah). New Age is defined as a recent, derivative eclectic Western belief adopting a holistic form of divinity including mind, body and spirit in synchronicity with the rhythms of the universe.

2.3 Islam: Levels of Purity and System (Religion, Philosophy)

Levels of Purity: System includes the gross and subtle planes—heaven (Jannah), gross universe and hell (Jahannam), with temporary abode, *Barzakh* (views vary), pending final judgement. And similar to Barzakh, there exists a belief also in an interim *A'raf* which is closer to the definition of Christian purgatory in terms of the chance of redemption. Islam believes in a permanent abode in multitiered seven heavens (e.g., Illiyin, Firdaws) and hell (e.g., Sijjin, Saqar), respectively; note earth is also considered to be multilayered. Islam provides a lengthy list of sins, categorized between major and minor sins; examples include *Dhanb* (heinous, major), *Ithm* and *Haram* (unlawful, heinous, major), *Khati'ah* (moral lapse, may be major or minor), etc. Staying away from the former will influence forgiveness for the latter. Note however that Allah may forgive any based upon their genuine repentance.

The Day of Judgement (Qiyamah) is ushered in by a sequence of volatile and variant events including corruption, chaos. Three periods (greater, lesser and major signs) include the appearance of the Antichrist *al-Masih ad-Dajjal*, with Isa (Jesus) and the Mahdi (Messiah) then descending to triumph over this false messiah as a precursor to final judgement. Note that the *Hadith* or records of the verbal teachings (acts, words) of Prophet Muhammad mentions that the return of the Mahdi coincides with the timing of Jesus during the final period before the Judgement Day. Final judgement by Allah includes annihilation, resurrection of the dead and final abode allocation in heaven and hell. Common names of heaven and hell include *Firdaws*, *Dār al-maqāmah*, and *al-Nar*, *Haawiyah* respectively.

System: Islam is centered around six sublime articles of faith (iman) including the oneness of God (Allah), belief in angels, divinely revealed religious texts, prophets, destiny, and the Day of Judgement. Note that these beliefs translate into daily actions by way of the five pillars of Islam mentioned in Item 1.3 above. Islam literally means submission to the will of God and peace. Note the traditional greeting "Salaam Alaykum" which means peace be upon you. And the customary response is "Wa-Alaikum-Salaam" or peace be also with you.

The two major branches of Islam constitute the Sunni (majority) and the Shia, with variations (including reform) such as *Ahmadiya, Ibadi, Wahabi-Salafi* and *Mahdavia*, emphasizing original teachings, promoting oneness of Allah, strict adherence to the five pillars of Islam, etc. Sufism is often mistaken as a branch of Islam; in fact it represents the more mystical aspects of worship. While all are unified by the primary belief in the Holy Quran, differences exist on the succession to Prophet Muhammad (the last Prophet), religious practices, views on derivative literature and interpretation of divine Islamic law (Sharia). The latter is an integral part of Islamic traditions whose principles also extend into law, derived from the holy Islamic books Quran and the Hadith. *Fiqh* is the human interpretation of Sharia law as revealed in the Quran and the *Sunnah*, the latter describing the traditions and model lifestyle practices of Prophet Muhammad for Muslims to follow. Interpretations of this divine law extend into rituals and social relations including recommendations or *fatwas* by jurists (called muftis), which can be mandatory, recommended, neutral, abhorred and prohibited (haram). Mecca and Medina are considered the holiest sites amongst others such as Jerusalem, Eyüp, Hebron, Harar.

Each branch has its derivative practices, spiritual leaders and beliefs. For example, the largest branch of the Shia is called the Twelvers, derived from belief in twelve designated leaders (imams) after Prophet Muhammad, and it holds that the last imam will appear as the promised Mahdi (messiah). The Sunnis on the other hand believe in the first four caliphs as the rightful successors to the Prophet. Derivative religious practices include variations on the five pillars of Islam. For example, while the Sunnis follow the five pillars as listed in Item 1.3, the Shias have ten acts called "Ancillaries of Faith." The Ismailis (subset of Shia) have seven pillars. *Jihad* is a term sometimes referred to as the sixth pillar of Islam. Used primarily for one's efforts to attain religious and moral perfection, variations to the theme include utilizing one's powers with the means available to take on negative influences including but not limited to restraining sinful desires and if necessary engaging in defensive struggle.

Some of the principles of Islam extend into derivative and other religions such as Sikhism, Druze, Bábi Faith, Nation of Islam and others.

2.4 Buddhism: Levels of Purity and System (Religion, Philosophy)

Levels of Purity: System includes cycle of *samsara* (birth-death-rebirth) typically through six major realms/planes of existence: gods, demigods, humans, animals, hungry ghosts including restless spirits with excessive cravings, and hell. The last one is also considered a form of purgatory until the being returns to Karmic cleansing cycle. Note that Buddhism rejects the notion of the permanent Self/Atman as in Hinduism, with belief in *anattā* or non-self as one of the three hallmarks of existence including *dukkha* (suffering) and *anicca* (impermanence), and that the belief in the soul is the very essence of suffering. Hence, the journey as per the scriptures (suttas) through cyclical life cycle samsara constitutes the development of the non-self *citta* or mind, heart and our emotional nature to reach realization, *nirvana*. This is achieved by understanding that everything is impermanent, interrelated; ultimately transcending to achieve divine Buddha nature of detached, infinite awareness or emptiness, *sunyata*, devoid of suffering.

Multiple philosophies (example Theravada, Mahayana) translate these six realms/planes of existence into three major realms (similar beliefs exist in other sects). They include dimensional and geographical zones in diminishing level of purity, called formless (arupaloka) with multiple heavens and highly evolved, subtle beings; form (rupaloka) including pure abodes with higher-level (dhyana) gods; and the desire realm (kamaloka) including lesser gods (devas) on the slopes of the mythical Mount Sumeru with malevolent gods (asuras) at its base, humans and animals on earth, hungry ghosts in deserts and wastelands, and errant souls in multilayered hot and cold hells (purgatory). Cumulative thirty-one planes of existence are sustained by the extent of the Karma of inhabitants in each plane. If Karma is exhausted in a particular plane, the plane disappears (converse is also true); hence the term "dependent origination."

Earlier Buddhist texts refer to an overall five realms rather than six. In the five realms, the god and demigod realms constitute a single realm. These gods are not indeed "perfect," but subject to varying degrees of imperfection, and hence bound to the cyclical life cycle of samsara.

Above these six are four additional realms (pure lands) beyond the rebirth cycle in increasing purity: "Sravaka" the abode of highly transcended disciples, "Pretyabuddha" for solitary Buddhas who understand dependent origination and the interrelated nature of existence, the famed "Bodhisattva" realm with the aspirant well on the path to attaining salvation but instead sacrificing and being reborn to help others, and finally the highest "Buddhahood" realm.

After a period of progressive societal degradation and consequent loss of spiritual knowledge, the coming of the *Maitreya* Buddha (the next future Buddha) rebalances the system. Fate (end) of the world is characterized by the Sermon of the Seven Suns in which the earth begins to get hotter until it is destroyed. Eventually, the samsara cycle of birth, death and rebirth continues, hence there is no beginning or end. This is represented by the Wheel of Life through the successive periods of time (kalpas), known as *Bhāvachakra* adorned in temples and monasteries. The aim is to purify the personality of the practitioner so that all moral and character degradation, defects (kleshas) such as anger, ignorance and lust are wiped away and nirvana (Buddhahood) is achieved.

System: Buddhism originated in ancient India from the teachings of Gautama Siddhartha, the Buddha, today representing a marvelous amalgamation of multiple philosophies stemming from progressive segregation of early Buddhist schools (Nikaya), cultural and geographical factors and religious traditions including derivative doctrines and Scriptures (Vinaya). Evolution commenced thanks to several Councils (after 400 BC), and also royal support from King Ashoka and his son Mahinda including efforts to create a formal orthodoxy which contributed to its creation during the third council in 250 BC. Through this council heretics were expelled, and Theravada was established as the orthodox school including the sacred text *Tripitaka* known as the "Triple Basket" which later expanded into derivative text such as the "Pali Canon" of the Theravada school. Buddhism progressively spread from India to Sri Lanka and Southeast Asia including Myanmar, Cambodia, Thailand, Malaysia, China, Tibet and the trade routes of the Silk Road. It is thought that as many as eighteen traditional schools resulted, with many more subsequently established (numbers debated) including some later becoming extinct.

The three main philosophies emanating out of the aforementioned which are prevalent today include *Theravada*, *Mahayana* and *Vajrayana*. Core tenets of *Theravada* or the teachings of the elders include the Four Noble Truths of which the Middle Way (eightfold path) is a means to transcending the three hallmarks of existence including suffering, impermanence and the non-self, and delusory attachments and ignorance leading to samsara. And from the third council, Theravada followed the original teachings of the Buddha, while *Mahayana* Buddhism (see below) reinterpreted/adapted the Buddha's teachings to a more modern lifestyle after 250 BC. Theravada includes understanding the dependent origination or the interconnected nature of existence, rising over our personality traits and levels of consciousness, persevering through the prerequisites and methodology for holistic improvement (concentration, meditation) leading to Nirvana. Prevalent in Sri Lanka and Southeast Asia, referred to as the only surviving school of early Nikaya traditions, today it includes many branches such as *Maha, Siam, Thudhamma* and *Sangharaj.*

Mahayana or the great vehicle which reinterpreted/adapted the original sutras (teachings) from the Buddha also constitutes multiple philosophies including *Zen, Pure Land* and *Nichiren,* prevalent in Japan and East Asia including Chinese Buddhist traditions. While affirming early Nikaya teachings (Tripitaka or Triple Basket), it also introduces its own derivative texts called the Mahayana Sutras. Mahayana also focuses on the multiple Buddhas and emphasizes on the lifepath of a Bodhisattva (or the path to Buddhahood) by ascending through multiple levels (expanded cosmology) or stages of awakening. It promotes the concept of divine luminous essence, *sunyata* or emptiness or pure knowledge while leveraging on the teachings of the divine Buddha nature and the primordial, detached empty awareness devoid of suffering—synonymous with belief in the non-self (anattā) aforementioned.

Vajrayana or the Northern or Indo-Tibetan Buddhism is prevalent in Tibet, Bhutan, Mongolia and parts of Russia. It also incorporates East Asian influence of other religions; for example *Shugendō* constitutes a hybrid of esoteric Buddhism, Shinto, Taoism and other religions. Vajrayana includes doctrines such as *Nepalese Newar, Shingon, Shugendō* and others while incorporating traditional Mahayana practices including virtues (Paramitas) like generosity, morality, patience, energy, meditation, and wisdom (note Theravada lists ten virtues). Additionally, it utilizes systematic doctrines or *tantric* practices from both ancient and modern schools such as the *Nyingma* (six classes of tantras, red hat sect denoting color of the hats of the monks), and *Sarma* (four classes of tantras) including *Sakya* (red hat sect) and *Gelug* (yellow hat sect) schools. These schools cumulatively include multiple levels of yogic practices (inner and outer tantras) called *Kriyatantra, Caryatantra, Mahatantra, Anutantra, Atitantra,* etc., as in *Yogatantra, Mother* and *Father* Tantras. Other esoteric practices include use of mantras, deity worship, use of statues and paintings, sacred spaces such as *mandalas* (symbolic pure lands), the combined bell and the *vajra* (divine spiritual weapon) implement aids synonymous with compassion and ultimate wisdom of emptiness in the universe, visualization of deities and Buddhas, chanting (dharanas), subtle yoga (Tummo) and advanced meditation (e.g., Dzogchen). Additionally, the use of symbolic seals gestures or poses (mudras) which positively affect energy flow in the body by cleansing the occult centers (chakras) and energy channels symbolizing divine manifestation. Esoteric practices include secret techniques. Students need initiation (abhisekha) and vows (samaya) solidifying their bond with the Guru. And like the other two philosophies, Vajrayana is seen as advanced practice to expedite the path to Buddhahood, the main text being the *Kangyur* and *Tengyur*, enriched by Mahayana scriptures, tantric doctrines and early Buddhism text.

2.5 Judaism: Levels of Purity and System (Religion, Philosophy)

Levels of Purity: The universe was created by God (Ein-Sof, Infinity) without any aid of another being. The system of judgement post-death from the material universe includes going to heaven or hell although concept of the latter is minimized in Judaism (as against Christianity), and rather considered to be an interim purgatory for cleansing before erring souls return to their path of progression. Belief in the coming of the Messiah as a future savior and ruler during Messianic Age and the world to come is integral to Judaism. This *Mashiach* will be a future Jewish king or high priest duly anointed. Belief in his coming includes a series of events including but not limited to resurrection of the dead, return to homeland (Promised Land), building the Third Temple, heralding a Messianic Age of peace and blessed existence.

As per esoteric principles called *seder hishtalshelus* including the teachings of the Kabbalah (see Item 4.5, Holy Books), eleven energy channels (one unmanifest, ten manifest) of light called *Sefirot*, both male and female, emanating from the undifferentiated, divine life force or consciousness (Ein-Sof, God) are responsible for continuously creating gross and subtle realms including life in God's image. Note that Ein-Sof constitutes multiple levels of God's divine essence of infinite light and self-revelation (Kabbalah mentions ten levels including "Atzmut" or absolute simple essence, "Aliyat Haratzon" or ascent of God's will to create the world, etc.). These lead to progressive creation of the five realms or planes of existence (our subtle, gross universe) in diminishing order of purity, each with a guiding energy or *Sefirah* (singular) as follows: (a) "Adam Kadmon" representing the first subtle, albeit unmanifest supreme, cosmic man (analogous to Hinduism's initial emanation of the cosmic ego or *Mahat* in Table B-1), with the first, highest, unmanifest divine Sefirah called "Keter" guiding; (b) "Atziluth" or emanation where the next ten Sefirot initially manifest but still in a highly subtle and formless state, with Sefirah "Chochmah" or wisdom guiding; (c) "Beri'ah" or world of creation comprising formless, subtle existence (non-gross) including angels, souls and the higher Garden of Eden, Sefirah "Binah" or understanding, intellect guiding; (d) "Yetzirah" or world of formation which takes shape and form, including souls and angels and the lower Garden of Eden, multiple lower Sefirot "Chesed to Yesod" (kindness to foundation, knowledge) guiding; and (e) "Asiyah" or world of action, including active angels and our material universe, Sefirah "Malchut" (humility, kingship) guiding. Note that the first two levels "Adam Kadmon" and "Atziluth" are closely linked to the divine Ein-Sof, with differentiated worlds following.

Cumulatively these five worlds include the overall system permeated with a higher degree of holiness and exclusivity. These range (in diminishing order of divinity) from the multiple seven heavens (Shamayim) including highest "Araboth", "Zebul to the Shehaquim", "Vilon" including the Gardens of Eden, with a hierarchy of celestial beings (archangels, angels and others) residing, culminating in the created universe followed by hell (known by Sheol, Gehinnom, Abaddon). Note hell (as in many other religions) is believed to have multiple levels comprising both geographical and dimensional zones.

System: Judaism is an ethnic religion with multiple philosophies/movements, most of which came out of Rabbinic Judaism of which those prevailing today includes Orthodox (such as Haredi/Chassidic strict Orthodox and Modern Orthodox), Conservative and Reform. Original beliefs constitute God as revealing his biblical laws and commandments (Mitzvah) to Moses on Mount Sinai as per the written and oral Torah. Judaism believes in a special covenant established between God and the children of Israel incorporating religious, cultural and legal traditions encompassing a wide body of texts, practices, theological positions and defined organization.

Orthodox Judaism stresses adherence to the original Torah, with emphasis on Jewish law (Halakha) and strict practices including dress, diet, purity and others. Modern Orthodox Judaism allows less stringent practices, within the confines of accepted Halakha in most cases where religion may interfere with opportunities of the modern world. Conservative Judaism (also called Masorti) considers Halakha to be more fluid and is therefore more open to interpreting Jewish law in ways that allow for greater inclusivity and tolerance of other cultures and religions. It also promotes acceptance of traditional and modern religious scriptures and observances. Examples include Shabbat (the seventh day of the week, day of rest) and Kashrut or dietary laws including preparation leading to Kosher foods.

Reform Judaism rejects a significant portion of the rituals and reinterprets original Jewish binding laws. It believes in continuous revelation (adapted to modern culture) and upholding moral and ethical values, while promoting broader prayer practices and developing direct connection to religion and God. It may be noted that Reconstructionist Judaism took root in the early 1900s as an alternative to Reform Judaism, its principles based on an evolving society as opposed to being strictly religion bound. By contrast, Humanistic Judaism is another modern movement whose principles extend into practices such as non-theistic ceremonies and rituals while continuing to reinforce the cultural and historical background of the Jewish people.

Other sects and derivative groups include Subbotniks (Russian origin), Sephardi (Hispanic), Mizrahi (Middle East and North Africa), Jewish Renewal (North America) with an esoteric approach focusing on Kabbalistic principles and meditation (including yoga) as part of the religious process, Karaites (Israel, Ukraine, United States) with strict emphasis on written Torah, Samaritans (of the Levant) or ethno-religious group from ancient Near East, etc.

A point of clarification needs to be made on references to "biblical" versus "rabbinical." Biblical laws are all of the authoritative laws and commandments that are either explicitly mentioned in written Torah, derived from written law through the act of exegesis (critical interpretation of scripture) using the thirteen tools of exegesis given to Moses at Sinai, including a handful of commandments (not included above) also given to him at Sinai. Rabbinical on the other hand have no direct basis in scripture and have been instituted from the times of Moses through the end of the era (at the end of the fifth century AD) where Jewish religious authority was centralized. Rabbinical uphold the existing biblical commandments and laws, refrain people from transgressing by way of ignorance, negligence or rebelliousness while promoting both individual and collective divinity through the ages. They support or complement the existing biblical laws by way of instituting decrees, precautionary practices and in a few instances new commandments and laws based on historical or relevant context.

3. System of Gods, Deities/Angels and Sages/Saints/Prophets

3.1 Hinduism: System of Gods, Deities/Angels and Sages/Saints/Prophets

Gods and Deities: "Ishwara" is Supreme God seen as the spiritual arm of impersonal Brahman or pure undifferentiated consciousness (Table B-1 and Item 2.1 above). Synonymous representations of Ishwara include aspects of the Holy Trinity (creator, sustainer, destroyer)—Lords *Brahma*, *Vishnu*, *Shiva*—including their respective goddesses (called energy or *Shaktis* of life, matter and mind)—Goddess *Saraswati* of learning and creation, Goddess *Lakshmi* for fortune and wealth, and Goddess *Parvati* for devotion, strength and children. Devout belief in these founder gods and goddesses also led to traditions (movements), for example, *Brahmanism, Vaishnavism, Shaivism, Shaktism, Smartas,* etc. Note that gender definition takes place for purposes of creation guided by vibrations and mantras. Each of the trinity have popular representations (avatars), for example Lord *Vishnu* include Lord *Krishna*, Lord *Rama*, Lord *Buddha*, etc. Lord Krishna is seen as a godchild, prankster, charioteer, warrior-diplomat, cowherd, disciple, guru and universal supreme being playing the flute of goodness for all to help them out of cosmic delusion.

Lord Brahma is represented by *Aditi* the mother of both creation and the twelve celestial gods (*Adityas*) governing zodiacal spirits, the fourteen *Manus* representing the progenitors of humanity and later cyclical heads of the cosmic governance cycles of time, the Seven Great Sages (Saptarishis) also linked to seven stars, and *Narada,* the popular Vedic sage. Lord Shiva is represented by Lord *Ganesha* (see next paragraph), Lord *Pashupati* presiding over animals, Lord *Nataraja* for dance and dramatic arts, etc. Goddesses are similarly represented. Goddess *Parvati* is synonymous with *Kali* representing creation, destruction, salvation; *Durga* is associated with knowledge, memory and wisdom; and so on.

In summary, there are four tiers. Tier 1 is for the trinity and their wives mentioned above; Tier 2 is for their incarnations and support gods such as Lord *Hanuman,* the monkey god symbolizing strength, who accompanied Lord *Rama* and his brother *Lakshmana* to Sri Lanka to overcome Lord *Ravana* and rescue Lord Rama's wife *Sita* as depicted in sage Valmiki's epic *Ramayana*; and Lord *Ganesha* (Ganapati), son of Lord Shiva and Parvati, fondly worshipped as remover of obstacles. Easily recognized by his elephant head, Ganesha is known for his intellect and wisdom, and as promoter of arts and sciences. Tier 3 includes thirty-three deities: the twelve *Adityas* (zodiacal deities), eight *Vasus* (gods of natural phenomena), eleven *Rudras* (gods of storms who follow God Rudra, one who roars and renews the soul and is associated with Lord Shiva), Lord *Indra* (god of heavens, lightning) and Lord *Prajapati* (god of progeny). Some of these deities are also referred to as Lokapalas or Digpalas who rule the specific directions of space (west, east etc.). It may be noted that many of the deities are also associated with presiding over various functions including speech, hearing, actions, travel, etc. Tier 4 includes local deities such as animal, nature, great sages, ancestral spirits and realized souls who assist in cosmic government and helping humans in spiritual ascension.

Collectively, the four tiers constitute a highly integrated system of gods and deities as representations of Ishwara, including timely cycling of deities commensurate with cosmic governance cycles of the universe (Item 12.1 below).

Sages: Include *Ved Vyasa,* author of the epic battle *Mahabharata* and the texts related to the original ancient scriptures, Vedas. Sage *Vishwamitra* is author of the revered *Gayatri* Mantra and *Mandala 3* (sixty-two hymns from the *Rigveda*) used for prayers and chanting. Sage *Adi Shankaracharya* was a proponent of *Advaita Vedanta* philosophy unifying the concept of soul and Brahman, also credited with unifying the principles of Hinduism. Sage *Patanjali* is the author of the *Yoga Sutras* which influenced other systems due to promotion of coordinated mind–body efforts. Recent sages (nineteenth century onwards) include *Sri Ramakrishna*, Swami *Vivekananda*, *Shirdi Sai Baba*, Swami *Chinmayananda*, Baba *Lahiri Mahashaya*, Sri *Yukteswara*, *Paramahansa Yogananda*, *A.C. Bhaktivedanta Swami Prabhupada* (ISKCON) who cumulatively promoted ancient scriptures of Hinduism through derivative texts and teaching. And a special mention to Jiddu Krishnamurti, the twentieth century philosopher. Jiddu, who was closely associated with Annie Besant, rejected any titles, religious and theosophical traditions while promoting action oriented, holistic practices in perfect communion with man and nature extending beyond geographical, social, political and cultural boundaries.

The threefold nature of God is represented by *Aum*, *Tat*, *Sat*. *Aum* represents and upholds all creation through vibration. *Tat* represents the Holy Trinity or Brahma-Vishnu-Shiva. *Sat* refers to God represented by the above, both the unmanifest and manifest nature of the universe.

3.2 Christianity: System of Gods, Deities/Angels and Sages/Saints/Prophets

God: The Holy Trinity—the Father, Son and Holy Spirit.

Father: God, absolute, unmanifested, who is responsible for all creation.

Son: Jesus Christ.

Holy Spirit: The divine power sustaining all creation.

Prophets and Saints: Are both seen as being close to God and having exceptional divinity. Prophets include those having the ability of prophecy though saints are also known to possess such gifts. System of formal recognition commences from the Bible (Old and New Testaments) leading into system of veneration and canonization (posthumous) varying by denomination. For example, the Coptic Church of Alexandria (Oriental) sets a minimum fifty-year pre-formal recognition of a saint. Interestingly, some beliefs fondly refer to any person who has passed as being "Saints in Heaven" although the traditional title of Saint includes formal recognition for those associated with divinity. Protestants tend to be the most conservative with respect to formal recognition given their direct approach to the Lord. The title of "Patron Saint" is also used for those indicating elevated status of one associated with representing a particular group, endeavor, region. For example St. Francis of Assisi was Patron Saint of Italy; St. Patrick (St. Patrick's Day) is Patron Saint of Ireland. Apostles are typically associated with being messengers of God, whereas monks are typically associated (across multiple religions) with ascetic, monastic living, although marriages are allowed in certain denominations. You will also hear synonymous terms such as friars, brothers, nuns, mothers and sisters, etc.

While Jesus is acknowledged as a prophet in Judaism and Islam, in Christianity he is divine, the son of God and the Savior who died for the sins of humanity and was resurrected. The twelve apostles are recognized as his primary disciples and included in the Holy Bible (for example, Acts of Apostles, Synoptic Gospels), spreading his gospel to all nations. Note that Eastern Christianity include as many as seventy apostles. The twelve include Simon (also called Peter), Andrew (brother of Peter), James (the Great, son of Zebedee), John (youngest apostle), Philip, Bartholomew, Thomas (doubting Thomas!), Matthew, James (son of Alphaeus), Thaddaeus (Judas the Zealot), Simon (Canaanite) and Judas Iscariot. These saints preached globally, for example in Spain, Syria, Greece and India. Their efforts commencing early in the first century AD to spread the teachings of Jesus are inspirational! And in some Christian traditions (as among the Catholics) the Blessed Virgin Mary (mother of Jesus) is considered holy and divine (also mentioned in the Quran).

Moses and Abraham are considered as prophets in the Judeo-Christian tradition along with many more, mostly in the Old Testament for Christians and the Tanakh for Jews. Other prophets from the Bible include Isaiah, Elijah, Ezekiel, David (David and Goliath), Jeremiah (weeping prophet); the list is long including the former, latter and minor prophets. Yet other examples of those synonymous with new movements and branches include the famous German reformist Martin Luther (Protestant). St. Loyola Ignatius was integral to creation of the Jesuits (branch of Catholicism).

Angels: In the Abrahamic religions are depicted as supernatural, celestial beings performing a number of roles including serving God, assisting humans. They usually possess great beauty including but not limited to winged creations, exhibiting divine light and/or halos. Classifications constitute three spheres with 9–10 subcategories, serving as servants of God in heaven, managing creation and forming cosmic government, with the lowest sphere entailing active management of humans as their spiritual guides and protectors. Commonly associated terms for the latter include spirit guides, guardian angels, archangels (for example, seven including Michael, Gabriel, Raphael, Uriel, Jophiel, Selaphiel and Barachiel). Also quoted are master guides, regarded as masters who ascend through human form and can assist with the highest stages of spiritual development.

3.3 Islam: System of Gods, Deities/Angels and Sages/Saints/Prophets

God: Allah is all-powerful, all-knowing, all-merciful, has no intermediaries, cannot be seen or heard, is omnipresent, omniscient. He is known by ninety-nine names, has no gender or plurality, is the sole creator of the universe and beings, with a divine purpose in mind. The entire nature of the teachings of Islam are based upon the singularity, oneness (Tawhid) of all-transcendent Allah.

Prophets: Twenty-five prophets are mentioned in the Quran, but it is believed there are about 124,000 prophets in total. They include Adam, Isa (Jesus in Christianity, Judaism), Nuh (Noah), Musa (Moses) and Ibrahim (Abraham). Ibrahim in Islam is not seen as the patriarch of the Abrahamic religions but rather as a link in the chain of prophets from Adam to Prophet Muhammad (the last prophet). The latter is considered the "Seal of Prophets" or designated prophet to whom Allah revealed the Quran in a series of revelations as his literal divine words. Some prophets are called *Rusul* or messengers of divine revelation passed through by angels. Prophets are considered champions of ideal living as per Islamic teachings, often forebearers of prophetic tidings to come. Miracles performed by them occur only through the will of Allah. A saint is called a *Walī*, famous Sufi saints include *Hasan* of Basra, *Junayd* of Baghdad, Imam *Muhammad-i Ghazali* and the Hanafi Faqīh *Jalāl al-Dīn Rūmī* of Persia.

Angels: Are integral to the six articles of Islamic faith. Examples of famous archangels include *Jibril* (Gabriel) as angel of revelation, holiness; *Mika'il* (Michael) governing forces of nature, mercy; *Azrael* the benevolent angel of death; and *Israfil* who blows the trumpet to signal Judgement Day (Qiyamah). Many including guardian angels are quoted in the Quran, and they originate from heavens (seven-tier) and high celestial spheres. They have specific functions including advising revelations of God and glorifying him, recording the actions of humans and taking our soul at the time of passing. Example may be cited of the two angels *Munkar* and *Nakir* who test the faith of the deceased in their graves (while in temporary purgatory Barzakh) to give them a chance for redemption. Angels are represented in supernatural forms, including with wings, clothed in heavenly attire and being devoid of bodily desires. However, pictorial depictions are minimalized as opposed to other religions (Christianity and Judaism). Benevolent angels are depicted as being created from cold light (Nur) as opposed to hot light (Nar) for meting out rightful punishment.

Threefold Nature: Islam doesn't believe in threefold nature, but in one God only.

3.4 Buddhism: System of Gods, Deities/Angels and Sages/Saints/Prophets

God: Buddhism primarily does not believe in existence of a creator God, but rather an impersonal high level of being defined by state of emptiness (sunyata) devoid of suffering. The lineage of the Buddhas are seen as the closest representation of God and universe. Early Pali Buddhist texts list seven including Gautama Siddhartha Buddha (founder), plus a future *Maitreya* or Laughing Buddha; later increasing to a total of twenty-nine Buddhas as recorded in Theravada Pali Canon's *Buddhavamsa* scripture. All the Buddhas are categorized in different ways, for example meditation, wisdom, celestial, historical, etc.

Spiritual Leaders and Sages—key leaders—constitute the Buddhas who are liberated; a *bodhisattva* who is training to become a Buddha is regarded as being liberated but remains in the cycle of samsara to help others reach enlightenment; and an *arhat* is one who becomes liberated by following the teachings of a Buddha.

Role of the Bodhisattva: Note that the sacrifice of the bodhisattvas is regarded in Mahayana as a superior path, and refers to one who has achieved *bodhicitta* or enlightened mind dedicated to the benefit of all beings. Theravada Buddhism refers to them as anyone who has made a resolution to achieve Buddhahood and has received such confirmation from a Buddha.

Role of the Arhat: An arhat is one who has gained insight into the true nature of existence and has achieved nirvana. Theravada states that arhat is considered to be the proper goal of a Buddhist, whereas Mahayana states that the arhat ideal is the lesser goal to pursue than that of the bodhisattva, given that the latter vows to become a Buddha in order to work for the good of others (see above).

Also, the *Brahmas*, a category of minor gods within the realm of the gods (devas) assist humans through counseling and advice. Note that these devas fall into three main classes of purity, are not considered immortal, and the lowest class exhibit human desires and joys.

In Tibetan Buddhism, the lineage of Dalai Lamas are considered to be reincarnations of the original Dalai Lama (born in AD 1351) who is said to be the reincarnation of *Avalokiteshvara,* bodhisattva of compassion. The current Dalai Lama is considered the fourteenth reincarnation. *Thích Nhất Hạnh* was a Vietnamese Buddhist monk and peace activist, founder of the Plum Village tradition. *Nagarjuna* was creator of Madhyamaka (Middle Way) path of Mahayana, considered one of their premier philosophers. *Padmasambhava* (Guru Rinpoche) was a key figure in spreading early Vajrayana Buddhism.

Angels, Prophets: There is no noted system of angels or prophets in Buddhism.

Threefold Nature (Trikāya): The Buddha has three bodies (kāyas): 1) *Dharmakāya*, the unmanifested Buddha nature signifying universal, boundless enlightenment (akin to unmanifest Brahman in Hinduism) from which Buddhas arise and return; 2) *Sambhogakāya* or boundless subtle body comprising light of divine intelligence to teach higher-level students including bodhisattvas, residing in the highest universe planes "Pure Lands" synonymous with the highest subtle (causal) planes described in Hinduism; and 3) *Nirmāṇakāya* representing the physical Buddha manifested within the created universe in time and space. It may be noted that beliefs vary on the number and types of bodies, depending upon the doctrine.

Another version of this threefold nature are the "Three Jewels," which are the Buddha himself, the "Dharma" (doctrine, or teaching) and the "Sangha" (monastic order or community).

3.5 Judaism: System of Gods, Deities/Angels and Sages/Saints/Prophets

God: There is one God only, impersonal in the sense that He cannot be seen or identified. However, it is deemed that one can develop a personal relationship. No gender, but gender references are used to emphasize message. God established a special covenant with the Jews who follow His laws to bring holiness in their lives in exchange for good deeds performed by them for their physical and metaphysical benefit, as well as the formula to live a complete, purposeful life. Sages emphasized in Talmudic (oral law) and Midrashic sources (interpretation of Torah or partial guidance by God to Moses) the oneness of God and rejected the existence of a higher or similar being. Note that the essential obligation in Judaism is to emulate, implement and manifest the traits and qualities of God (the ones that we can emulate) in order to achieve the highest level of human existence one can strive for. The scriptures use different names and genders to describe God. Oral tradition interprets these as manifestations of His "character" such as compassionate, etc., to bring out the essence of His teachings for purposes of transcendence.

Prophets, Angels: Per oral tradition, many prophets mentioned in the Bible were capable of achieving this level of divinity including the power of prophecy which evolved over time, but for all intents and purposes came to an abrupt end after the passing of the Prophet Malachi, around 460 BC. The sages revealed, however, that prophecy is still a true mode of transcendentalism, although it is less frequent and less obvious. Abraham is considered as the founding father of the "Covenant of the Pieces" where God revealed Himself and advised him of the special relationship between God and the Hebrews, and that his descendants would later inherit the land of Israel. Abraham is also considered a patriarchal figure in Christianity, Islam and other religions, notably the Abrahamic religions.

Moses is perhaps the most important prophet in Judaism, receiving the spiritual guidance (Torah, see Item 4.5 below on Holy Books) from God at Mount Sinai. He was also chosen as leader of the Jewish nation in Egypt because of his propensity to seek out God despite his circumstances. His communication with God is referred to in scriptures as "face-to-face" and "as clear as light through crystal." His successor Joshua is fondly compared to Moses as the difference between the sun and the moon, the sun imposing light on the moon so that it can be seen at night. Tens of subsequent prophets are mentioned in the "Book of Prophets" which is split into early/late prophets. The Talmud records forty-eight prophets and seven prophetesses, and records stories of great sages and even righteous (and not so righteous) Gentiles or "Ger toshav" that achieved prophethood by following the "Seven Laws of Noah" or universal moral laws (like refraining from cursing God, adultery, theft, etc.) for all humanity. It is important to note that no prophet ever contradicts the words of the Bible (Old Testament) or that of Moses. If they do, this is considered as the sign of a false prophet.

As for angels, the involvement of the metaphysical beings are kept very localized and controlled, without the ability to "do" beyond what their assigned task demands of them. Angels have assigned tasks and carry out the will of God, such as assisting in prayer, healings, defending the good, carrying messages and teaching. Mentioned in Rabbinic literature including the holy books (Tanakh, etc.), angels are segregated by levels of purity based upon their understanding of God. Maimonides who wrote *Mishneh* or *Mishnah* Torah defined ten levels. The Talmud describes the physical appearance of certain winged angels including seraphim and cherubim with multiple faces including those of birds and animals which are prevalent also in Islam and Christianity. Many religions believe that angels appear as birds to give us divine messages.

Threefold Nature: Judaism does not believe in threefold nature, but only in one God.

4. Holy Books

4.1 Hinduism: Holy Books

Hinduism originated from the experiences and teachings of sages, saints (rishis); the holy texts are known as the *shastras* which contain answers to such questions as to who is God, where does He dwell, and how is His appearance. These shastras teach us multiple methods by which we can reach Him, utilized by many sages through the centuries. Hence the reason for the numerous shastras perfectly attuned to differing levels of consciousness in the community capturing every aspect of religious and social life including fields of law, medicine, art, architecture, etc. And all of these originate from the ancient Vedas (Shrutis) which have no author but are based on the direct experiences and revelations these sages passed down over the years, eventually recorded in Sanskrit text. After exhaustive analysis, debate and verification on the various theories emerged these sublime scriptures—rational, impersonal in approach, and hence universal in spirit as a timeless, perfect amalgamation of science, philosophy, religion, ethics, and music for all humanity. As an example, take music. The *Sama Veda* has some of the world's earliest text on musical science, as a subset of Aum. Music, painting and drama are considered divine arts reinforced by the Holy Trinity of Gods (Tier 1 in Item 3.1). Note that Lord Brahma's wife Saraswati is known as the goddess of wisdom playing the Veena, mother to all stringed instruments globally!

In effect, all of the teachings of Hinduism originate from the four *Vedas*, namely *Rig, Sama, Yajur* and *Atharva*, each roughly subdivided into four sections:

1. Mantras: Lyrical chants adorning the beauty of nature, spoken with realization and concentration and having materializing value.
2. Brahmanas: These contain description of rituals.
3. Aryankas: Prescribing various methods of subjective worship.
4. Upanishads: Referring to the highest philosophical truths, also known as Vedanta or end of the Vedas given that they contain their essence summarized at the end of the scripture.

Related texts to the Vedas constitute:

- Brahma Sutras: Sage *Veda Vyasa* revealed the identity of Brahman or pure consciousness in 555 aphorisms (sutras) and 192 topics cumulatively summarizing all spirituality.
- Puranas: These deal with history cumulatively symbolizing illustrations of philosophical principles, written to popularize the Vedas. They are in the form of inspiring stories about lives of saints, great men and historical events.
- Itihasa (literally meaning history): The *Ramayana*, written by Sage *Valmiki*, and the *Mahabharata* by Sage *Ved Vyasa* are categorized as Itihasa. These are great, popular and useful epics in India to emphasize teachings used to introduce people to religion.
- The *Bhagvadgita* is the central portion of the Mahabharata and contains the cream of the Upanishads, the end of the Vedas.
- Tantra: They dwell on the energy (shakti) aspect of God and present numerous courses of ritualistic worship of the Divine Mother in many forms.
- Smritis: These are codes or manuals of social, ethical, moral and domestic laws of conduct, and embrace a substantial portion of the shastras.

4.2 Christianity: Holy Books

The Bible or the Old and New Testaments are the central biblical canons, acknowledged and established holy scriptures as the divinely inspired word of God compiled by multiple authors over several centuries.

The Old Testament is synonymous with the Hebrew Bible, comprising four sections: (1) the Pentateuch or five books of Moses (from Jewish Torah) called Genesis, Exodus (including the famous parting of waters), Leviticus, Numbers and Deuteronomy; (2) history of the Israelites from conquest of Canaan to Babylon struggles (exile); (3) poetry and wisdom books in multiple forms addressing good and evil; and (4) the books revolving around the prophets including recommendations and consequences of straying from the holy path. Number of books vary by denomination and interpretations: Catholic forty-six, Eastern up to forty-nine, and thirty-nine in Protestant; all share the twenty-four books of the Hebrew Bible.

The New Testament (twenty-seven books) revolves around the life and teachings of Jesus including the first century AD events comprising (1) the four canonical gospels of Matthew, Mark, Luke and John; (2) the Acts of the Apostles on the progressive roots of the Christian Church and its message across the Roman Empire; (3) the twenty-one Epistles including the fourteen Epistles of Paul, and seven general Epistles—note that Epistles are educational, inspirational and instructional text typically for select groups (religious, other); and (4) the Book of Revelation or message (Epistle) to the seven churches of Asia leading into prophetic messages as a precursor to the second coming of Jesus.

There are several versions of the Bible, for example, Catholic, Protestant, King James Version, Orthodox, New World translation of holy scriptures (Jehovah's Witnesses). Given the prevalence of Greek scriptures to offset the understanding of Hebrew around the time of Jesus, the Greek Old (Septuagint) and New Testament feature heavily in the development of the Christian Bible. Amongst many derivative religious texts and scriptures that followed, creeds (Nicene, Apostolic, etc.) and catechisms (doctrine manuals) feature strongly to drive the development of global Christianity.

4.3 Islam: Holy Books

The Holy Quran is the central religious text of Islam, considered to be the verbal, direct, literal revelations of God (Allah) to Prophet Muhammad via the Archangel Jibril (Gabriel) over a period of around twenty-three years. Constituting 114 chapters (surahs) containing 6,236 verses (āyāt or miracles or signs), the Quran represents a summary of a series of divine teachings commencing from those given to Adam, including the Torah, the Book of Psalms (Hebrew Bible) and the Gospel of Isa (Jesus). Chapters are either "Meccan" or "Medinan" depending upon when verses were revealed pre/post-migration of the Prophet to Medina, although the verses from each period are intermixed.

The Quran deals with fundamental Islamic beliefs including (but not limited to) God, early prophet narratives, prayers, code of charity and ethics, legal subjects, nature, resurrection and Day of Judgement, historical events in the life of Prophet Muhammad. The surahs are integral to reciting in daily prayers, manner of recitation of Quranic verses is specific (rules are called Tajwid) for divine effect; note the similarity concepts in other religions, e.g., Sanskrit mantras in Hinduism. Islamic verses are also an integral part of art and architecture, adorning buildings, pottery, literature, paintings, etc.

As described in earlier sections, notable ancillary religious texts and commentaries to the Quran include the *Hadith*, the records of the verbal teachings of the Prophet, derivative divine Sharia law, the *Fiqh* which constitutes interpretation of Sharia law as revealed in the Quran, and the *Sunnah* or exemplary practices of the Prophet. Additionally, the *Tafsir* contains broad supplementary commentary across the multiple schools of thought elucidating the meaning of Quranic verses.

4.4 Buddhism: Holy Books

Buddhist scriptures are a collection of sacred texts (sutras). They are also known as *suttas*, and are canonical scriptures, many of which are regarded as records of the oral teachings of Gautama Buddha. They are not aphoristic, but are quite detailed, sometimes with repetition.

The sutras have been embraced by multiple doctrines. Mahayana and others evolved from the original teaching used by Theravada, and while there are some overlaps and usage, they do not share a centralized consensus as in Hinduism, Christianity and other religions. Original text of the early Buddhist schools (Vinaya) established around the third council (third century BC) post-Buddha are called the Tripitakas (literally Triple Basket) constituting a) the "Vinaya Pitaka" or moral discipline monastic rules and ethics of the *Sangha* or community; b) "Sutta Pitaka" including Buddha sermons and teachings, religious poetry and aphorisms; and c) "Abhidhamma Pitaka" expanding upon extensive Buddhist doctrines, interpretations about systematic philosophy and psychology.

Initially taught orally by monastics, these texts including derivative interpretations and doctrines made their way into several Indo-Aryan languages including Sanskrit, Pali, Buddhist Chinese (Agamas), Classical Tibetan, Gandhari and Khotanese, promulgated by the spread of Buddhism. Note that the Theravada version of the Tripitaka is the *Pali Canon* in Pali language, considered sacred text constituting a mix of several *Prakrit* (mid-Indo-Aryan) languages from the third century BC with roots in Sanskrit. Ancillary derivative commentaries including old Sinhala manuscripts emerged in Sri Lanka rein-forced by their *Mahavihara* monastery traditions which were later integrated by the famed Theravada scholar *Buddhaghosa* which also supported sacred texts in other sects such as Mahayana.

Mahayana Buddhism reaffirms the original Tripitaka, and also developed derivative canon texts considered *Buddhavacana* (Buddha word), including the Lotus Sutra or White Lotus of True Dharma which formed the basis for schools such as *Nichiren*, *Tendai*, *Cheontae*, etc. Acceptance of these later texts varies amongst the other doctrines and schools of Buddhist thought. For example, they were adopted in overall Chinese and Tibetan canons, and the famed Mahayana scholar *Asaṅga* (founder of Yogacara Buddhism) classified them as part of "Bodhisattva Pitaka" collection of texts for bodhisattvas. Conversely they were questioned by Indian Buddhist schools and Theravada Buddhism.

Vajrayana canons incorporate early Buddhist, Mahayana, and tantric sutras into an amalgamation of loosely defined canons covering its multiple schools. Main texts are defined in two broad categories called "Kangyur" and "Tengyur," the former containing original Buddha teachings, and the latter constitut-ing commentaries and dissertations including "Abhidharma Pitaka" works (Mahayana, etc.). Cumulatively, they deal in subjects including Sangha or com-munity monastic rules, perfection of wisdom, metaphysics, virtues of the bodhisattvas, original Tripitaka teachings. Additionally, tantric materials are extensively covered including mantras, rituals, commentaries, poems, songs and *termas* or hidden esoteric teachings. Vajrayana texts constitute a combination of diverse verse and prose heavily weighted in Sanskrit while drawing from middle Indic dialects. Examples of influential texts in Chinese Esoteric Bud-dhism which later formed a central basis for Japanese *Shingon* Buddhism are the *Mahāvairocana* Sutra (Dainichi-kyo in Shingon) and *Vajrasekhara* Sutra (Kongocho-kyo in Shingon).

4.5 Judaism: Holy Books

The Tanakh (Ta-Na-Kh) or the Hebrew Bible summarizes the original, cumu-lative relationship with God. It comprises a threefold compilation of the Old

Testament (Ta: Torah), the Book of Prophets (Na: Nevi'im) and divinely inspired writings (Kh: Ketuvim):

1. Old Testament Torah is divided into Written Torah (Torah Shebikhtav) and Oral Torah (Torah Sheb'al peh). Note that the Christian Old Testament corresponds with the Jewish Torah. The Written Torah constitutes the first five books of Moses called Genesis, Exodus, Leviticus, Numbers and Deuteronomy, and provides the blueprint for moral and ethical living through the revelations of the 613 commandments of which the "Ten Commandments" are epic. The handwritten (manuscript) Torah is called the *Sefer* Torah or the Sacred Torah scroll, the book version being called the *Chumash*.

   The written Torah can only be understood through the lens of the Oral Torah which is often referred to as the Moses Torah since Moses was verbally introduced to it by God Himself which he passed on orally to the congregation of sages (Anshei Knesset HaGedolah), and to subsequent religious leaders. The Oral Torah was mostly transcribed and redacted into the Mishnah at the beginning of the third century (AD) and elucidated by the Talmud in the sixth century. Accordingly, this written version of Oral Torah (Talmud) constitutes part of rabbinical works comprising both the Mishnah and subsequent analyses and commentaries called the *Gemara*.

2. Nevi'im or Book of Prophets is broken into two parts: four books of former prophets and fifteen books of latter and minor prophets.

3. Ketuvim or writings including psalms, proverbs, and history in eleven books.

Complementary, derivative texts to the above cumulatively falling under Rabbinic literature include the following:

- Halakha or cumulative body of religious laws derived from the Oral and Written Torah, both considered integral to achieve a complete understanding, as otherwise these religious laws may be easily misconstrued. It examines judicial laws, both civil and religious, consisting of behavior codes, religious procedures including marriage, divorce, charity and ethics.

- *Aggadah* or non-legal interpretations of Rabbinic text particularly in Talmud and Midrashic sources represented in the form of wise sayings of sages, parables, folklore, anecdotes and practical advice in multiple fields (like medicine, business, etc.). Note that Midrash or Midrashic literature and sources do not imply a specific book but rather a compilation of religious (biblical) exegeses by ancient authorities including but not limited to Halakha and Aggadah as methodology to inspire high morality and related practices. Examples include the Midrash Halakah and Midrash Aggadah.

- Maimonides's "Thirteen Principles of Faith" or various logical, hermeneutical principles put forth by this great medieval sage. Maimonides took a novel approach in an attempt to codify the teachings of oral and written laws with regard to faith. He also codified the 613 commandments and was seen as a pioneer in Jewish philosophy. While Maimonides was not the first to expound on Jewish philosophy, he certainly popularized it, and incorporated elements of Greek philosophy to explain complex concepts of religion, morality and life. His drive to codify stemmed from the same reason the oral law was put to writing, namely that people were forgetting and/or misconstruing the teachings of God.

- Kabbalah constitutes the esoteric path and beliefs also known as *Kavanot* or mystical philosophy. Elements of Kabbalistic teaching provide profound insight into God's ways. Legend has it that a third or hidden Torah was also revealed to Moses as contained in "Sefer ha-zohar" (book of Zohar) with related literature through the ages. It covers all aspects including theoretical study to understand the divine system of God, practices to reach Him (meditation), and theurgy. Note that Sefer ha-zohar is a Midrashic text that is attributed to the holy sage Rabbi Shimon Bar Yochai, who disseminated the Torah mysteries to his students. However, earlier Kabbalah texts exist, namely, *Sefer Yetzira* and *Sefer HaBahir*, but Sefer ha-zohar is central. There are many theories as to who was the first to transcribe Sefer ha-zohar, thus making it available to the public. Kabbalah is considered part of the oral tradition, and most of what we have today (text and teachings) are a mere fraction of what was actually revealed to Moses.

Some of the earliest Hebrew Bible manuscripts that exist today that were discovered archeologically include the Dead Sea Scrolls, Silver Scrolls, Masoretic Text, etc. These texts, although thousands of years old, are practically identical to those used today.

5. Mantras/Devotional

5.1 Hinduism: Mantras/Devotional

Mantras are associated with sacred vibrations, whereas prayers are more about devotional practice, although the latter can also be a mantra with dedicated focus. Special mantras are also given by gurus for individual needs.

Aum (Om) originated in scriptures and represents universal energy sound (Sanskrit mantra), the manifested part of pure consciousness (Brahman). In other words, Aum is the resonant frequency sound upholding and representing the created universe as we know it, including nature and life in all its myriad variations. It must be recited with focus, meditating upon its meaning. This mantra can be traced through the annals of history, utilized in an almost universal sense representing God via this basic, all-enveloping sound. *A* is the root, first sound produced without touching any part of the tongue or palate, *U* rolls from the very root to the end of the sounding area of the mouth. And *M* represents the last sound produced by the closed lips. Hence, Aum represents the complete sound promulgation encapsulating the experience of the pulsating universe, audible or otherwise (thoughts and emotions). Chanting Aum gets you into synchronicity with the subtle laws of creation, thereby enabling inflow of healing energies. Mantras and verses (ślokas) are used alongside perfected breathing techniques by advanced yogis/sages for transcendence. Examples of other powerful mantras include the *Gayatri* mantra, *Om bhūr bhuvaḥ svaḥ* . . . , on universal knowledge, divine sun (light); *Aham brahma asmi*, I am Brahman; *Pavamana*, purity (from darkness into light); *bhaja govindaṁ bhaja govindaṁ, govindaṁ bhaja mūḍha-mate* . . . , worship Govinda, worship Govinda, worship Govinda oh deluded mind; *Har Har Mahadev,* destruction of evil by Lord Shiva; *Jai Bajrangbali,* Lord Hanuman evoking bravery and strength; *Jai Mata Di,* glory to goddesses; *Om Namo Shivaya,* praise of Lord Shiva and universal consciousness; *Om Sarve Bhavantu Sukhinah,* may all be happy, healthy and free of suffering; *Shanti,* peace recited at start/end of rituals and sermons. And how about the legendary *Hare Rama Hare Krishna,* the sixteen-word mantra, cornerstone of ISKCON (International Society for Krishna Consciousness) devotion!

Integral to devotional practice is the singing of hymns and chants in majority of religions, and Hinduism is no exception. Reverential (bhajan) singing composed of *ragas* or classical Indian emotive rhythm accompanies rituals at home, temples and religious ceremonies, reinforced by temple pandits, pujaris (priests), swamis and even professional musicians.

5.2 Christianity: Mantras/Devotional

Christianity does not use mantras as understood in other traditions, but repeated prayer may work as a mantra. Hymns, antiphons, psalms, chants (such as Gregorian and Ambrosian chants), and others constitute an integral part of diverse church and personal prayers. These may be spontaneous or textual which are read from a breviary containing canonical hours (liturgy of hours) marking divisions of the day with respect to fixed prayer times. Note that ancient traditions promoted prayers seven times a day. Naming of prayers varies by tradition including lauds (morning), vespers (evening), major and minor hours, weekly timings for prayers, etc. Other types of prayer include the Lord's Prayer (Jesus Prayer), mealtime prayers, sign of the Cross, intercessory (on behalf of others), being a witness for Christ (glorifying Jesus given one's personal transformation through him), short exclamations or praises (such as Hallelujah), listening, child's prayer, etc. Focusing on Jesus, "Maranatha" meaning "Our Lord has come," or "Abba" meaning Father, may also be seen as equivalent to a mantra. Note that the latter is considered an intimate term in ancient Aramaic which was spoken by Jesus and his disciples.

Note that Amen (Āmīn in Islam) is usually said at the end of a prayer or to assert strong confirmation about a prayer or hymn, or blessing. Amen means "it is so" or "so be it," and is derived from the Hebrew "āmēn" which means "certainty," "truth," and "verily." It is not a mantra.

Speaking in tongues occurred in ancient Greece, also mentioned in Acts of the Apostles in the New Testament. It is often associated with Pentecostalism (sect of Protestantism), and can be interpreted as people in a trance channeling the words from divine source, albeit not understood. Sometimes it involves others dancing and spinning around in circles to attain a state of communion with the divine.

Singing is also very popular, including singing and chanting of hymns (sacred songs) and Gospel music (popular modern music). Note "a cappella" singing (i.e., without any accompanying instrumental music) is also very popular.

5.3 Islam: Mantras/Devotional

Chanting prayers and mantras in Islam are integral to getting closer to Allah.

The surahs (114 chapters of the Quran) are used in reciting daily prayers (namaz, salah or salat) five times a day. Some of the more important verses include the *four Quls* or small sections at end of the Quran. For example, reading the surah "Al-Kafiroon Qul" is equivalent to reading a quarter of the Quran. The four Quls are also considered to protect against evil influences. Other common chants and mantras, short remembrances (dhikr) typically used at the end of prayer include "Allahu Akbar" or God is Great, "Bismillah Al-Rahman, Al-Rahim" or "in the name of Allah, most merciful and compassionate." The latter is also associated as per numerology (Arabic Abjad system) with the number 786 which is considered fortunate by Muslims. "Ya Salaam" is equated with divinity and equanimity, "Allaahumma Innee Asaluka Bi ismika" meaning "Allah, I beseech thee in thy name" seeking forgiveness. "Inshallah" and "Mashallah" are also very common, referring to "if God wills" and "God has willed" in the future and past tense respectively. Others include "Subhanallah" (Glory be to Allah), "Alhamdulillah" (Praise be to Allah), etc. Islam also promotes the use of personal supplication, invocation or request prayers (called dua), meant for reinforcing personal relationship with Allah by saying these at any time of day and night. Variations include short and long duas. Typically at end of each prayer, Shias raise their hands three times saying "Allahu Akbar", whereas Sunnis look at the right and then left shoulder saying "Peace and blessings of God be unto you", this being the "Taslim" or the concluding part of the prayer.

Practice of worship at Mecca (holiest site in Islam) constitutes circumambulating seven times counterclockwise around the "Kaaba," the central building in the Great Mosque of Mecca. This act is called "Ṭawāf," performed as a fast walk three times, then slowly for the remaining four. It signifies oneness in worship to God. Several forms of Tawaf can be performed. The circumambulation entails worshipping at pre-designated points around the Kaaba, the four corners coinciding with the points of the compass. In fact, worshippers the world over face the direction of Mecca while doing their daily prayers five times a day. This consists of a series of cyclical bows, kneeling and touching the ground with forehead called *raka'āt,* the number varying by the time of day. For more on this, see notes on Hajj in item 14.3 below.

5.4 Buddhism: Mantras/Devotional

Mantras, chanting and discourses are highly prevalent in Buddhist practices. Buddhism refers to the term "Dharani" which may be a chant, mantra, or recitation, with protective powers. All these are very popular as preparatory acts for, or as integral acts in meditation. The most common mantra is, of course "Om" or Aum, which is said to be the sound of the vibrations of the universe. Repetition contains the potential of spiritual connection. By reciting a mantra, you can clear your mind. Examples of popular mantras include the mantra of compassion "Om Mani Padme Hum" (Vajrayana) and "Namu Myoho Renge Kyo" (Japanese Nichiren Mahayana) to meet challenges by adopting the Buddha nature. "Kun Byed Rgyal Po" is a Vajrayana Tibetan mantra. In its roots lies its meaning, i.e., the supreme ordering principle in the universe. Mantras can also be personal and private. One can select one that resonates or is given to one by the guru. Whether using the universal Om or one chosen or given, the mantra includes all and everything we have amazing awareness of. That something which beckons our awareness never ebbs or goes away, to include God, the Christian Lord, consciousness of the Buddha, and of course "Param Atman" or the supreme spirit synonymous with Brahman of the Hindus. They are all inseparable from each other as a oneness, wholeness, inseparable universe. Once realization truly opens, one's bias and opinions dissolve into nothingness.

Other examples of mantras and chants include Theravada's "Buddhabhivadana" or preliminary obeisance for the Buddha, "Tiratana" or the three refuges, "Pancasila" or five precepts, "Buddha Vandana" or Buddha salutation, and "Dhamma Vandana" or salutation to his teachings. Pure Land Buddhism (Mahayana) uses "Namo Amida Butsu," "Namo Amituofo" or "Namo Nianfo" or repetition of "Amitabha" Buddha's name. Sutras and discourses include "Prajñāpāramitā Hridaya Sūtra" or Heart Sutra for Zen, Shingon and other Mahayana Buddhists. The Diamond Sutra is popular in Zen temples, Lotus Sutra in Tendai temples, and the Metta Sutta or loving kindness in Theravada. Ancillary practices include specialized throat singing (Tibetan), form of chanting called "Shomyo" (Japanese), "Shigin" or recitation of poetry in Zen, sitting in a "Seiza" (kneeling) position while singing from the gut (seat of power). Also, the singing bowl is used to aid meditation in many sects of Buddhism, also used in Taoism and Western holistic practices. And the portable, twin-headed drum (*damaru*) is popular in Tibetan Buddhism and Hinduism, linked with sounds/vibrations of creation (OM). In Hinduism, it is also linked with the union of cosmic, creative male/female (Shiva/Shakti) energies popularized by the Shiva Langa statue (*murti*) adorned with ash (*tilak*) and a female (*yoni*) base.

5.5 Judaism: Mantras/Devotional

Judaism does not specifically have mantras but tools and aids to communicate with God. For example, cumulative effort by a group of ten people (minyan), traditionally ten males over the age of thirteen and speaking certain words effects communications. Deep in the annals of esoteric thought there are specific phrases that can achieve a more immediate connectivity with God, for example, the seventy names of God (Yahweh, Elohim, Ein-Sof, Hashem, Yah, Adonai, etc.) that can only be uttered by the purest of human forms. Additionally, praying or speaking to God in Aramaic as opposed to Hebrew is said (as per Oral tradition) to penetrate the seven stratospheres without manipulation and reach God unadulterated. This is because angels "do not relate" to Aramaic and will not be able to contest it.

As with Christianity, Judaism has a full court of hymns (Zemirot), prayers, a range of religious music including Hebrew cantillations (chants) from varying traditions, "Piyyut" (liturgical poems), "Nigun" (songs, tunes) sung by groups, recitations, psalms, etc. Prayer is one of the most central elements of Jewish devotion, in which the mindful recitation of texts composed by the Anshei

Knesset HaGedolah, the institution of Torah sages that led the Jewish people at the beginning of the Second Temple period (c. 516 BC to AD 70) is considered essential to everyday life. Spontaneous, non-text-based prayer, in any language, is also valued and encouraged, as prayer is also intended to foster a personal and intimate relationship with God. And one of the central philosophies of Judaism revolves around "Avodah" or service which is accomplished through prayer. Hence, prayer serves a dual purpose, Avodah and fostering a relationship with God. And the aim of a Jew (derived from Judah or pertaining to the kingdom of the tribe of Judah) is to develop devotion from the heart through a combination of focus on divinity through philosophy, contemplation, education and esoteric theology. *Kavanah* is a mindset (focus if you will) that helps elevate the service of prayer beyond the simple words being uttered, to steer the prayer in a direction in which the participant can connect to the *Avodah* or prayer on a completely personal and unique level.

A complete roster of timing and events for prayers entail daily (three times) for "Shacharit" (morning), "Minha" (afternoon), "Arvit" (evening) for "Yom khol" (ordinary day of the week). With special additions on "Mo'adim" (holidays), "Rosh Chodesh" (first day of the new month), and the Shabbat. The "Siddur" is the traditional prayer book, and many versions of "Siddurim" (plural) are available, reinforced by the same underlying theological principles. Examples of these prayers include, but are not limited to, "Modeh Ani," "Reishit chokhmah yirat Adonai" for arising, awakening to the Lord, "Mah Tovu" while entering the synagogue, "Birkat HaTorah" for Torah blessings, "Kaddish" expressing longing for earthly kingdom of God and for timely mourning of loved ones, "Barekhu" for call to worship at synagogue, "Ahavah Rabbah" for the blessing of the great love that God bestows upon His creations and for His gift of the Torah (bible), ending with "Aleinu," "it is our duty to praise." The "Shemoneh Esrei" or "Amidah" constitutes eighteen blessings including praise, petitions and thanks, and is perhaps the most important synagogue prayer recited standing facing the "Aron kodesh" (the Torah ark, an ornamental chamber housing the Torah scrolls), with alternate versions for weekdays and Shabbath/holidays. Note that it is essential to face Jerusalem, the location of the Temple Mount while praying, and thus most synagogues are built facing Jerusalem. Additional prayers called "Musaf" are recited by Orthodox or Conservative Jews on holidays (Chol Hamoed and Rosh Chodesh). "Ne'ila" (special closing service) is recited only on Yom Kippur (Day of Atonement). *Shuckling* or swaying during prayers is customary but not mandatory.

6. Beliefs in Single and Cyclical (Birth-Death-Rebirth) Life Cycles

6.1 Hinduism: Cycle of Birth

Belief in reincarnation via countless life cycles exceeding a million years to cleanse through the law of Karma into realization. The soul (jiva) journeys through the gross/subtle, subtle/subtler, and causal planes to achieve realization. There are multiple interpretations on whether the realized soul (the Self) unites with the creator, or stays amalgamated in the causal plane (sea of causal cosmos) which is the highest achievable level within manifest Brahman.

Transmigration to different species (like animals): Yes, it is there to bear out previous Karma only, which enables the soul-cleansing process. Note that this is not decision based. Animals work by instinct which limits their condition, hence transmigration does not influence future life cycles.

6.2 Christianity: Cycle of Birth

While some theologians of Early Christianity debated reincarnation and related Gnostic beliefs, they were firmly rejected. Belief in one life only, with a defined heaven or hell, and an interim (purgatory) which is debated. One must be "born again" spiritually with Christ to go to heaven. "Born again" has great credence, achieving a new birth, spiritually speaking, as opposed to physical. Note comments also on "grace" in this analysis. It is essential to believe in Christ as redeemer to go through the final judgment to heaven. Formal practice of induction includes baptism, believer's baptism varying by age and conscious profession of faith (example infants, professing believers).

Transmigration to different species (like animals): No, it is not there. Animals exist as part of God's larger plan.

6.3 Islam: Cycle of Birth

Belief in one life only, with minor variations. For example, the Druze faith which is an offshoot of the Shia subsect called Ismailism believe in reincarnation.

"Barzakh" and "A'raf" are temporary afterlife abodes (debated) pending final judgement, leading into defined areas of hell and heaven. Interestingly, the Quranic verse 40:11 has led to inferences by some scholars of two lives and two deaths. The interpretation is that our earthly life constitutes our second life, our previous life in the heavenly kingdom came to an end, given negative influences by Satan (himself a fallen angel), resulting in Allah (all-merciful) giving the earth-bound souls a second chance to redeem in our current (second) existence.

Transmigration to different species (like animals): No, it is not there. Animals exist as part of God's larger plan.

6.4 Buddhism: Cycle of Birth

In Buddhism, the continued cycle of birth, death and rebirth is called *samsara*. Once one reaches enlightenment, samsara is broken. Note that the concept of a permanent Self/Atman is rejected in Buddhism; rather the belief in soul is the very essence of suffering. Hence, the journey as per the Suttas (scriptures) through samsara constitutes the development of empirical self "citta" or mind, heart, emotional nature reaching nirvana by gaining the understanding that everything is selfless. Defined in the first of the four noble paths, dissatisfaction (dukkha) leads to suffering and rebirth cycle of samsara, to eventually attaining salvation, nirvana, via purification (meditation) and release from ignorance and desires.

Transmigration to different species (like animals): Yes, it is there to bear out Karmic deeds into eventual purification. It is said that when the Buddha attained enlightenment, he saw all his previous lives as all sorts of animals, from bugs to higher mammals.

6.5 Judaism: Cycle of Birth

Per esoteric beliefs in the Kabbalah (further articulated by Isaac ben Solomon Luria Ashkenazi), the soul can be reincarnated to progressively achieve completion of specific goals (example, to fulfill God's commandments) in pursuit of perfection and consequent liberation, or to perform assigned tasks to help others as part of God's larger plan. The process is called "Gilgul Ha Neshamot," Gilgul meaning cycle or wheel and Neshamot, souls. The soul can thus be employed as a vehicle to help man ultimately ascend the gross and subtle created worlds comprising the ten spiritual levels (Sefirot per Item 2.5) as a variation of light energy (Ohr) vested in a spiritual vessel (Kli); the process is driven by the latter persuading the former to descend to fulfill Karma including God's will to ultimately create a world to reside in bliss leading into the messianic age. This light energy (Ohr) in each vessel (Kli) adapts to the spiritual level of each of these levels of Sefirot, while being governed by the integral characteristic or desire (Ratzon) of the soul to return to higher realms; the said characteristic can be described as metaphysical attributes of God. It may be noted that Ratzon is synonymous with the term "Chefetz" for which multiple interpretations exist. Ratzon is deemed as the more positive characteristic of the soul with a subtle desire to do the right thing, held back by Chefetz as being associated with a more physical (hence negative) type of desire. Alternatively, Chefetz has been interpreted as positive in that it is construed as being closer to perceivable reality, harnessing a more powerful motivating drive (than Ratzon which is more abstract) to execute the will of God.

Transmigration to different species (like animals): Yes, it is there to bear out Karma, to complete tasks left unfulfilled in this world.

7. Cosmic Delusion, the Devil and the Discarnate

7.1 Hinduism: Cosmic Delusion, the Devil and the Discarnate

"Maya" is a term used to describe both the powers of universe creation and cosmic delusion, the latter causing our selfish attachments and confusion. Confusion of our ego limits our ascension through the multiple universe planes, structured in order of increasing purity (see Item 2.1), to achieve salvation. This thrusts us into the continued birth and rebirth cycle.

We also continually hear many stories of fallen angels, and of human masters, who achieved a certain spiritual level (albeit still reversible) and then gave in to their temptations to remain trapped within the lower realms of gross creation.

Representations of fallen demigods include the names *Rakshasa* and *Rakshasi* (female) and *Asuras*, although some of the last named also fought on the good side along with gods (devas) against evil. These supernatural beings are personified as fierce warriors possessing great strength and size with powers to create illusions to overcome their foes, all the way to extreme physical demonic characteristics including having fangs, red eyes, claw-like fingernails, multiple heads, arms, etc. Rakshasas are popularly represented in art, dance, festivals, architecture and literature. And on the lighter side, *Panvati* is a female jinx who bears negative astrological influences and changes expected good tidings, to much collective sighs and groans!

Lord *Yama* (Yamaraja) is a pious deity mentioned in the original holy scriptures *Rig Veda* as the son of the sun god *Surya*. Along with his assistants (Yamadutas), he presides from a subtle plane (called Pitriloka) as the Lord of Death driving impartial justice in the Karmic cycle by sending aspiring souls into the realms of the multi-layered hells (Naraka) or heavens (Swarga).

7.2 Christianity: Cosmic Delusion, the Devil and the Discarnate

"He who sins is of the devil, for the devil has been sinning from the beginning."[4]

The Devil (Satan) is a fallen angel symbolized with tempting Jesus for a period of forty days and nights in the Judean desert. He is also symbolized as the devious serpent tempting Adam and Eve in the Garden of Eden; and as being a prime mover of sin, dualism (confusion) and delusion creating great sorrow through the ages, after his expulsion from heaven following a war with Archangel Michael.[5]

Possessing great temporary powers (allocated by God), these fallen angels and their derivatives are symbolized in multiple classifications as the source of physical and mental vices, causing mass suffering (sickness and other), and targeting vulnerable souls in many ways (including possessions). Amongst many, Lucifer, Beelzebub, Belphegor, Leviathan, Behemoth are names synonymous with the Devil, representations including characteristics of animals like the goat, ram and pig, and popularly of dragons.

---

[4] 1 John 3:8.
[5] Book of Revelation 12:7–9.

Numerically, the number 666 is associated with the Devil based on classi-fication and organization of the number of demons into legions. Ultimately the Devil, his demons and followers are defeated at eventual Judgement Day and relegated to eternal fire.

7.3 Islam: Cosmic Delusion, the Devil and the Discarnate

Satan, the Devil in Islam is regarded as a fallen angel; associated names include *Shaitan*, *Iblis*, malevolent spirits (Jinn), *Ifrit*, *Div* and false gods (Taghut). Representation in the holy scriptures (for example, Hadith) also include the anti-Christ (Al-Masih ad-Dajjal) who will be defeated by the Mahdi (Messiah) and Isa (Jesus) in the events leading up to Judgement Day. The Devil is mentioned several times in the Holy Quran and Hadith, but belief in these forms of evil is not mandated by faith. Satan is seen more as luring humans to sin, and not as a malevolent force as seen in Christianity as the cause of evil itself.

Powers vary, for example the *Div* possesses huge physical strength, size resembling ogres and fiends with animal characteristics capable of creating powerful illusions to overcome their foes and possessing humans. Spirits (Jinn) on the other hand are akin to humans with similar needs and temptations, but have significant lifespans equaling hundreds of years. Jinn are also subject to death, hence must procreate. They cannot ordinarily be seen and are also capable of acts such as possessions and bringing diseases. But they are known to be both good and bad given they have the power to choose (free will). Another evil spirit such as the *Shaitan* is associated through the ages commencing with tempting Adam and Eve, and all meet their eternal fate and defeat at the time of the final judgement. Any attempts on their part to reach heaven are thwarted by the forces of good such as the angels and shooting stars. They are also called *Waswas*, and are not ordinarily known to possess humans but rather incite by imposing themselves through negative emotions directly into their minds. It may be noted that a *Kafir* denotes a person who is a non-believer. *Harut* and *Marut* are two fallen angels commonly cited, although their status (as fallen) is debated. The angel *Maalik* is the stern chief of the forces of hell supported by nineteen angels called *Zebaniyah*.[6] These are angels being created from fire as opposed to angels of mercy created from cold light.

7.4 Buddhism: Cosmic Delusion, the Devil and the Discarnate

Ignorance reinforces our condition in impermanence (existing life cycle) through duality or "Yin and Yang," and these continued opposites trap our ego and veil the real essence of higher existence. In Buddhism, the god of desire and unenlightened existence leading to continued life cycles (samsara) is called *Mara*. When the Buddha achieved enlightenment (nirvana) while sitting in a lotus meditation pose, Mara tried to draw the Buddha into temptation with his three daughters called Tanha (thirst), Arati (discontent) and Raga (desire), but to no avail. When Mara challenged Buddha to produce a witness as to his enlightenment, the Buddha with his left hand in his lap, palm upright, and his right hand touching the earth asked the Goddess of Earth (Prithvi) to confirm, which she obliged. That is, the earth was his witness. This act of the Buddha, in lotus pose touching the earth, is one of his famous personifications, indeed considered a form of ritual gesture (mudra) associated with transcendent flow of energies aiding enlightenment. A point to note is that Mara as personification of evil in Buddhism is not at the same level as that of Satan in Christianity, given that Mara comes from only the lower level, the desire realm (Kamaloka, see Item 2.4), and is consequently considered a relatively minor figure in the overall scheme of things. Mara is the god of desire, not evil.

Buddhism (like Hinduism), especially the Tibetan Buddhism tradition, also believes in anti-gods and demonic entities such as *Asuras* and *Rakshasas*, who also reside in the aforementioned lower Kamaloka of the universe. They are in turn countered by righteous deities (Dharmapalas) as defenders of Buddhist values and teachings (Dharma), who are indeed often considered as fierce forms of Buddhas and bodhisattvas themselves. Note that the god of death (Lord Yama), is also considered a righteous deity (Dharmapala) and protector of Buddhism presiding over hell (Naraka), and distributing efficient, fair justice in the cycle of Karma and rebirth. Both the demigods (Asuras) and deities (Dhar-

---

[6] The Quran 66:6.

mapalas) are depicted in wrathful forms including multiple heads and arms, the latter being personified in blue, black or red skin with fangs.

7.5 Judaism: Cosmic Delusion, the Devil and the Discarnate

While similarities exist in Judaism and Christianity on the definition of Satan by being categorized as a celestial force or fallen angel, in Judaism the Devil wields only limited power. The Devil does not have the ability to contradict or act beyond its assigned tasks, and is seen as subservient to God. The larger belief appears to be about Satan being synonymous with the baser, congenital struggles of man such as the free will to perform negative acts ("yetzer hara"), and not being a major demonical force to contend with. Same principles apply for spirits and demons, seen as minor entities.

Two classes of spirits (as per Tanakh) include the "Shedim" and "Se'irim." Shedim are beings that channel forces of evil and are capable of interacting on a physical and metaphysical plane, though interpretations vary. Shedim are also viewed as foreign gods (hence evil by default), all the way to being seen as helpful at times to humans. Physical traits of Shedim vary including partial traits of angels (wings) and humans, with feet and claws of roosters. They are also seen to take the form of a serpent, and possess powers to assume human form. Se'irim are symbolized as spirits or demons with goat-like appearance. "Mazzikim" are another example of minor, invisible demons making nuisance of themselves in our daily lives.

And as with other religions, the concept of dualism is recognized by Judaism, the struggle between good and evil to overcome cosmic delusion—represented as confusion ("Olam Ha Tohu") and rectification ("Olam Ha Tikun").

8. Spiritual Centers within the Body, Meditation and Transcendental States

8.1 Hinduism: Spiritual Centers within the Body, Meditation and Transcendental State

Spiritual Centers: It is said that there are seven main centers of consciousness in the human body called chakras or light lotuses channeling our subtle life energy (prana). These are in ascending order of purity: coccygeal, sacral, lumbar, dorsal, cervical, medullary and the crown or thousand-petaled lotus of light. This subtle-life pranic energy is also called *kundalini* energy, which is compressed and coiled, sitting at the base of the spine in this central space awaiting its release—in turn dependent upon our level of spirituality through concerted meditative or equivalent practices. There are three main energy channel flows in the body called the *ida* (left), *pingala* (right) and the central *sushumna*. Once this central channel is opened up through spiritual practices, this leads to an all-enveloping, eternally blissful spiritual experience as the kundalini energy released strikes the chakra centers causing progressive degrees of enlightenment. Note that the opening of the chakras is an involuntary process; trying to manipulate them can be very dangerous resulting in grievous harm to oneself, given that the contained energy is very powerful and cannot be sustained by the untrained body.

Animals and plants also have chakras, and even inanimate objects have their own set of vibrational energies. And given that every being or object is in process of evolution, it consequently follows that the earth itself as a minuscule part of the universe is considered a living entity in its own right with chakras. It is said that when one meditates on the universe and starts to become one with it, one realizes that the universe is contemplating itself as pure energy in its natural state.

Meditation and Transcendental State: The Yoga Sutras were substantially integrated by Sage Patanjali (c. second century BC), Yoga constitutes one of the six systems of Hinduism; with related treatise also included in the end of Vedas scripture called *Upanishads*. Integrated into the eightfold path (similar to Buddhism) with structured yoga processes and breathing practices (pranayama), its philosophies remain highly prevalent today, given its influence over modern-day yoga practices and continued evolution. These include harmless breathing for calming the mind and advanced processes including natural stoppage of breath while transcending into progressive levels of concentration and meditation to achieve transcendental bliss and realization. The holy scriptures state there are five levels of bliss on the earth plane (see Table B-1) culminating in the superconscious Nirvikalpa Samadhi state, and that true life begins after this fifth level (Nirvikalpa Samadhi) is achieved.

After this commences the ascension through the non-gross planes (see Item 2.1 above) including progressive cycling to the highest levels of purity achievable, that is, the Sea of Causal Cosmos in Table C.

The Yoga Sutras have influenced myriad systems of meditation globally given its methodical manner to combine improvements physically, mentally and spiritually.

8.2 Christianity: Spiritual Centers within the Body, Meditation and Transcendental State

Spiritual Centers: "The mystery of the seven stars which you saw in my right hand, and the seven golden lamp stands is this: the seven stars are the angels of the seven assemblies. The seven lamp stands are seven assemblies."[7]

Author's Note: Paramahansa Yogananda mentions in his book *Autobiography of a Yogi* an equivalent quote from the King James Bible referring to the seven lotuses of light, described by yoga treatises as the subtle spiritual centers along the spine, or chakras.

"The lamp of the body is the eye. If therefore your eye is sound, your whole body will be full of light."[8]

Author's Note: Paramahansa Yogananda mentions in his book *Autobiography of a Yogi* an equivalent quote from the King James Bible referring to the third eye (sixth chakra) in the center of the forehead representing the center of willpower, intuition. Note that Hinduism believes in the subtle divine light (life) energy, prana, naturally entering the body through the base of the sixth chakra at the medulla (back of neck), which is directly connected through positive/negative polarity to this third eye (positive pole).

Meditation and Transcendental State: The term "meditation" in Christianity in fact is a mid-step process between prayer (vocal) and contemplation, the latter being synonymous with terms like "Theoria" ("Theosis" in Eastern Orthodox), gazing, sensing that magical (mystical) union with the divine. Meditation is a form of structured prayer including reflection while utilizing the Bible as opposed to mantras, with contemplation as the intuitive result. Contemplation

---

[7] Revelation to John 1:20.
[8] Matthew 6:22.

is also subcategorized as purgative (cleansing), analysis/reflection and the vision of God. Cumulatively, Western and Eastern Christianity include these as steps to salvation, be it through liturgical prayer and reception of the sacraments, or by faith and grace alone ("sola fide" and "sola gratia," respectively).

The defined boundary between meditation and contemplation is blurred; ancient customs included varying practices. Examples discussed below are of St. Augustine (seven stages), St. Teresa of Avila (four stages), and Hesychasm (esoteric contemplation) in Eastern Orthodox. St. Augustine spoke of preliminary stages of contemplation leading into purification ("Katharsis"), followed by mastery of passions, then entering the divine light and union into mystical contemplation. St. Teresa similarly promoted four levels of contemplation (union) including incomplete, semi-ecstatic, ecstatic and transformational, leading to merging with God. Eastern Orthodox developed a methodology of achieving mystical contemplation called Hesychasm through intense focus on the "Jesus Prayer" given great emphasis on his inner conscience, awareness and humility.

Central to the transcendental state is the belief in Jesus Christ as the Son of God, as the savior of humanity, that he died for their sins. Note some of my favorite verses:

". . . neither will they say, 'Look, here!' or 'Look, there!' for behold, God's Kingdom is within you."[9]

"Be still and know that I am God. I will be exalted among the nations. I will be exalted in the earth."[10]

". . . I am the first, and I am the last; and besides me there is no God."[11]

"Jesus said to them, 'Most certainly, I tell you, before Abraham came into existence, I AM'."[12]

---

[9] Luke 17:21.
[10] Psalms 46:10.
[11] Isaiah 44:6.
[12] John 8.58.

8.3 Islam: Spiritual Centers within the Body, Meditation and Transcendental State

Spiritual Centers: The esoteric Islamic Sufi order believe in chakras known as "Lataif-e-Sitta" or "Latifa," numbering five to seven depending upon the school of thought. Belief varies from potential to actual psycho-spiritual centers associated with multiple levels of divine, spiritual growth. Each chakra is associated with certain colors and is located at certain points in the body with a governing divine Islamic prophet from corresponding cosmic realms. For example, the Sufi order called *Naqshbandi* mentions chakras such as (a) Heart (Qalb), yellow, location left side of body, Prophet Adam; (b) Spirit (Ruh), red, location right side of body, Prophets Ibrahim/Noah; (c) Secret (Sirr), white, location below navel, Prophet Moses; (d) Mystery (Khafi), black, location forehead, Prophet Jesus, etc. Teaching methods vary, including direct Sufi teacher-to-student transmission and joint receptivity of chakra energies, focus and visualization on specific names of God, chakra points in the body, etc.

Meditation and Transcendental State: Meditation is an esoteric practice mainly prevalent in Sufism, and is synonymous with the word "Muraqabah" or achieving complete awareness of God. Initial steps include (but are not limited to) incorporating knowledge of Allah and Satan, transcending our carnal desires and ego through humility and modesty, abstaining from wealth while performing good deeds, practicing equanimity and contemplation, observing silence and stillness by abstaining from non-essential acts, maintaining a mindfulness and constant awareness of the state of our being in relation to our purity, and ability to please and create a relationship with Allah. Note that there are seven equivalent "Maqaams" or stations that one must work through including repentance (Tawba) for one's sins, watchfulness (Wara'), renunciation (Zuhd), abstaining from riches (Faqr), patience (Sabr), trust (Tawakkul), and satisfaction (Riḍā) or acceptance of one's condition.

Further broad steps of ascension (with sub-tiers) include becoming spiritually tuned with the divinity of one's guru, Prophet Muhammad, the Quran and ultimately with the essence of God. Stages of meditation include sleepiness or drowsiness overcome by wakefulness and increased perception to spiritual eye activation. This leads to the person merging with the experience (as distinct from experiencing) and gaining progressive intuition as one gains higher creation knowledge involuntarily. The meditator transcends space and time, well on the way to understanding the ultimate reality and will of Allah and the universe. Ultimate stages incorporate mystical union and absorption in divine essence called "Fana" followed by "Fana-al-Fana" (oblivion), then their re-emergence as God-appointed guides to help humanity. A point to note here is that one cannot merge with Allah; any such belief is an unforgivable sin (Shirk) akin to having a belief in multiple gods.

Note that Sufism incorporates multiple teaching styles and meditative techniques for differing levels of students. Examples include in ascending order: (a) Beginners: focusing on light energies, the cosmic universal sound, names of Allah, (b) Mid-level: focusing on life after death, Allah's will of creation, the subtle universe, and (c) Advanced: focusing on knowledge transfer through one's master, focus on Prophet Muhammad, Allah, perfection of faith. Sufis also perform devotional practices including short remembrances (Dhikr), supplication prayers (Duas), music including devotional (Qawwali) singing and dance and rituals effecting "Sama" or physical meditational listening to achieve perfection (Kemal). Note their famous "whirling dervish" dance in symbolic dress by the *Mevlevi* order of Sufis originating in Turkey. This entails transcending one's ego and lower desires (Nafs) by focusing on music, God and repetitive, symbolic body spinning akin to that of the motion of planets in the solar system.

8.4 Buddhism: Spiritual Centers within the Body, Meditation and Transcendental State

Spiritual Centers: Multiple philosophies in Buddhism attest to the chakras, numbers ranging from three to six depending upon doctrine. For example, Vajrayana generally mentions four main chakras in increasing order of purity including navel, heart, throat and crown. Similarly, a five-chakra system exists in a certain class of tantras ("ma rgyud" or mother), each with an associated Buddha (similar analogy in Hinduism), a nature element and a related source characteristic mantra called "Bija." Another interesting version of chakras is the link to the universe planes in increasing purity: gross (Nirmānakāya), subtle (Sambhogakāya), causal (Dharmakāya), and non-dualistic (Mahāsūkha-kāya). This is as per the Nyingma school of Tibetan Buddhism.

Chakras are integral to attaining Buddhahood via meditative practices by aligning subtle life energies to achieve unity of individual consciousness and wisdom. The Chinese practice of "Qigong" involves the circulation of "Qi" or subtle life energy called prana, flowing through our psychic energy channels called meridians (nadis) to awaken the chakras to achieve progressively increasing levels of transcendence. An equivalent practice is the spinning of prayer wheels (often clockwise) adorned with auspicious symbols (Ashtangamala or eight signs) and mantras such as "Om maṇi padme huṃ" resonating with the core of Buddha teachings as a path to purity and liberation. Such an act is equivalent to reciting/visualizing mantras revolving around the *nadis* and the chakras. These mantras are also inscribed in landscape such as rocks (Mani stones), on prayer flags and on the sides of hills. Related terms to chakras and energetic channels include *sushumna* nadi (Hinduism), *Avadhuti* (Buddhist tantra), *Chong Mai* and *Taiji Pole* (Taoism, Chinese medicine), Caduceus staff (Greek medicine) and mid-path of Sefirot in esoteric Judaism.

Meditation and Transcendental State: Good deeds, tolerance for all, discipline and detachment leading to meditation are integral steps within the larger umbrella of Buddhism. Prevalent also are wonderful practices such as prostration, paying reverence to the triple gem or jewels—the Buddha, his teachings (dharma) and the spiritual community (sangha), with additional benefits such as improving Karmic balance, developing humility, etc. Sometimes an entire pilgrimage is completed by prostrating oneself forward in the direction of intended religious or spiritual journey. Imagine the dedication! Further techniques include mindfulness, reflection, focus, recollections and advanced breathing techniques.

And as mentioned in Item 1.4 above, the noble eightfold path, which must be followed to avoid suffering and achieve enlightenment, includes (1) right view, (2) speech, (3) thought, (4) behavior, (5) livelihood, (6) effort, (7) mindfulness, and (8) concentration (meditation). The path also includes the five precepts.

You will come across related terms with respect to various levels (states) of the mind and techniques. These range from the beginner to the advanced practitioner, including *Mushin* (no mind), *Wu Wei* (effortless action), *Zanshin* (relaxed awareness), *Shoshin* (a mind devoid of preconceptions), *Fudōshin* (immovable mind), *Vipassanā* (calmness, mindfulness of breathing), etc. The popular Zen (philosophy of Mahayana) incorporates rigorous self-restraint and meditation practices towards perceiving the true nature of the mind (*Kenshō*) and things; with supporting arts such as poetry, painting, calligraphy, tea ceremony and flower arranging as part of training. These yogic practices (both physical and mental) are integral to this effort, with derivative prowess extending into martial arts in some schools. They represent multiple paths to developing that intuition or experienced spiritual guidance to a relaxed mind to promote daily activities with concerted precision (devoid of our ego and emotions) to transcend. Tantrism focusing on religious rituals for gods emphasizes mystic symbols, chants and other esoteric techniques, the last named being analogous to Shamanic beliefs. Advanced meditation practices include "Tummo" or inner fire meditation, "Dzogchen" which entail practices such as "Trekchö" and "Tögal" focusing on divine luminous essence (see Item 9.4 below).

Core to the principles of enlightenment, nirvana, is realizing the three marks or reality—*dukkha* suffering or pervasive dissatisfaction, *anicca* or impermanence, and *anattā* or non-Self; and also that one is able to discern and no longer be fooled by them. Nirvana is not some blissful place that one goes to, it is the cessation of feeling and suffering (Nirodha) and the cessation of craving (Tanha). One must blow out or detach from the three poisons (kleshas): greed, hatred and delusion. For example, training in Theravada commences at the level of lay persons (Upasakas) leading to four levels of aspirants called: (a) "Sotāpanna," one who has reached an initial stage of enlightenment, (b) "Sakadāgāmin" or partially enlightened aspirant, (c) "Anāgāmin," one who has transcended rebirth on the earth plane and resides in the pure abodes, and (d) "Arhat" who has achieved or is near to achieving nirvana.

A couple of clarifications on words like "Arhat," "Pretyabuddha" and "Bodhisattva." An arhat achieves Buddhahood with the guidance of a Buddha, whereas a bodhisattva (also guided by the Buddha) is one who has willingly accepted to be reborn to help others, and will achieve Buddhahood at some point. Prety-abuddhas on the other hand are solitary Buddhas who do not teach others.

8.5 Judaism: Spiritual Centers within the Body, Meditation and Transcendental State

Spiritual Centers: The ten manifested "Sefirot" or energy channels mentioned in esoteric text "Kabbalah" are modes with which God manifests himself. These are translated into humans as characteristics called "Partzufim." Each one of these modes have a differing level of spirituality or consciousness, associated with different parts of the human body. These are called "Chochmah'" or wisdom, "Binah" or understanding, "Daat" or knowledge, "Chesed" or kindness, "Gevurah" or strength, "Tiferet" or beauty, "Netzach" or victory, "Hod" or splendor/glory, "Yesod" or foundation, and "Malchut" or kingship, humility.

Note there is another (first) Sefirah called "Keter" representing unmanifest or divine knowledge, which is represented in the manifest condition as "Daat" (Sefirah mentioned above). A man's soul possesses this divine attribute at the core because he is a divine being, and progressively takes advantage of connecting to these modes and transcending to achieve godliness.

Meditation and Transcendental State: The concept of prophecy (nevu'a), as well as other forms of divine communication (ruach hakodesh) and direct or indirect contact with celestial beings who take on anthropomorphic features to convey messages, are areas in which one can appreciate the hierarchy of the transcendental states. In order to become primed to receiving the ruach hakodesh or divine messages expressed through force or inspiration, an individual must be fluent in spiritual knowledge and understanding of God's ways. It is also imperative that one achieve levels of complete bliss and exaltation, as this manifestation of happiness increases the expansiveness of the human mind. On a smaller scale, it is possible for one to momentarily transcend through the completion of God's commandments (mitzvot), where the person leaves the trappings of purely material existence and subjects himself or herself to a higher power. Thus, following the many laws and commandments, as well as teachings that are echoed throughout the written and oral law, one can transcend to a certain degree. While these levels may not be necessarily quantified, the Talmud (oral law) does occasionally speak of those who engage in specific mitzvot as actively moving up closer to the divine presence.

Consequently, Jewish meditation constitutes many forms of practice stemming from biblical times. Keywords in the Old Testament include terms such as "hāgâ" (connect with) or murmur, meditate, and "sîḥâ" to muse, converse, rehearse mentally. Practices range from structured prayer such as "Amidah" to contemplation or concentration on prayers with sincere devotion (Kavanah), including theurgy or focus on secret meanings on certain words, divine names to achieve unity with God, to esoteric practices and also euphoric and ecstatic "Devekut" or altered trance-like states, and theosophical Kabbalistic practices utilizing the concept of Sefirot, channeling mystical energies between our being to the divine realm. Other practices include "Musar" or a series of contemplation techniques to focus and eliminate the barriers precluding release of the divine essence centered within our being. Chassidic (Hasidic) philosophy constitutes secluded, silent meditation (hitbodedut) as a means to transcendence.

9. Significance of Light Energies

9.1 Hinduism: Significance of Light Energies

Heaven has its own divine light, translated into our daily lives by way of holy illumination integral to our religious and spiritual activities. Examples include lighting of oil lamps (diyas) placed in temples, homes, shops, used in religious events, processions, festival fireworks including *Diwali* the festival of lights, and celestial representations. Juxtaposed against science, light energy or electromagnetic radiation constitutes the fundamental basis of all creation at its core commencing at subatomic levels, for example, photons or heated packets of energy which have no mass. And light energy is the only constant in an evolving universe with factors such as time and gravity being proven impermanent. Ancient sages understood this constant phenomenon of light. Through their powers of concentration, meditation and concerted yogic practices including use of herbal dietary aids to purify their bodies, they learned to control the resident, subtle life (light) or pranic energies within the psychic energetic system (chakras). They were hence able to convert their physical bodies or electromagnetic subatomic energies into weightless light energies, thereby achieving feats such as teleportation, levitation, etc.

Similarly, these great sages also came to fully understand the universe planes (gross, subtle) as vibrational energies in increasing levels of purity (variations of light energy) driven by superconscious, divine power (God) culminating in heaven. And they also understood that these principles were the path to break out of our endless chains of confusion and cosmic delusion (maya) to eventual redemption.

9.2 Christianity: Significance of Light Energies

Keywords associated with light include the divine presence of God and Christ, purity, goodness, radiance, inspirational, as opposed to Satan, the prince of darkness epitomizing evil. Indeed we even use derivative terms such as the "light of knowledge," "light at end of tunnel" in our everyday lives.

Divinity associated with light is strongly emphasized across all philosophies within Christianity; for example Quakers (Protestant) refer to inner light as symbolizing presence of Jesus within our being, Eastern Orthodox refers to the transfiguration of Jesus in divine radiant light at Mount Tabor, etc. Church design places strong emphasis on illumination including sunlight, for example in atrium design, use of octahedron and star shape to represent celestial light. Use of candles is strongly prevalent in religious and personal services including "lighting a candle for someone else," baptism, prayers for the deceased, and myriad other festivals. Votive candles are indeed common in both homes and churches as a sign of faith. And as with other religions, Christianity emphasizes the radiance of angels and the glory of Heaven through divine spiritual light.

9.3 Islam: Significance of Light Energies

According to the Quran,[13] God is the Light of the heavens and the earth. This means that everything has come into existence, everything occurs as a result of

---

[13] An-Nur 24:5.

the manifestation of His Light. Light, in the absolute sense, belongs to Him exclusively, starting with the *light* of Prophet Muhammad, upon him be peace and blessings, about which the Prophet himself said that "the first thing that God created is my *light*, everything is the manifestation of His Light at different wavelengths and its appearance in different forms in the external world."

Note the use of capitals to differentiate between the "Light" of God, versus the derivative *"light"* from Him. "Light" herein is construed as something immaterial which cannot be comprehended, and can be the immaterial essence of *"light"* which is the material aspect. Examples of the latter in the physical realm of existence constitute the inner radiance of our soul and power of intellect, *light* of nature (sun, moon, etc.).

Nur has multiple interpretations (depending upon beliefs), including but not limited to the guiding light at resurrection, the commandments of Allah, the authoritative guidance of the Quran, divine faith in Islam, the light of day, etc. Note also references to God creating angels of mercy from Nur or cold light of night or light of the moon, in contrast to *Nar* for angels of punishment which are created from fire or the solar light (see Item 3.3 above). Angels commonly dwell in the heavenly spheres and are generally considered to be the first creation of God.

As an additional point, it may be noted that Islam utilizes light sources (candles, lights) to aid efficient religious practices only.

9.4 Buddhism: Significance of Light Energies

Integral to the threefold nature (see Item 3.4) of Buddha is the astral or subtle body called "Sambhogakāya" where the Buddha manifests in boundless subtle form comprising the light of divine intelligence to teach higher-level students such as bodhisattvas. Multiple religious texts including early Buddhist and mother tantras all refer to an enlightened meditative mind blazing with perfected, absolute knowledge of the nature of emptiness (sunyata) shining with a radiance translated as "clear light." Many advanced meditation practices such as "Dzogchen" utilize techniques such as "Trekchö" and "Tögal" incorporating the use of light energies to manifest as a "Rainbow Body" whereby an advanced practitioner transforms his body into light noted as a rainbow phenomenon witnessed both before and after death depending upon the level of the practitioners. Indeed advanced practitioners (such as Bon tradition) have been able to achieve similar light energy state without undergoing the process of death.And as mentioned in Item 8.4, chakras are integral to achieving Buddhahood via meditative practices by aligning subtle life (light) energies to achieving nirvana.

In Buddhism, the use of light aids such as candles and butter lamps are an integral part of rituals at monasteries, shrines and homes. Indeed there is even a candle festival called "Ubon Ratchathani" in Thailand celebrated on/around the time of "Āsāḷhā Puja" (see Item 14.4) associated with Buddha's first sermon after achieving nirvana.

9.5 Judaism: Significance of Light Energies

The eleven Sefirot or energy levels aforementioned (in Item 2.5) emanate from the "Ohr Ein-Sof" or "Light of the Ein-Sof" or divine, unmanifested God to create the subtle and material worlds. And the journey of the soul consists of a light "Ohr" housed in a vessel "Kli" adapting to the spiritual levels of divinity in the said worlds (universe), which ranges from undifferentiated to differentiated creation including both the inanimate and the animate. Thus light energy is an integral derivative part of creation, with heaven having its own divine light. In Genesis the light that was created on the first day refers to the light of "ultimate knowledge" or divine connection that God reserves for his righteous followers in the world to come (olam haba). In that vein, light can also be seen as the emanation of divinity. "Nitzotzot" or sparks are representative of these emanations that are inherent in creation. At a lower level, light rays of the sun or other sources are seen as anthropomorphic representations of higher divinity. That being said, the context in which many Tannaitic (views of rabbinic sages recorded in the Mishnah between AD 10–220) and Talmudic texts contrasting light and darkness may allude to a slightly different focus, which is presence versus absence of divinity. This can be appreciated in the way candlelight is used symbolically in the temple, as well as during the celebration of Hannukah, a festival where eight candles are lit in increasing order, over eight days.

10. Creation by God, Nature and Science

10.1 Hinduism: Creation by God, Nature and Science

The universe commenced from the merger of spiritual (male, Purusha) and material (female, Prakriti) energies of God, from the unmanifest Brahman (pure consciousness) to initial macro-level differentiation (cosmic ego or "Mahat") through to the multiple stages of creation, i.e., macro-to-micro (as per Table B-1). Initial subtle involution commenced leading to parallel streams of creation both subtle and gross, including combinations thereof resulting in the inanimate coming to life—from cells to plants to animals to humans. Note that the ancient religious representations of deities on earth substantially follow the creation of life explained by science.

Physical nature also evolved as part of this creation, its gross elements including ether, air, fire, water, earth constituting a critical part of our being, thereby playing an integral role leading to our natural attraction for it. We are involuntarily fascinated by plants, planets, stars, mountains!

Hence, nature is deemed sublime, with pilgrimages (Tirth Yatra) to sites associated with gods, deities, and sages. Note the ancient towns of Rishikesh and Vrindavan on the banks of the holy Ganges and Yamuna rivers respectively; and mountains like Kailash (Lord Shiva's abode), Trikuta Hills (Vaishno Devi temple), Tirumala Hills (Tirupati Sri Venkateshwara temple), and Garhwal (Badrinath, Kedarnath temples). Vrindavan has over 5,000 temples and is where Lord Krishna (born in nearby Mathura) spent much of his childhood. Mount Kailash is also considered holy in Buddhism, Jainism, etc. Also, respect and food offerings "Bhuta-yajna" towards animals are an integral part of silent love for God's creation. The cow is revered for its gentleness and giving nature, associated with Goddess Aditi, the mother of creation.

Religious practices integrally utilize the use of plants and fruits such as the holy basil (tulsi leaf) and coconut renowned for their medicinal benefits, and are also given as holy gifts (prasad) from God to us. The practice of "Satsang" incorporating religious, holistic and meditative acts includes the plantation of trees. And how about the divine lotus flower symbolizing meditative postures, chakras or light of infinite knowledge. Note that the lotus posture locks in the back and spine (upright) when yogis go into a deep trance during meditation. Some interesting pieces of information: did you know that the much beloved character E.T. in the science fiction movie *E.T. the Extra-Terrestrial* was closely associated with botany, the study of plants. I was once on a trip to Goa (India) and happened to meet a remarkable chauffeur who told me that the use of the holy basil (tulsi) leaf is so spiritual that its benefits emerge in subliminal fashion when least expected! Note that the tulsi and lotus are both integrally linked to Goddess Lakshmi.

It is said that science is catching up with religious/spiritual explanations of creation, with confluence of the two once we get past the question of what the actual initial conditions were for kick-starting creation (for example the big bang theory), or what precisely caused the creation of living cells.

10.2 Christianity: Creation by God, Nature and Science

"God said, 'Let's make man in our image, after our likeness. Let them have dominion over the fish of the sea, and over the birds of the sky, and over the livestock, and over all the earth, and over every creeping thing that creeps on the earth.'"[14]

As per Biblical sources, God created the heavens and earth, the plants, the beasts, and eventually man over a six-day period through progressive differentiation (examples darkness and light, land and sea), resting on the seventh (Sabbath). In the first five days, God created the universe including light, sea and land, plants, fruit trees, marine and flight-based creatures, and finally land animals and humans (Adam in His image, with Eve following) on the sixth day.

For relative confluence of religion and scientific theories on creation, note the basic belief in Abrahamic religions that God created the universe ex nihilo (out of nothing) in stages. Modern science considers this timing (see Item 12.2 below) as symbolic.

As for nature, Christianity places great responsibility on humans with respect to stewardship, i.e., playing a key role to respecting and protecting nature as a means to glorifying God's creation. Communities such as the Amish and the Anabaptists have incorporated holistic living in rural communities close to nature reinforced by the belief that service to plants and animals, and harmony with nature, soil and weather are integral to pleasing God. And the

---

[14] Genesis 1:26

Book of Genesis states that God called upon Noah to bring with him unto the Ark all animal representatives to preserve their continuity in the future of his creation. Note also similar references in Hinduism, Zoroastrianism, Greek and Chinese mythology (the Gun-Yu flood).

10.3 Islam: Creation by God, Nature and Science

Islam believes that God is the sole cause of creation as described in the Holy Quran. All aspects of Allah's creation including the gross and subtle universe with its multiple heavens, earth and hell, nature, derivative forms of life, and achievements including science are all representations of His divine purpose and love.

Consequently, it is the duty of all Muslims (given free will) to respect all forms of nature and life while aiming to excel in meritorious endeavors such as science, as a means to praising God by achieving harmony for all beings. Theories ranging from the six-day account of creation, ex nihilo, Adam and Eve, Sufi cosmology describing progressive differentiation or emanations from subtle to gross planes, to scientific theories such as the big bang and progressive evolution all fall under the umbrella of God-guided evolution.

Nature plays a significant part of this larger equation; in fact more than 500 out of Holy Quran's cumulative 6,236 verses provide specific related guidance. These include conservation practices, charity, precluding cruel treatment of animals (halal meat consumption is as per specific dietary laws, similar to Jewish Kashrut laws allowing Kosher), scientific study of nature while translating our beautiful planet into an abode similar to the Garden of Eden.

Allah is all powerful and merciful Who creates and sustains our universe resplendent with all its signs (āyāt) continually glorifying His existence in every aspect, reinforced by His message and revelations to mankind through anointed prophets to provide universal balance and harmony.

10.4 Buddhism: Creation by God, Nature and Science

Buddhism does not believe in an overall creator or immortal God, instead teaching that the universe emerges out of a primordial state of pure infinite awareness and knowledge called sunyata (emptiness) or *Tathātā* (thatness or suchness), terms used interchangeably based upon doctrine. Buddhism does not specifically delve into what caused the first spark of creation. The Buddha reportedly did not answer related questions about the origin of the universe. Buddhism however promotes creation as a chain of related events, "dependent origination," which are impermanent with no beginning and no end, with cycles eventually repeating (samsara) for those who do not transcend into the highest four planes (see Item 2.4).

To explain further about this dependent cycle, the existence of a subtle or gross plane is dependent on the Karma of the beings inhabiting it, and disappears when their Karma is exhausted, or they pass away. The goal is hence to transcend this by achieving nirvana via Buddhahood, which is a state free of all disturbing emotions and obstructions to knowledge.

Note also that the reference to gods in Buddhism are also subject to this cycle of dependence. The early schools of Nikaya, Hinayana Buddhism, discuss the gods (such as Mahabrahma) existing in heavens within the cycle of samsara, and that they are misconstrued as creation gods.

Ultimately, the Buddhas are seen as the closest concept of a creator God given that they emerge from the said sunyata also known as "Tathagatagarbha" (womb of all Buddhas). Examples include the first or primordial Adi Buddha (note Gautama Buddha was not the original) worshipped in multiple Mahayana and Vajrayana traditions as Vairocana or Amitabha Buddha and Samantabhadra or Vajradhara Buddha respectively.

The philosophies of Buddhism welcome and accepts science, astrophysics and scientific theories for the origin of the universe, such as the big bang theory. It is constantly adaptive and encourages experimentation.

Indeed, the Buddha himself urged disciples and followers to not take his word, but to only believe when they experienced for themselves. Confluence of Buddhism and science begins with recognition of four primary material elements of creation including solidity, fluidity, temperature and mobility; equating to the basic elements of earth, water, fire, and air as an integral part driving nature's involution.

Buddhism and nature go hand in hand commencing from the Buddha achieving nirvana under the Bodhi tree. Nature indeed was integral to Buddha's life and teachings, and as a future venue for peaceful meditative practices the world over. The Pali Canon cites examples of the close relationship of the Buddha with animals. Indeed, ancient martial art practices incorporate the movements of animals for protection and spiritual transcendence.

10.5 Judaism: Creation by God, Nature and Science

As with the other Abrahamic religions, Judaism shares the Biblical views on God creating the universe ex nihilo in stages, i.e., six-day (Yom) period. Note however that Yom can pertain to multiple time representations. For example, while a day represents twenty-four hours, according to another interpretation this one day may represent thousands of millions of years as per the religious theory of creation.

And as described in the *Levels of Purity* (under Item 2.5), according to the esoteric teachings of the Kabbalah, eleven energy channels called Sefirot (one unmanifest, ten manifest) of light, both male and female, emanating from the divine undifferentiated life force of Ein-Sof (God) were responsible for continuously creating five subtle and gross realms of the universe in varying levels of purity. This includes life commencing from angels to the inanimate to the animate including humans created in God's image. Science is closely correlated with God. It is important to note that as per Jewish beliefs, God is present even within the scientific descriptions of natural progression to the most infinitesimal degree. Furthermore, Judaism places great emphasis on acknowledging and respecting nature as a means to its creator.

Last but not the least, the divinity of nature is acknowledged universally across the myriad cultures and religions, commencing from ancient civilizations, including but not limited to gods of the heavens, sun temples, belief in astrology (although Islam differs), use of land topography to revere the elements and deities, the hailing of agricultural and other seasons, partaking in religious events honoring nature, and as a natural setting for relaxation and meditation practices.

11. Miracles

11.1 Hinduism: Miracles

In addition to miracles by the gods which are acknowledged across most religions including Hinduism, *siddhi* powers or the ability to perform these are a natural by-product of growing spirituality. This is achieved by way of intense focus and practice leading into progressive levels of concentration, meditation and realization cumulatively called *samyama*.

In essence, this is an innate ability within us (some exhibit from childhood) curtailed by the relative strength of our ego. Through intense religious and spiritual focus we are able to convert willpower into thought to understand the inner, energetic workings (prana) of the object of our focus, thereby gaining control over the same; one can suddenly develop these powers including healing, telepathy, regression analysis, etc. Indeed, advanced yogis can perform levitation, involuntary stoppage of breath and other feats. Note that some of these lesser feats are sometimes experienced temporarily with the use of drugs and alcohol (focus temporarily enhanced) but the after-effects are catastrophic on our mind and body. Our sages also continually de-stress the importance upon such abilities given that they can also attract temptations of misuse and abuse.

Instead, as an example look at the collective ability of people to focus on humanitarian efforts globally; get involved and you will see a series of miracles taking place!

11.2 Christianity: Miracles

Among many examples,

> "A certain one of them struck the servant of the high priest, and cut off his right ear. But Jesus answered, 'Let me at least do this'—and he touched his ear and healed him."[15]

In addition, Jesus is known for performing seven miracles including changing water into wine at Canaan, restoring the eyesight of the blind man, his Resurrection at Mount Tabor in radiant divine light, raising St. Lazarus of Bethany from the dead four days after his entombment, etc.

---

[15] Luke 22:50–51.

Indeed, miracles are accepted in Christianity for betterment, not selfish gains, including but not limited to practices of Theoria or contemplation leading to direct experience with God, attaining beatific vision via God's grace seen as the purpose of man and angels. Others include faith healing including "laying on of hands" eliciting divine presence, speaking in tongues, communicating with angels and spirit guides, receiving gifts from the Holy Spirit, the Eucharistic miracle. As with Hinduism, many saints of Christianity the world over are reported to have performed or experienced aforementioned divine experiences. Read also about the fascinating October 1917 "Miracle of Fátima" in Portugal, given credence by the Catholic Church.

11.3 Islam: Miracles

Miracles in Islam are divine gifts from Allah performed by prophets, saints and chosen designates on His behalf. The Holy Quran is considered a miracle given that Allah's divine teachings illustrated by the *āyahs* (or *āyāt*) or signs complete with scientific revelations on universe origin and involution/evolution, metaphysics, nature and geology, biological sciences were passed on directly to Prophet Muhammad by the Archangel Jibril (Gabriel) over a period of about twenty-three years. Indeed the Quran is considered to be Prophet Muhammad's greatest miracle in addition to which he performed many others in his lifetime including healing of the needy, control over nature, enhancement of natural resources, etc. Miracles by prophets and saints (for example, Sufis) are referred to as "Mu'jiza" and "Karamat" respectively. Note that prophets are generally regarded as the most divine within all humanity.

Related terms with respect to miracles include "Baraka" or a flow, transmission of blessings and grace from God through prophets and saints; one receiving the same in turn can perform miracles including healings, levitations, reviving the dead, etc. Indeed, pilgrimages (Ziyara) are undertaken to receive Baraka from holy shrines such as mosques, or tombs (Maqām) associated with Prophet Muhammad and other venerable prophets and saints. Baraka is also passed on by Sufi saints (Murshids) to students (Murīds) by passing of an initiatory cloak (Khirqah) representing deep esoteric knowledge of the Sufi chain of spirituality. Communications with spirits (jinn) is also considered as a lesser form of miracle, according to the Quran. Sulayman ibn Dawood (Solomon, son of David) was the third king and prophet of the Israelites with a God-given gift of the ability to speak to the jinn spirits and animals.

11.4 Buddhism: Miracles

Buddhism does not believe in a creator God, hence there are no divine miracles as in other religions. Buddhism attributes miracles as a result of progressive holistic living (for example, the eightfold path) following concerted religious and spiritual *dhyana* (in Sanskrit) or meditative practices (for example the nine-fold stages of form, formless dhyana) or *Jhānas* (in Pali). The resultant higher knowledge (Abhijñā) gained leads into six types of supra-normal perception including psychic and higher powers (iddhividhā) such as levitation, teleportation, clairvoyance (dibba-sota), knowledge of the minds of others (ceto-pariya-ñāṇa), regression analysis (pubbe-nivāsanussati), divine eye (dibba-cakkhu) including seeing one's Karma and multiple life path, and eliminating all mental vices (āsravakṣaya).

All these powers were initially attained by Gautama Buddha, and later by his disciples and monks following these intense paths of knowledge and divine learning. As also mentioned, advanced monks are masters of meditation practices such as Dzogchen and Tummo, even to the point of preparing for their future life transition via rainbow body manifestations.

A wonderful point to note is how the Dalai Lamas of Tibetan (Vajrayana) Buddhism are chosen. Given that His Holiness chooses his next reincarnation (new identity), the high monks (Lamas) set off on a concerted trail looking for clues, armed with high visions and dreams, culminating in a series of tests once the likely candidate (child) is found. These traits include whether the child will identify his toys or everyday objects used in his previous life and such others. Once satisfactorily ascertained, intense spiritual training ensues through scriptures and progressive meditation. Author's note: I have had the pleasure of meeting His Holiness the Dalai Lama twice, and have gained a certain understanding as to his all-encompassing spiritual nature. I never cease to marvel at his humility while trying to hide his divinity gained from aforementioned practices under the cloak of his bubbly humor!

11.5 Judaism: Miracles

Miracles are accepted in rabbinic literature including but not limited to the Talmud, esoteric Kabbalah, Chassidic and other scriptures. Miracles are either brought about through God's will without human involvement, or through human involvement (prayer). Examples include achieving divine communications utilizing special names of God, via the minyan or combined prayer, silent meditation (hitbodedut), the Sefirot (Partzufim) as means of spiritual transcendence, gifts from God, the powers of prophets such as Moses parting the Red Sea (called Yam Suph, Reed Sea) following the exodus from Egypt. And last but not the least, the strength and endurance of the Jewish people reinforced by their belief in the natural order of the universe, their special covenant with God leading to perseverance, compassion, love, hope, and systemic advances all constitute miracles in their own right. Interestingly, Oral tradition maintains that occurrences are set forth by God Himself at a macro level, thus minimizing the belief in luck and chance.

12. Cyclical vs. Historical Patterns of Time in the Universe

12.1 Hinduism: Cyclical vs. Historical Patterns of Time in the Universe

Readers are requested to see the diagrammatic presentation under the subheading "Timeline of the Universe" following the discussion on Table C later under the heading "Overall System of Spirituality."

The universe cycles in and out of periods of cosmic governance (yugas) within the lifespan (100 years) of the creator Lord Brahma, translated into human years as follows: One day and one night each of Lord Brahma is equal to 4,320,000,000 human years, totaling to 8,640,000,000 human years for a whole day. Consequently, the 100-year lifespan of Lord Brahma in human terms is 8,640,000,000 x 360 days x 100 human years, or 311.04 trillion years.

Within the said period (one day) are subsets, recurring Yugas or defined time periods (X, 2X, 3X and 4X) where X=432,000 human years; each with a set of prevailing guiding energies (positive and negative, see below) that we have to contend with and grow from: (a) Kali Yuga (X) Period of difficulty or moral degeneration, (b) Dvapar Yuga (2X) Period of compassion, honesty offset by some challenges, (c) Treta Yuga (3X) Period where the power of humans diminishes slightly because of the tussle of materialism versus spirituality, and (d) Krita or Satya Yuga (4X) Period of golden age when humanity prevails.

These four periods of yugas combined are called a Mahayuga, cumulatively totaling 4,320,000 (or 4.32 million) earth years. One day of the creator is 1000X of this Mahayuga or 4,320,000,000 (or 4.32 billion) human years! Same period for one night. The scriptures further state that the day of Lord Brahma (creator) promotes projection and manifestation of the universe. Night is the reverse when the cosmos merges back into the unmanifest condition. And given that these sequential worlds are limited and conditioned in time and the knowledge of this creation is ever retained within pure consciousness (Brahman), this knowledge is utilized periodically for the continued cycles of creation and dissolution. Consequently, our individual Karmic cycle also continues when cyclical creation re-emerges (day), and we continue in our action/reaction cycle where we had left off in prior creation. A swami also mentioned that given the holy scriptures like the Vedas are eternal as also are certain gods including Lord Krishna, they manifest with each positive cycle of creation.

At present, we are in the fifty-first year in the life of Lord Brahma the creator. The overall cycle repeats itself after 100 years of Brahma's life (311.04 trillion earth years) with a new Brahma in place. Synonymous terms associated with Lord Brahma include Hiranyagarbha, meaning "golden womb," from which the cosmos manifests.

Last but not the least, Brahman or pure undifferentiated consciousness itself is never destroyed. Akin to waves rising and subsiding in an ocean, all the created worlds noted above come in and out of this ocean of pure knowledge whereas the ocean never ceases to exist.

12.2 Christianity: Cyclical vs. Historical Patterns of Time in the Universe

An interesting historical categorization of Six Ages based upon religious events was formulated by Saint Augustine of Hippo. Commencing from the creation of Adam to the events of Revelation, each age lasted 1,000 years (interpretations on time periods vary). The First Age is from the time of Adam (first man) to Noah building the ark pre-flood. The Second Age then follows until the advent of Abraham (patriarch). The Third Age follows to David the king (keywords David and Goliath), with the Fourth Age extending up to the Exile to Babylonia during the Chaldean Empire. The Fifth Age goes from the Exile into Babylonia to the all-important coming of Jesus Christ, with the Sixth Age following (currently ongoing).

Multiple interpretations exist on the timing of the Seventh Age—either running parallel to the Six Ages, or following after the Six Ages; both are associated with lasting bliss and heaven. Cumulatively, these ages represent the seven days of creation. Note that the last day is symbolized in our lives as Sabbath, a day of rest in the week to be spent on worship and praise of the Lord. It may be noted that the ancient Greeks also had historical time categorizations such as Iron, Bronze, Silver and Golden Ages.

Accordingly, these represent historical and/or symbolic categorizations of time. Note that there are additionally multiple interpretations of time including Gap, Cosmic, Day-Age versus Progressive Creationism, whereby translations of symbolic time to science are reconciled. As an example, Day Age reconciles the six-day biblical creation to thousands of millions of earth years with respect to creation according to science. Further theories include dispensationalism (similar to Hinduism) with periods of time, for example, ages of innocence, conscience, grace and promise, allocated by God with certain guiding principles prevailing for us to contend with.

12.3 Islam: Cyclical vs. Historical Patterns of Time in the Universe

Islam follows the broad umbrella of historical, linear (not cyclical) patterns of time as laid out in the Abrahamic religions, with a messianic age leading up to eventual final judgement. According to the Quran, the universe was created in six days (Ayyam), verse 70:4 defining one day as around 50,000 years on earth. This equates the concept of six days of creation to six distinct periods/eons. The length of these periods and specific developments within them are loosely defined.

The Quran and the Hadith contain three periods in which events before the Judgement Day constitute several minor and major signs including negative periods (corruption, etc.) on the earth thanks to the Antichrist al-Masih ad-Dajjal, with Isa (Jesus) and the Mahdi (Messiah) then descending during the final period to triumph over this false messiah as a precursor to the final judgement and Resurrection. Another interpretation of these three periods leading up to the Judgement Day constitute the first period commencing with the passing of Prophet Muhammad, the second period beginning with the passing of all his companions and lasting nearly 1,000 years and the final period to commence with the advent of the Mahdi (Messiah).

12.4 Buddhism: Cyclical vs. Historical Patterns of Time in the Universe

In Mahayana, religious and spiritual development is segregated into three periods of time following the Buddha's passing: (a) Period of the right teachings (dharma) for about 500–1,000 years where the teachings of Gautama Buddha were followed, (b) Middle period for next 1,000–2,000 years where the Buddha's original teachings were not taken as seriously by people—only pretending to accept the dharma, and (c) Final period commencing about 2,000 years after Gautama Buddha's passing and lasting for 10,000 years when moral corruption precludes attaining enlightenment through the Buddha's teachings.

Ultimately a Maitreya (future Buddha) eventually emerges to rebalance the system. Note that similar cycles exist in other Buddhist streams of doctrines. And the aforementioned is a subset of the Buddhist belief in the cyclical patterns of the universe working through creation, sustenance and dissolution over defined time periods which are lengthy.

According to one belief, four time periods exist: "Kalpa" or a time period of around sixteen million earth years. A Small Kalpa equals 1,000 Kalpas or sixteen billion years, a Medium Kalpa is twenty-one times a Small Kalpa or 336 billion years, and a Great (Mahakalpa) is four times a Medium Kalpa or 1.344 trillion years. Another definition of Kalpa time delineation is by the number of Buddhas born during these periods. There are two types: (a) Suñña-Kalpa and (b) Asuñña-Kalpa. The former signifies a condition/period where no Buddha is born, whereas the latter is where at least one Buddha is born. There are five types of the latter, Asuñña-Kalpa: Sāra-Kalpa (one Buddha born), Maṇḍa-Kalpa (two Buddhas born), Vara-Kalpa (three Buddhas born), Sāramaṇḍa-Kalpa (four Buddhas born), and Bhadda-Kalpa (five Buddhas born).

Our mission is to break these continued cycles of life by ascending through the ten cumulative levels of subtle and gross existence (see Item 2.4) to achieve nirvana.

12.5 Judaism: Cyclical vs. Historical Patterns of Time in the Universe

The similitudes between Christian and Jewish traditions are fascinating. Jewish scriptures state that the Era of the Messiah is timed to 6,000 years post-creation, and a Talmudic reference also describes 2,000 years of chaos, two thousand years of Torah (bible) and 2,000 years of Mashiach (prophet of redemption).

Furthermore, a Kabbalistic (esoteric) tradition also equates these periods to six days of the week, with Shabbat, the seventh day, for rest corresponding to the seventh set of thousand years of other-worldly life (olam haba) in which no evil will exist, and man will follow the path of God without hindrance. Note that this latter period is referred to in the Abrahamic religions as the messianic age in which brotherhood and peace reign. And last but not the least, refer to the time definition of one day (Yom) in Article 10.5 equating to thousands of millions of years as measured per the religious theory of creation.

13. Temples, Churches, Mosques, Monasteries, Synagogues and Their Clergy

13.1 Hinduism: Temple—Structure and Clergy

Structure: As with all religious and spiritual establishments the world over, Hindu temples represent the symbolic, harmonious confluence of God and the created universe (gross, subtle planes) as a beacon of inspiration for the community and economy, and to pursue goals and transcend desires to achieve realization. Temples preserve ancient Vedic scriptural knowledge and traditions, our communion with nature and the interconnectedness of the universe and God. Retreat temples (called "ashrams" in Indic religions) were also built in serene locales such as mountains, caves, forests and alongside rivers to benefit from the influence of nature, the sun and the earth's magnetic fields. Architecture was also based on ancient Sanskrit textual knowledge linked to the Rig Veda, such as the Vaastu Shastra. Many were also built in zones of high vibrational pure (sattwic) energies, for example, where realized sages left behind their residual energies enabling people to get purified by visitation.

Temple designs utilize both circles (creation) and squares (divinity, light) to represent the principles of the multiple philosophies of Hinduism both visually and subliminally. Keywords in design are "Vaastu-Purusha-Mandala": Mandala meaning circle, Purusha representing spiritual essence (God), and Vaastu meaning dwelling structure. Temple axes follow the four cardinal points of the compass, with the square divided into sub-squares or quadrants (paadas), each representing a deity. Numbers of sub-squares vary from one to 1,024, with sixty-four being the most prevalent. The central square (comprising four squares) for the latter represents Brahman or pure consciousness housing a statue (Murti) of the resident deity, and is without decorations. This innermost space of spiritual energy (Purusha) of God is the purest, with the outermost squares incorporating negative symbolism such as evil, demons (Rakshasha). Practice of circumambulation (Pradakshina) around this central square is an integral part of "darshana" or religious practice to achieve transcendent knowledge. Note that Pradakshina is also performed in marriage ceremonies around a sacred fire.

Circumscribing the overall square with its sixty-four sub-squares is the circle of Mandala representing elements of the gross universe. A conical or equivalent towering structure (Shikhara) or *Vimana* utilizing principles of concentric circles and squares with a dome adorning the top of the temple is thought to be inspired by the holy Mount Kailash (in China). Larger temples have pillared halls (Mandapa) including waiting areas.

The overall layout is open on all sides, except for the innermost space. Paintings and sculptures symbolizing deities, religious, astrological and esoteric (yantra) designs aiding tantric practices, meditation and spiritual principles are integral to all temples, including complex recurrent design symbolizing universal essence. Temples are also hugely decorated with flowers, statues of gods and deities, holy *diyas* or lit clay pots filled with oil and wick. Another example of interconnected universal creation is the *Kalasha*, an ornately decorated pot (clay or copper) with a green coconut placed on top with mango leaves at its mouth—a welcome sight at multiple rituals including worship in homes. The Kalasha is filled with water or rice, the former symbolic of the inherent primal pure force of creation, with the coconut and leaves representing creation. A holy thread tied around the neck of the Kalasha symbolizes the interconnect-edness of it all. The Kalasha also represents the purest form of knowledge gained from ancient scriptures. Temple bells are also highly prevalent, and ringing the bell is very popular given that it represents Aum, the holy vibrations of the divine cosmic motor for all creation. The same principle applied for blowing the conch in battlefields to preserve unity while vanquishing evil.

In the larger complexes, the main temple is supplemented by shrines also following grid principles of symmetry and mathematical precision.

Clergy: There is no centralized system. It follows the origins of Hinduism con-stituting the direct experiences and revelations of sages (rishis) translating into ancient Sanskrit texts (the Vedas). Consequently there is no formal system; instead Hinduism has many spiritual leaders (see Item 3.1), some considered as achieving almost godly status. There are however many gurus, swamis and swaminis (female), pandits and acharyas who may be considered equivalent to formal clergy. Other titles for ascetics include *muni, rishi* (or *ruesi*), *rishi muni, maharishi, sadhu,* etc. Every temple typically has a pandit/*pujari* or *purohit* who performs prayers (puja) and special sacrifices, worship or *yajna* including home visitations for prayers and purification. Practices extend to marriages, perform-ing final rites, and others collectively known as "dashakarma"—ten rituals from birth to death of an individual. A highly popular ceremony (out of these ten) is the "mundan" ceremony or first shaving of the baby's hair, typically per-formed between the age of four months to three years. This is performed for reasons of purification, promoting good health, etc. It may be noted that equiv-alent ceremonies (to mundan) are conducted in Islam, Judaism, etc.

13.2 Christianity: Church—Structure and Clergy

Structure: Biblical wisdom is symbolized in the basic, traditional architecture of the church. Highly prevalent to interior design is the shape of the Cross. A lengthy central rectangle runs typically east–west, with a cross rectangle in front for the altar, complete with a dome or interior vaulted space envisioning the heavens. Use of circles or octagons and star designs commonly represent eternity and divine light. Variations to design including central-style plans (also including mausoleums) exist. Common terms for these designs include the Latin Cross (longitudinal) and Greek Cross (equal length arms).

Typical church architecture include the porch, the atrium (courtyard, skylight access), the vestibule/lobby (narthex), the nave or central lengthy part of the cross-shaped church lined with seating and aisles (double), the bema or elevated platform for clergy extending into the transept or the transverse section completing the arms of the cross; and a semicircular recess or apse covered by the vault or semi-dome. The facade constitutes the external rising feature such as domes, central tower, two western towers or towers at both ends. Spires atop steeples are common, which is a tall tower on the west end of the church or over the crossing (junction of the cruciform), including church bells located inside the belfry. Other key features include Stations of the Cross (mainly Western churches) dealing with the crucifixion of Jesus, the altar or the table where traditional bread and wine are consecrated representing the body and blood of Christ. The chancel is the space around the altar including the choir (seating for clergy) and the sanctuary (sacred space) synonymous with the term presbytery. There is also the cathedra (raised seat or throne of presiding bishop) and an ambulatory or covered processional passage around the east end of a large church and behind the altar. Additionally, the sacristy is a room for keeping vestments (garments, records).

Many churches face east (west–east axis), symbolic with the direction from which Jesus emerges on the Last Day,[16] with external architectural emphasis on the west side (entrance), and internal emphasis on the east including enhancing illumination by the sun. Architectural decorations both external and internal include but are not limited to columns, arcades, moldings, sculpture, mosaic, stained glass, illustrations of the life of Christ including crucifixes, prophets and saints, symbolic animals reinforcing Christ's affection for the church.

Churches vary in size, design, regional and period influences, such as Early Christian, Byzantine, Romanesque, Gothic, Baroque, Revival and Modern. Classification ranges from house (home), local parish, shrine, abbey and priory, collegiate, cathedrals and basilicas. Cathedrals are typically Roman Catholic,

---

[16] Matthew 24:27.

Protestant (including Anglican), Eastern or Oriental Orthodox, housing a cathedra for a presiding bishop. It can be large, lavish with certain liturgical rights. Basilicas are generally associated with the Catholic Church and are of two types— typically of rectangular design with a central nave and two or more longitudinal aisles, or a church designated by the Pope which may be an abbey, parish, shrine or cathedral with special privileges granted by the Pope and segregated into four major basilicas in Rome (including St. Peter's in Vatican City) and some 1,800 minor basilicas. Such designation is due to these sites being major pilgrimage destinations with relics of saints or preserving revered artifacts.

Clergy: Ecclesiastical church governance broadly falls under episcopal, connectional, presbyterian and congregational polity, each with a defined structure and jurisdiction. Note familiar terms related to the latter such as diocese, archdiocese, metropolitan sees, ecclesiastical province, councils, etc. The Pope is the supreme pontiff and the appointed worldwide leader of the Catholic Church with rights to interpret the scriptures as God's representative here on earth. He is also the bishop of Rome (as per jurisdiction of the Holy See) and sovereign of the Vatican City state. The formal system includes cardinals, archbishops, bishops, priests, deacons, etc. Non-clergy members are called the laity. Protestant leaders constitute senior pastor or similar clergy (minister, pastor, reverend), elders, deacons, etc. Note that the title of priest is largely absent in Protestantism.

In Eastern Orthodox, the patriarch of Constantinople constitutes the nominal head of the autocephalous and autonomous churches, each with their own administration (for example, patriarchs and archbishops). A similar system exists in six autocephalous churches in Oriental Orthodox with their own apostolic succession including patriarchs, bishops, catholicos, abunas or popes. Note that both systems have holy synods or group of bishops who elect the head patriarch, typically the primus inter pares or first among equals. Examples of Eastern and Oriental Orthodox range from the churches of Constantinople, Jerusalem, Bulgaria, Greece, Sinai, China and Japan to Oriental Orthodox such as the Coptic Alexandria, the Armenian Apostolic, the Ethiopian Tewahedo, the Eritrean Tewahedo, the Malankara Orthodox Syrian in India. Specific institutions associated with all branches of Christianity such as religious orders, institutes—both secular and religious (segregated)—clerical and lay, societies of apostolic life and other monastic orders have their own naming and leadership. Whether formally ordained or otherwise—note that a pastor may be "ordained" as leader of a church, as opposed to a priest who is formally "ordained" into a particular faith—we all rejoice in hearing familiar titles such as reverend father, reverend mother, priest (also padri, padre), pastor (which means to lead to pasture), chaplain, deacon, dean, bishop (including diocesan), pope, provost, etc. We offer our deepest respect towards this wonderful global community who have dedicated their lives in keeping us whole.

13.3 Islam: Mosque—Structure and Clergy

Structure: Mosques (Masjids) serve as larger community centers for prayers, religious teachings, Ramadan fasting, marriage and funeral services, place of business, tending to the poor, etc. The definition of a mosque constitutes any venue where worship ensues including informal open spaces (Musalla). Like many religions, mosque architecture has evolved to include the marvelous confluence of cultures, regional influences and dynasties, examples of the last named including Persian, Mughal, Byzantine, etc.

Initial (traditional) design was square and rectangular, with covered (flat roof) prayer halls with column supports within enclosed courtyard, with progressive inclusion of magnificent gardens, domes and arched entrances (Iwans)—fourfold with huge gateways on each side symbolizing entrance into spiritual realms. Central domes, symbolic of the heavens, were introduced over prayer halls, with smaller dome offshoots in other parts of a mosque; balconies were also common in some mosques. Minarets at each corner of the mosque were added, in many cases turning into bell towers as highest point of the mosque (and the surrounding area) calling people to prayer. Note that places of worship for Friday prayers are called Juma. Several mosques were built at the burial places of prophets and saints, treated as places of pilgrimage.

Cumulatively, these designs incorporated and completed the iconic mosque look, for example, with its onion or hemispherical shaped dome, minarets and significant gateways. During prayer, men organize themselves into parallel lines facing the semicircular niche (Mihrab) in the wall which indicates the direction (Qiblah) of Kaaba (Mecca). Note that the Qiblah is typically at opposite end of the prayer hall entrance. Women pray in separate spaces in the mosque. Incidentally, women don the *Hijab* to cover their heads and neck in society, synonymous with the expression *Khimār* (from the Quran) used for such head dress, veil, scarf, etc. A raised platform (Minbar) is used by the leader (Imam) for prayers, sometimes with an offshoot platform in the front left corner of the mosque for ancillary preaching and speeches. Ritual purification (Wudu) is important before commencement of prayers and reading scriptures, with related facilities being provided. Furniture is largely absent allowing for maximum number of occupants. Islamic calligraphy and verses expanding upon the beauty of the Quran adorn the walls for decoration. The design also includes images such as cosmic spirals and fruits/vegetables signifying eternal heaven with no boundaries. Conversion of religious establishments also influenced architecture. Note that Hagia Sophia in Istanbul was initially a Greek Orthodox Cathedral, world famous for its central dome, which was later converted to a mosque under the Ottoman Empire. And as mentioned, mosque architecture has been heavily influenced by regional designs—from examples of pagoda style in eastern China to the sacred pyramidal roof style in Southeast Asia.

Clergy: There is no centralized system or formal ordination. Titles of leaders and teachers are typically academic, scholastic. Typical titles include (a) Imam (Sunni), leader for worship at a mosque or community. Note that this title is also selectively used in Shia Islam for the highest leaders of the Twelvers (Imāmīyyah) branch who are directly associated with the Prophet, and also by the Ismaili and Zaidiyyah branches of Shia Islam, (b) Qadi (Qazi), a magistrate for Sharia law, (c) Mullah, commonly recognized name for clerics and mosque leaders, (d) Mufti, jurist qualified to provide a non-binding opinion (Fatwa) of the Sharia law, also providing guidance on rituals and life, and (e) Ayatollah, an honorary title of high esteem for Shia clergy, including Marji (Grand Ayatollah) who also writes treatises or Resalah which provide practical guidance and ruling on approach to life under the auspices of Islam. Other common names for clergy include Ulama in matters of jurisprudence and philosophy, Faqīh as an expert on Fiqh (interpretation of Sharia law), and Sheikh and Akhund as clerics in Afghanistan, Iran, Pakistan, etc. A Hafiz is a scholar who has memorized the entire Quran and who can intercede for ten people on Judgement Day, and a Khatib is one who delivers the sermon (khutbah) on the customary Friday prayer and Eid prayers. Sufi clergy are called Marabout, Murshid, Dervish, etc. The role of women in clergy is limited to date. A madrasa is a school of elementary and higher learning where the Quran memorization is taught including teachings of Arabic language, Quran interpretation (tafsir), Sharia law, teachings of the Hadith, Muslim history and logic, and courses for the scholar to be integrated as respected member of the community.

13.4 Buddhism: Monastery, Temple—Structure and Clergy

Structure: Buddhist temples or monasteries symbolically represent the pure, peaceful and realized inner and outer world of the Buddha in perfect harmony with natural elements—fire, earth, water, air and wisdom/ether. While designs vary by cultures and region, they range from the earliest rock cut and the circular designs in ancient India such as the Mahabodhi temple (built c. 250 BC) in Bodhgaya protecting the Bodhi tree, the site of Buddha's realization, to the iconic tiered structures of Southeast Asia.

Buddhist temples typically consist of a network of structures (central and outer) with enclosing walls visualizing the universe utilized as a sacred space including teaching and residential facilities. It is said that many temples have been inspired by Meru, the holy, cosmic mountain at the center of the universe surrounded by the elements. It is interesting to note that mountains feature in many cultures as sacred, such as Mount Olympus of the Greeks, Mount Kailash in China and Mount Fuji in Japan inspiring pilgrimages. Indeed many temples are constructed in mountains and forests, and while direction varies upon beliefs, many face east to harness the rising energy of the sun. Key design elements typically include a stupa or hemispherical mound or similar bell-shaped structure containing relics (śarīra), including remains of spiritual masters, which may be enclosed within a prayer hall (Chaitya). The stupa is synonymous with the later, famous, tiered, eaved pagodas of the Far East (Japan,

China, Korea, etc.), also known as "chörten" in Tibet. These are also seen in Taoism, Shinto and other religions. Particular styles become typical to a region. In Japan, for example, the five-story pagoda is common, with each story representing one of the five elements: earth, water, fire, wind, and sky (heaven). Pagodas, however, always have odd-numbered roofs.

Circumambulation or Pradakshina practice is also common around this inner space including a pathway provided for walking. A monastery (vihara) also constitutes living quarters with open, shared courtyard for the temple monks, also known as the "Wat" for Buddhist and Hindu temples in Southeast Asia. These temples can be multi-storied with steeply sloping roofs supported by marvelously decorated eaves and brackets. Many are capped by a spire. The overall structure represents a symbolic, pure pathway from the earth to the heavens. Temples usually contain sacred scriptures including fine copies of the sutras and canons, and numerous Buddha statues and deities (devas) including a large Buddha; bells and shrines are also prevalent. Religious events for gatherings are typically conducted outside in the courtyard. Building large Buddha statues is very popular. Examples of rock-cut include the 233-foot Leshan (Sichuan, China), the 180-foot Western and 125-foot Eastern (Bamiyan, Afghanistan); and the concrete 80-foot Walking (Kandy, Sri Lanka). Temples also have outer and inner gates. The outer adorns paintings and statues of gods, beasts and warriors to ward of negative energies, and the inner often have the four guardian kings representing cardinal directions equipped with symbolic weapons of purity to ensure protection from evil. Note that the practice of feng shui or energetic harmony of man and space exercises a large influence in the design of these temples to confuse and fend off evil spirits.

Of special mention is the Angkor Wat, Cambodia, which is the largest Buddhist religious temple complex in the world. This was built in the twelfth century originally as a Hindu temple, but was later converted to a Buddhist temple. Angkor Wat marvelously represents architectural design from both religions by way of universe representation via mandala design (see Item 13.1) including square and circle grid structures, and the mountain temple representing the mythical mountain Meru.

Clergy: Generally fall under the umbrella of the Sangha constituting ordained male and female monks (Bhikkus and Bhikkunis), formal structure varying by diversity of beliefs, cultures and regional and political influences. Clergy are largely monastic (with exceptions), with defined practices (Vinaya) promoting the highest standards of conduct including austerity, meditation, service to community, minimal personal possessions and receiving alms in lieu of manual labor, although some sects allow the latter. No centralized governing body exists. Examples of senior clergy under different philosophies include (a) Vajrayana: Lama including the Dalai Lama and the Panchen Lama in Tibetan Buddhism; also Guru, Ayya and Tulku, (b) Theravada: Acharya and Luang Por, and (c) Mahayana: Rōshi and Sensei. Note that the Sensei in Japanese ("Sen" meaning before, "sei" meaning living) implies one who has gone before, hence a highly knowledgeable master. They are spiritual, centered and equanimous, their teachings easily extending into martial arts and principles of corporate leadership.

13.5 Judaism: Synagogues—Structure and Clergy

Structure: Synagogues serve as sacred places for prayer, reading holy scriptures and community centers promoting holistic living for the Jewish people.

According to the Talmud, a synagogue had to be the tallest structure in a town, and had to have windows. Integral to all synagogues on the east end (opposite entrance) is the Ark or the Ark of the Covenant (Aron Kodesh or Hekhal) for keeping scriptures. Other key features include a Bimah or elevated platform for reciting prayers by a Hazzan (cantor) from the lectern (amud), with a "ner tamid" or chancel/altar lamp eternally lit as a constant reminder of the eternal flame that existed on the altar in the ancient Temple of Jerusalem. Note the ancient seven-lamp Hebrew lampstand "menorah" was often associated with this eternal flame to honor divine presence. The elevated platform ranges from simple tables to structures integrally linked into building design including pillars. Synagogues range from nondescript buildings built away from the street (given earlier anti-Semitism constraints) to magnificent structures including arches, domes and towers, incorporating designs and decorations from different styles and cultures including Italian Renaissance, Chinese, Gothic, Moroccan, Byzantine, etc. Artwork is optional, Hebrew inscriptions are seldom utilized, while figured subjects are not utilized. One may see the lion of Judah, the interlacing triangles, flower and fruit forms in Orthodox synagogues, the "shofar" or ancient musical horn and the "lulav" or closed frond of date palm tree.

Synagogues are typically built to ensure that the congregation face towards Jerusalem, and while they are considered as sacred spaces for praying and reading of the Tanakh, communal worship can also take place at other locations conditional upon the presence of the minyan or ten males traditionally above the age of thirteen. Synagogues typically have a large place for prayer (main sanctuary) and may have smaller study facilities and offices. Some have a separate room for study of scriptures called "Beth Midrash." Seating ranges from floor mats and cushions to benches and tables, typically facing the Ark. Synagogues are also used by Samaritans (ethno-religious group) albeit with some variations in principles of worship and design. Special mention is made to the Temple in Jerusalem (Temple Mount) as a holy site of Judaism, Christianity and Islam alike, which are part of Abrahamic religions acknowledging God revealing himself to Abraham. Note that Christianity and Judaism trace their roots to Abraham's second son Isaac, Islam to his older brother Ishmael. The current site includes a flat plaza with retaining walls including the Western Wall or the Wailing Wall, last remnant of the ancient Holy Temple (First and Second), the al-Aqsa Mosque, the Dome of the Rock and the Dome of the Chain, including four minarets, walls and gates. Note the marvelous confluence: (a) it is the holiest site in Judaism where the First and the Second Temples (now destroyed) stood and the venue of the "Holy of Holies" or inner sanctuary of the Tabernacle where the Ark of the Covenant was held; (b) as per the New Testament (Christianity) it is the Temple of Herod or the Second Temple which is associated with events in the life of Jesus; and (c) it is the third holiest site in Islam as majority of Muslims considered it as the Noble Sanctuary marking Muhammad's journey to Jerusalem and ascent to heaven.

Visitors from all parts of the world come to walk the Via Dolorosa or processional route ("Way of Suffering" including nine Stations of the Cross) representing the path Jesus was taken on the way to his crucifixion. The winding route (of about 2,000 feet) culminates in the Church of the Holy Sepulchre which houses the remaining five Stations of the Cross.

Clergy: The clergy in Judaism constitutes ordained rabbis and cantors (Hazzan). It may be noted that women cannot participate as clergy in Orthodox Judaism. Training includes intense study of scriptures such as the Torah, Tanakh and Talmud including ethics and laws. Rabbis today may provide interpretations of these laws and customs. Continued research of scriptures to pass on knowledge (Mesorah) is expected of the rabbis, teaching in multiple venues including schools, synagogues and other communal facilities incorporating multiple levels of knowledge—"heder" or elementary, "yeshivah" or mid-level and "kollel" or advanced. Many have also produced related literature including interpretations of the scriptures.

Rabbis also provide limited jurisprudence for certain matters including divorce and conversion, and may also serve in arbitrations. Cantors support rabbis by typically leading prayers, singing and chanting in synagogues including marriage and other civil functions. It may be noted that the role of cantors has diminished over the years and today is shared by any individual of the congregation that is picked by the "gabbai," or manager, to lead the services.

Among other clergy, a Posek is a legal scholar on Jewish laws (Halakha) providing final decisive position where required. A Mashgiach is associated with Torah laws of Kashrut who supervises a Kosher establishment, and may or may not be an ordained rabbi. Conversely, not every rabbi may be qualified to perform this specific function.

A *Mohel* (who may or may not be a rabbi) performs the religious ceremony of *brit milah* or circumcision, typically eight days after birth. It may be noted that a similar practice called *khitan* exists in Islam, which is debated (binding or otherwise) amongst scholars, and timing of such rite may vary. Reasons for performing the rites of circumcision are associated with purity, cleanliness, health, etc.

Dynastic priests such as a *rebbe* are also present in modern-day clergy. They are an offshoot of Hasidic (Chassidic) faith which is a subset of Haredi Strict Orthodox, are not ordained but are seen as leaders of congregation and sometimes community. They are relied upon for guidance, decision-making and inspiration, but not always for interpretation of Halakha (religious law). Earlier patrilineal priests included *kohanim* dating back to the time of Moses, but their prevalence has since become limited (mostly to prayer service).

14. Calendars and Festivals

Introduction to Festivals and Calendars

Festivals are celebrated on a set of fixed and variable dates yearly. Some are fixed to simply have everyone celebrate (e.g., Christmas) at the same time irrespective of calendars, others have variant dates given the type of calendar used. Historically, different calendars with varying time periods have been utilized globally depending upon the needs of the myriad cultures to organize time as per fixed astronomical cyclical patterns, astrological studies and future forecasting, planning seasonal and agricultural activities, migrations, religious and secular events. Christianity utilizes the Gregorian calendar derived from a solar calendar; all the other religions herein utilize lunisolar calendars other than Islam which has a lunar calendar. The Gregorian is the most prevalent with standard 365 days including a leap year of 366 days once every four years (one additional day in February) in synchronization with the astronomical timing of equinoxes and solstices falling in the periods of spring and fall, including rotation of the earth around the sun. Conversely, the lunar calendar is synchronized with a fixed length of the month in tune with the cycles of moon phases, hence the Islamic Hijri calendar has around 355 days in a year. The lunisolar calendar on other hand has lunar months but the years are based on sun cycles, hence interjects intercalation adding a day, week or even a month in some cases to align with the solar year. The Hindu calendar comprises multiple lunisolar calendars, follows the lunar cycles but introduces an additional month once every 32–33 months to ensure that harvest and festival dates are maintained in tune with appropriate seasons. Some calendars borrow from others to ascertain the date of a festival. Take Easter, for which the Gregorian calendar borrows from the Hebrew (lunisolar) calendar leading to a movable date, given that this marvelous festival as per religious edict falls on the first Sunday following the first full paschal moon after the spring equinox. Hence, the lunar rotation cycle (about 29.5 days) contributes to the variant Easter date yearly with respect to the Gregorian month.

Given the aforementioned, you will now understand just why the dates of so many festivals keep changing on a yearly basis! Enjoy the festivals, I tried to pick some major ones from each religion. Cumulatively, their rituals promote the highest ideals with humility, morals and a sense of duty while celebrating historical, religious and scriptural events, extending into national and regional themes. For easy reference, included herein are 2021 dates (as per Gregorian calendar) for each festival including typical range (months) of when they are celebrated.

14.1 Hinduism Festivals—Lunisolar Calendar (Multiple)

January: *Lohri* or *Lodi* is primarily observed in north India as a crop season celebration on/around 13 January (Gregorian); this fixed date equates into the tenth month of *Pausha* of the Hindu Calendar (hereinafter HC). Lodi marks the end of the winter solstice and remembering the sun god *Surya* (the Makar Sankranti festival dedicated to Surya follows the next day marking the first day of the sun's transit to Capricorn). People light bonfires on Lohri to honor the god of fire (Agni), singing songs asking for heat and thanking Surya's return. Similar celebration is observed in the south called *Pongal* (on/around 14 January) including communal prayers, processions and offerings to gods and goddesses the specially prepared sweet dish Pongal (among others) prepared from the first rice harvest, milk and raw sugar. Note all three festivals aforementioned are coined harvest festivals. Hindus also take part in festive celebrations whilst renewing friendships and thanking God, the sun, earth and cattle.

March: *Holi*, the festival of colors, marks the arrival of spring, typically in February/March lasting two days starting on full moon (Purnima) in the twelfth month of *Phalguna* in HC, which in 2021 fell on 28 March according to the Gregorian calendar. Date and length of celebrations vary geographically, albeit with common roots borne of the legends of Lord Krishna, Shiva, Vishnu, Kama (god of love) including symbolic victory of good over evil. Marked by a day to forgive and forget, people meet and celebrate friendship even with strangers by marking one other with colors—typically powders but also watercolors. Mock fights take place all over including on the streets to the accompaniment of good nature and laughter! And yes, it is customary to take an intoxicating drink called *bhang* made from cannabis, followed by social visits to friends and family once exchanges of colors are completed.

July: *Rath Yatra* or chariot festival which takes place in June/July on the second day equating to the fourth month of *Ashadha* in HC, falling on 21 July 2021 in the Gregorian calendar. These are public processions including large statues of deities, highly prevalent in the east with emphasis on Lord Vishnu, Lord Shiva and related deities such as Lord Rama, Krishna, Jagannath. Among others the Rath Yatra of Puri in the state of Odisha is very popular. The message of these processions promotes a sense of duty, community, humility and service to humanity while reinforcing cultural values.

September: *Ganesh Chaturthi* celebrates the birth of Lord Ganesha, the remover of obstacles, avoiding natural calamities and giver of success in new ventures, travel, etc. Hence, Lord Ganesha is popularly included at commencement of new ventures. Typically occurring in August/September equating to the sixth month of *Bhadra* as per HC, falling on 10 September in the year 2021 as per Gregorian calendar. Prayers and celebrations can last up to ten days culminating in the idol of Lord Ganesha being carried in a procession to the accompaniment of chanting for immersion in water (lake, sea). The city of Mumbai (India) is well known globally for celebrating this festival with an estimated 100,000 or more statues being immersed in the Arabian Sea.

September/October: Navaratri is a ten-day (nine nights) festival celebrating Goddess Durga's triumph over evil, celebrated four times a year, of which the following two are the most popular: September/October in the seventh month of Ashvin as per the HC, and also in the first month of Chaitra equating to March/April. The Ashvin festival is called Sharada Navaratri. Celebrations include recitals and enactments of Lord Rama's story and chanting scriptures, with classical and folk dances and joint celebrations. The timing of the Sharada festival coincides with the traditional *Durga Puja* and *Dussehra* (final day of celebrations), when the Durga statue is immersed in a waterbody such as a river or pond and also the statues of Ravana (the rakshasa king), his son and brother are burnt with fireworks. Additionally, the festival of Diwali is celebrated twenty lunar days (tithis) after Dussehra.

October/November: *Diwali* is the festival of lights, amongst the most popular Indian festivals signifying triumph of good over evil, light over darkness including ignorance. Celebrated on the fifteenth lunar day of the dark fortnight (Amavasya or the night of the new moon) in the eighth month of *Kartika*, one of the holiest months in the HC, in 2021 it fell on 4 November as per the Gregorian calendar. With the lighting of oil lamps (diyas) placed in temples, homes, shops while indulging in a wide array of fireworks, celebrations and rituals last several days accompanied by wearing the finest clothes, distributing sweets and gifts. Diwali honors the return of Lord Rama, his wife Sita and brother Lakshmana after a period in exile of fourteen years described in the epic *Ramayana* (see Item 4.1). Another tradition links good triumphing over evil symbolized by Lord Krishna killing the demon *Narakasura*. Many Hindus also associate Diwali with Goddess Lakshmi, the goddess of wealth and prosperity.

Miscellaneous: The marvelous festival of *Thaipusam* (Tamil month: Thai, Star: Pushya or Pusam) is celebrated typically in January/February in south India by the Tamil and Malayali communities and in other countries such as Malaysia, Sri Lanka and Myanmar, venerating Goddess Parvati giving her son Murugan, the brother of Lord Ganesha, a spear to vanquish demon Surapadman. Wonderful dance, devotional offerings, processions and self-penance ensue for purification. *Saraswati Puja* (note puja means prayer) is popular in the east, celebrated for the blessing of Saraswati, goddess of wisdom and the arts. Also in the January/February timeframe equating to the fifth lunar day in the bright fortnight of the eleventh month *Magha* in HC, this puja heralds the arrival of spring, with the festival of colors *Holi* following forty lunar days later. *Guru Purnima*, observed on the full moon day of *Ashadha*, the fourth month in HC, June/July in the Gregorian calendar, is dedicated to spiritual and academic teachers.

Festivals for highly popular deities include (all HC/Gregorian dates): (a) *Shivaratri* for Lord Shiva celebrating knowledge over ignorance, at night on fourteenth lunar day in the twelfth month of *Phalguna* or February/March; (b) *Ram Navami*, the birthday of Lord Rama (seventh avatar of God Vishnu) on the ninth lunar day of the bright fortnight of *Chaitra* or March/April; and (c) *Janmashatmi*, the birthday of Lord Krishna (the eighth avatar of Lord Vishnu) on the eighth lunar day (Ashtami) in the fifth month *Shravana* or the sixth month *Bhadra*, August–September. Cumulative celebrations include all-night temple prayers, pilgrimages, fasting and meditation, chanting devotional songs (bhajans), bathing statues and placing/rocking these statues in cradles within decorative mini-temples and reciting popular stories associated with these deities. Celebrations may span over many days.

Other important festivals include the following: Karva Chauth is celebrated by married Hindu ladies from north and west India on the fourth day after Purnima (full moon) in the month of *Kartika* (as per HC), typically October/November in the Gregorian calendar. Women fast for the day (until the moon is sighted) and perform rituals (typically at start and end of the day) for the long and healthy life of their husbands. Author's note: It is typical for families to congregate at temples. I have always chuckled at the sight of various bands of husbands being sent out politely but firmly by the wives to look for the errant moon (if hiding behind the clouds) for a first sighting so that these gracious and devoted ladies can complete their prayers and break their all-day fast! And an ancillary popular custom associated with Hindu marriages is "Mehndi" or temporary artistic henna decoration, typically paste derived from the henna plant applied on the hands and feet of ladies attending the marriage. It may be noted that men also selectively apply henna, additionally the henna plant has medicinal properties. Similar practices of decoration extend into many countries in South Asia, North Africa and the Middle East.

Another highly prevalent custom is *Raksha Bandhan*, celebrated on the last day of *Shravan* (fourth month as per HC, typically August in the Gregorian calendar), where sisters tie a *Rakhi* or colored string (typically red orange) around the wrists of their brothers thereby protecting them and receiving a gift in return, while reinforcing the continued duties of the brother to protect the sister. Indeed a heart-warming experience for all.

Other types of functions include special prayers in front of a religious fire at a temple or home, such as "Pitri-yajna" (practices include *shraddha, tarpana*) devoted to departed parents and ancestors and "Nri-yajna" offering food to strangers and the poor. Mantras are chanted while saying "Swaha" (so be it) and throwing grains, seeds and flowers into the fire, normally an act of great fun for gleeful children and smiling adults alike! Similar prayers in front of the holy fire are called *havan* or *yajna* and are performed to mark occasions like birth, marriage, blessing a new home and other rituals.

Last but not the least is the *Kumbh Mela*, the single largest gathering of pilgrims globally. Held at four separate locations (each site hosts every twelve years) associated with holy rivers such as Allahabad (now Prayagraj) at the confluence of rivers Ganges and Yamuna, Haridwar (river Ganga), Nashik (river Godavari) and Ujjain (river Shipra). Pilgrims and priests in millions come together over a two-month period to pray and wash away their sins. Ascetics of all walks include yoga practitioners and those performing extreme austerity, naked ascetics (Naga sadhus or sages) descend from the mountains complete with their ash-covered bodies signifying removal from all worldly desires. Origins of the mela (gathering) are associated with the astrological sign Aquarius where good and evil forces (gods and demons) confronted each other over a pot (kumbh) of nectar synonymous with immortality. There is some conjecture over later legend that one of the victorious gods spilt nectar in the proximity of the four locations where the melas are held. Note that around 130,000 "lost and found" cases of people were reported at one of these melas! Think about the scale of logistics and support services for this event!

14.2 Christianity Festivals—Gregorian Calendar

February: Ash Wednesday or Day of Ashes marks a day of repentance for Christians to confess their sins and profess their repentance to God given that Jesus died for them on the Cross for their sins. Celebrated forty-six days before Easter, this movable feast fell on 17 February in 2021. During the Mass a priest marks ashes on the worshiper's forehead in the shape of a cross often quoting "Remember that you are dust, and to dust you shall return," or "Repent and believe in the Gospel." Fasting is typical by Catholics, including avoiding non-vegetarian meals on each Friday during the Lent. Religious services are also performed by certain Protestant groups including Anglicans, Episcopalians, Lutherans, Presbyterians and United Methodists. Ash Wednesday marks the first day of Lent commencing the Lenten sacrifice while acknowledging the forty days Jesus spent in the Judaean Desert resisting temptations by Satan. This is a time for fasting and discipline as a precursor to Easter when Jesus was resurrected. Ash Wednesday is preceded by Shrove Tuesday marked by confession, forgiveness and ritual burning of the previous year's Holy Week palms including the preparation for the Lenten sacrifice.

March/April: Holy Week is the last week of Lent before Easter, held in March/ April (commenced 28 March in 2021), and includes important days such as Palm Sunday, Holy Tuesday, Holy Wednesday, Maundy Thursday, Good Friday and Holy Saturday. Palm Sunday is the first day of Holy Week recalling the last week of the life of Jesus on earth, including his triumphant entry into Jerusalem marked by processions carrying symbolic branches of trees and palm leaves shaped as a Cross. Holy Tuesday venerates the Parable of the Wise and Foolish Virgins on benefits of vigilance, symbolism of Christ as the bridegroom, and one's blessed state on the Day of Judgement. Holy (Spy) Wednesday marks the betrayal of Christ by Judas Iscariot with the chief priests (the Sanhedrin). Maundy Thursday marks reflection on the Last Supper of Christ (Passover Meal with disciples) and "Washing of the Feet" exemplifying message of humility for all to pursue. Good Friday commemorates the crucifixion of Jesus for blasphemy (Pontius Pilate presided over the trial) outside the walls of Jerusalem and his sacrifice for humanity. This is observed as an integral part of the Paschal Triduum as per the canonical gospels, when cumulatively a period of three days are marked by prayer in the evening of Maundy Thursday to Easter Sunday recalling the Passion, Crucifixion, Burial and Resurrection of Jesus in the old City of Jerusalem (Church of Holy Sepulchre). Holy Saturday (Great Sabbath) marks the last day of the Holy Week where the body of Jesus lay in the tomb and his triumphant descent into hell (Harrowing of Hell) pre-Resurrection given that he achieved salvation for all through his sacrifice. The Holy Week is considered the most solemn week of the year with respect to religious festivals. Easter Sunday (Pascha in Eastern Orthodox) celebrates the resurrection of Jesus on the third day following his crucifixion, and marks the end of the forty-day period of prayer, fasting and repentance. Note that Easter and related events fall on movable dates, the date varying between 22 March and 25 April; Easter was celebrated on 4 April in 2021. Easter celebrations are marked by early morning services, the decorations of Easter eggs signifying an empty tomb including Easter lily church decorations (chancel area), citing of the Paschal greeting "Christ is risen," Easter parades, egg hunting, etc. Easter symbolizes the triumph over evil and death, a new life eternally salvaged through belief in Jesus leading to blissful existence marked by the Kingdom of Heaven.

May/June: Ascension Day (Feast of the Ascension) is a celebration on the fortieth day after Easter marking the physical ascension of Christ into heaven in presence of his apostles. This is traditionally celebrated on a Thursday, and also on a Sunday in countries where it is not designated as a public holiday. Traditionally marked by an all-night vigil in Eastern and Orthodox Churches, it is also associated with specific hymns and church music.

Pentecost (Whit Sunday) signals the end of Eastertide celebrations and marks the descent of the Holy Spirit upon the apostles fifty days after Easter while they were celebrating the Feast of Weeks in Jerusalem. Marked by special liturgy, it is also one of the twelve Great Feasts in Eastern Orthodox.

August: Transfiguration of Jesus is a major festival celebrated on 6 August (fixed date) by many denominations and is also included in the twelve Great Feasts of Eastern Orthodox Church. It marks the miracle when Jesus became divine light, radiant with bright rays shining from his being when he went to pray with three disciples John, Peter and James, at the mountaintop. Moses and Elijah also then appeared next to him, where the voice of God called Jesus "Son." Symbolically it represents the connection between humans and God, heaven and earth, with Jesus as the bridge. This event is considered one of the five major events in the gospel narrative in the life of Jesus including baptism, crucifixion, resurrection and ascension.

Assumption of Blessed Virgin Mary is celebrated on 15 August (fixed date) by the Catholic Church, Eastern Orthodox, Oriental and Church of the East, marking the ascension of Mary into heaven by the power of God. Celebrations include religious processions, parades, public worship and votive offerings.

September: Nativity of Mary (see December below).

October: Halloween is celebrated on 31 October (fixed date) marking a three-day window of "All Hallowtide" comprising All Saints Eve (Halloween), All Saints Day (All Hallows) and All Souls Day, paying respects to the departed including saints, Christian martyrs and all faithful Christians. Borne primarily from Western Christianity including Celtic roots (harvest festivals), the celebrations include trick or treating, apple-bobbing, carving pumpkins into jack-o-lanterns, etc. Church services also take place on the eve of All Saints Day.

October/November: Thanksgiving is celebrated on the fourth Thursday of November (fixed) in the USA, and second Monday in October in Canada. In other countries including the Caribbean, Liberia and Brazil, this constitutes a day of thanks (prayers) and ceremonies (prayers, festive meals) for the harvests of the current and the previous year. It stems from historical, religious, cultural and regional traditions, with similar festivals and celebrations in the UK (Harvest Festival, Guy Fawkes commemorating the failed 1605 Gunpowder Plot), Germany, Japan, India, etc. In the USA it is associated with the arrival of the pilgrims (English settlers and Puritans [Protestant reformation]) in the seventeenth century.

December: Feast of Immaculate Conception (primarily Catholic) followed by Nativity of Mary (birth) are two fixed-date celebrations occurring on 8 December and 8 September, respectively. Cumulatively it rejoices in the belief of Virgin Mary born free of Original Sin leaving her sinless including the birth of Jesus, the latter occurring through the power of the Holy Spirit. The birth of Mary is also mentioned in the Quran, and is one of the twelve Great Feasts of Eastern Orthodox Church called "Nativity of Theokotos." While Immaculate Conception is debated, the Eastern Orthodox does celebrate the Feast of the Conception by Saint Anne (mother of Mary) of the Most Holy Theotokos on 9 December.

Christmas (X'Mas) commemorates the birth (Nativity) of Jesus Christ at Bethlehem marked by the Christmas Star, celebrated globally on 25 December (fixed) as both religious and cultural festival. Related celebrations around Christmas include (a) Advent, preparatory activities including penance, fasting up to forty days in anticipation of his birth and Second Coming; (b) Christmastide (or X'Mas season), a twelve-day period commencing 24 December evening (X'Mas Eve), it includes a series of celebrations including Christmas Day, St. Stephen's Day (first Christian Martyr) on 26 December, also Boxing Day in the UK, Childermas (28 December), New Year's Eve, Feast of Circumcision of Christ or Solemnity of Mary (1 January), and Feast of Holy Family (Jesus, Mary and St. Joseph) for which the date may vary. It culminates on

Twelfth Night (Epiphany Eve) on 6 January. Christmas is one of the most celebrated religious festivals, including but not limited to church services, Bible reading and prayers, Christmas tree decorations and lights, traditional meals, completing Advent calendars and wreaths, exchange of gifts and cards, Christmas music and carols, enjoying the age-old tradition of Santa Claus (Saint Nicholas) rewarding well-behaved children with gifts on the night of Christmas Eve. And it is customary for people from other beliefs the world over to join and make merry in the festivities!

14.3 Islam Festivals—Lunar Calendar

March: Muhammad ibn al-Hasan al-Mahdi's birthday is celebrated within the Twelver Shia community on 15 *Sha'bān*, the eighth month in the Islamic calendar (hereinafter IC) which in 2021 fell on 28 March as per Gregorian calendar. He was born c. AD 870 and will re-emerge as the Messiah Mahdi (debated amongst Sunni scholars) together with Isa (Jesus) during the final period leading up to pre-Judgement Day to defeat the Antichrist. Celebrations highly prevalent in Iran include public adulation through acts of generosity, distributing food, charity, fireworks and lights; also distributing sweets to strangers and enjoying picnics.

Lailat al Miraj is celebrated on 27 *Rajab*, the seventh month in IC which fell on 27 March in 2021 as per Gregorian calendar. This marks a two-fold night-time journey (Isra' and Mi'raj), considered both physical (Isra' being night journey) and spiritual (Mi'raj) respectively by Prophet Muhammad on a winged *Buraq* or mythical animal (akin to a winged horse) from Mecca to what the Quran describes as the farthest mosque in Jerusalem (later Al-Aqsa mosque). Prophet Muhammad then ascended (Mi'raj) to heaven where Allah advised him of the need for Salah (prayer) five times daily. Here he also examined the seven stages of heaven including meeting with Jesus (Isa), Moses (Musa), Abraham (Ibrahim) and John the Baptist (Yaḥyā ibn Zakarīyā); and was taken to the sacred tree *Sidrat al-Muntaha* on the seventh Heaven. Muslims celebrate this festival through prayer at the mosque, reciting prayers at night and relating the story to children, lighting candles and partaking in festive meals.

April: *Ramadan* or *Ramzan* is celebrated on the first day of the ninth month (Ramaḍan) of IC, which fell on 13 April in 2021 as per Gregorian calendar. Ramzan celebrates the first revelations of the Quran to Prophet Muhammad by the angel Gabriel (Jibril) near Mecca. The festival is marked by thirty days of fasting, prayer and introspection from sunrise to sunset between two meals, *Suhur* or *Sehri* in the morning and *Iftar* in the evening. This is considered to accelerate one's spiritual progress during this period marked by one moon sighting to the next. Additionally, Laylat al-Qadr (Night of Power) is considered by many as either the twenty-third or the twenty-seventh day of Ramadan when Allah revealed the first verses of the Quran to Prophet Muhammad.

May: *Eid ul-Fitr* is one of the two official Islamic holidays celebrating the end of thirty days of Ramadan fasting, commencing on the first day of the tenth month (Shawwal) of IC which fell on 13 May in 2021 in Gregorian calendar. Celebrations commence at sunset on the first night of sighting of the crescent moon (Chaand Raat). Fasting on the day of Eid is not permitted. Specific prayers (Salah) are conducted communally in a mosque, large hall or field. These include two units of *raka'āt* or specific movement and words and chants, including *Takbirs*, raising hands to ears while chanting Allahu Akbar (God is great). Eid lasts for one to three days (varies by country), partaking in delicious festive meals, reveling in sense of community, wishing each other "Eid Mubarak." Acts of charity are common before Eid prayers.

July: *Eid al-Ghadir* constitutes a significant Shia celebration coinciding with Prophet Muhammad's farewell pilgrimage, his sole visit to Mecca shortly before his demise (AD 632) while appointing his successor Ali ibn Abi Talib. The said date is also associated with the final verse of the Quran being revealed, thereby cementing the perfection of Islam. Celebrated on the eighteenth day of the last month (Dhu al-Hijjah) of IC which fell on 28 July in 2021 in Gregorian calendar. Celebrations include fasting, taking ritual bath, distributing food, making pilgrimages.

Hajj is the annual pilgrimage to the holiest city of Mecca at the Kaaba (House of Allah) lasting for about five to six days. It is a mandatory religious duty to be carried out at least once in the lifetime by devout Muslims. The pilgrimage is performed between the eighth and thirteenth day of the final month (Dhu al-Hijjah) of IC which fell during 18–23 July in 2021 in Gregorian calendar. Gender separation is absent, special attire must be worn; for example, men wear two white unhemmed sheets before entering into the purified state of *Ihram* to perform this major pilgrimage. Note that Ihram also applies to minor pilgrimage (Umrah) to Mecca at any other time of year. Hajj is integral to the five pillars of Islam. Millions converge during Hajj performing series of acts including but not limited to walking seven times counterclockwise around the Kaaba, walking briskly to and from the hills of Safa and Marwa (part of the complex), drinking from the Zamzam Well (20 meters east of the Kaaba), standing vigil at the plains of Mount Arafat (20 km southeast of Mecca), spending a night in the plains of Muzdalifa (near Mecca) including stoning the devil, followed by shaving or trimming one's hair.

Eid al-Adha or the Feast of Sacrifice is one of two official Islamic holidays, celebrated on the tenth day of the last month of IC (Dhu al-Hijjah) which coincided with 20 July in 2021 in Gregorian calendar. This festival commemorates Abraham's willingness to sacrifice his son Ishmael as per Allah's command, who in turn replaced his son with a lamb for the said sacrifice. Lasting for around three to four days, the festival celebrates the intervention and devotion to Allah. It is customary to share the meat of the animal with family, friends and the poor. Communal prayers at the mosque are followed by the traditional greetings "Eid Mubarak," exchanging gifts, visitations to friends and family, reinforcing the culture and the principles of Islam.

August: *Al-Hijra* is an annual festival commemorating the Islamic New Year on the first day of the first month of *Muharram* in IC which fell on 9 August in 2021 in Gregorian calendar. This festival celebrates Muhammad's journey from Mecca to Medina.

Ashura is observed on the tenth day of Muharram falling on 18 August in 2021, recognizing multiple events. Sunni Muslims regard this as the day that Moses and the Israelites were saved from the Egyptians by God creating a path in the Red Sea; also the day Prophet Noah left the Ark. It is treated as a recommended fasting day. Shia Muslims observe the day in a solemn manner as the martyrdom day of Hussein, grandson of Prophet Muhammad at the battle of Karbala, through multiple rituals including memorial services and processions. Note that Ashura is also considered synonymous with Yom Kippur (Judaism).

October: *Mawlid* or *Eid-e-Milad un-Nabi* is the birthday of Prophet Muhammad which is celebrated in the third month (Rabi' al-Awwal) of the IC. Sunni Muslims consider this to be on the twelfth day which in 2021 fell on 18 October as per Gregorian calendar whereas Shia Muslims accept the seventeenth day which was on 23 October in 2021. It is celebrated in most Muslim-majority countries (except Saudi Arabia and Qatar) by way of candle-light feasts, recitation of poems on the Prophet, parades, food and charity.

Note that in general, Islam minimizes the use of aids such as bells, lamps, lights, etc., in conducting religious practices.

14.4 Buddhism Festivals—Lunisolar Calendar (Multiple)

January: The Buddhist new year is celebrated between January and May depending upon the doctrine or school (Mahayana, Theravada, etc.) on the first full moon day of the chosen month for one to three days. It is called Losar in Tibetan Buddhism. Buddhists joyously celebrate the new year with gusto. It is customary to attend monastery lectures, meditate and introspect on the five precepts (part of the noble eightfold path), and refrain from vices and wrongdoings. Buddhists offer food to the monks, alms to beggars, clean their houses, exchange greetings, present gifts and partake of delicious meals with family members and friends. It is also customary to attend the ceremony of circumambulation three times around a stupa as a mark of respect to the Buddha, the Dhamma/Dharma or existence of phenomena as per teachings of the Buddha, and the Sangha (community) in the Three Jewels. It is interesting to note that *Dhamma* comes from Pali language whereas *Dharma* originates from Sanskrit, but both are synonymous within the teachings of Buddhism. Statues of the Buddha are also bathed in reverence.

It may also be noted that the Buddhas, bodhisattvas, etc., are popularly depicted in Buddhist art including paintings and statues amongst the different branches/sects as being seated, reclining, laughing, emaciated, standing, etc.

February: *Magha Puja* or Sangha Day commemorates an event early in the teaching life of Gautama Buddha when 1,250 Arhats or enlightened saints who were his disciples assembled spontaneously to pay respects and accept his teachings. Also known as the Fourfold Assembly, this took place at the Venuvana Monastery (India) donated by King Bimbisara to the Buddha. The festival honors the Sangha, enabling reinforcement of their commitment to Buddhism and takes place on full moon day of *Māgha*, the eleventh month in Pali (Buddhist) calendar, typically January–February in Gregorian calendar (dates vary by country/doctrine).

April: *Hanamatsuri* celebrates the birthday of Gautama Buddha. The date varies according to the multiple Buddhist lunisolar calendars used in different countries, typically April/May as per Gregorian calendar. For example, it is celebrated as a flower festival on the eighth day of the fourth lunar month in Chinese calendar, and also celebrated as part of *Vesakh* (see below) in South and Southeast Asia. It includes lighting of candles and lanterns to symbolize the Buddha's enlightenment. Celebrations vary by country, including prayers, chanting, alms giving, study of the five precepts and focus on the Three Jewels, large fairs near temples, festive meals, carrying the Buddhist flag and so on. National holidays are common, with recognition from officials of governments. The Buddha's birth is beautifully symbolized by the accompaniment of flowers, depiction of singing by celestial birds and sweet gentle rains bathing him.

May: *Vesakh* or Buddha Day or *Saga Dawa* is a major Buddhist festival as it cumulatively celebrates the birth, enlightenment or nirvana, and passing of the Buddha on the first full moon day of *Vesākha* (second month) in Pali calendar, typically May in Gregorian calendar. A special part of the festival is at night when the statue of the Buddha is taken outside. People walk around it three times, carrying candles. They pour scented water and sweet tea over the statue symbolic of cleaning one's sins. Celebrations of the Three Jewels are also conducted.

July: *Āsāḷhā* Puja (prayer) or *Dharma* or *Dhammachakka* Day is celebrated in Theravada Buddhism as the Buddha's first sermon post-enlightenment on full moon of Āsāḷhā or the fourth month of Pali calendar, typically June/July in the Gregorian calendar. It symbolizes the initial Turning of the Wheel incorporating the four noble truths including eightfold path, etc. It is also known as *Chök-hor Düchen* in Tibetan Buddhism.

December: *Bodhi* Day celebrates Gautama Buddha's threefold stages of enlightenment under the peepal tree in Bodhgaya (India), the famous Bodhi tree, after years of asceticism, dedicated effort and meditation to achieve nirvana after understanding cyclical rebirth, Karma, noble paths, etc. It is celebrated on the eighth day in the twelfth month in Chinese calendar, typically December/January in the Gregorian calendar by many countries in Mahayana including Zen, Pure Land sects, etc. It is called "Laba" in China, "Rōhatsu" in Japanese Zen, "Jodo-e" in Tendai and other sects.

Miscellaneous: Festivals include the *Ulambana* Ghost Festival held during the fifteenth day of seventh month or ghost month in Chinese calendar, August-September in the Gregorian calendar. Religious ceremonies are performed to honor the dead (both young and old) and pray for relieving their circumstances. Prevalent in Mahayana and Theravada, festivities include inviting and making seating arrangements for the deceased spirits, prayers and food offering, burning incense, offering clothes and other items, floating lanterns and paper boats in the water symbolic with providing directions to lost souls. Synonymous festival includes the Qingming for older generations only. *Kathina* or Alms-giving ceremony is celebrated at the end of the monsoon period (Vassa) in October–November. Highly popular in Theravada Buddhism, it also marks time for the wandering monks to move on to another location. Ceremonies include giving cloth offerings to two monks, symbolic with providing this to the entire Sangha or community, including meals and other gifts being provided. Following Kathina is the wonderful *Loy Krathong* festival which venerates the Buddha's footprint on the river Narmada (India) and takes place on the full moon day of *Kattika* in Pali calendar (October–November in the Gregorian calendar) where bowls made of leaves containing flowers, candles and incense are floated in full waters (post-monsoon) inviting good fortunes and tidings to come. The *Ploughing* Festival honors the Buddha's first moments of enlightenment, celebrations popular in Southeast Asia. It marks the start of rice-growing season (typically May–July) with two white oxen pulling a gold-painted plough with two girls sprinkling rice seeds from decorated baskets. There are also many regional festivals. The highly popular Elephant Festival of Thailand which honors these much-loved gentle giants is held on the third Saturday in November in Surin province. Held with great pomp including some 100-odd elephants, dances, cultural and historical performances, this festival symbolizes the Buddha's taming of an elephant with integral relationships between older and younger monks to preserve the transition of knowledge. Elephants also prominently feature in Sri Lanka's fifteen-day Tooth Festival (Esala Perahera) held in August (full moon) in the town of Kandy by honoring the Buddha's tooth signifying Buddhism's entry into this island nation. Celebrations are complemented by performers, musicians, lights, parades and decorations. *Higan* is celebrated in Japan twice a year for seven days around the spring and autumn equinoxes, with special prayer services while reinforcing one's vows towards Buddhism. *Abhidhamma* Day is primarily celebrated in Myanmar on the full moon day of *Thadingyut*, the seventh month in the Burmese calendar (October in the Gregorian), associated with the Buddha's ascent to *Tushita* (one of the heavenly realms) to teach his mother the Holy Abhidhamma Text of the Sutras.

And last but not the least, while this is not a festival, the ancient, marvelous practice of debating in Tibetan Buddhism in idyllic settings (monasteries) draws onlookers from all parts of the world to come and collectively rejoice. Different formats of debate are used, for example, one monk sitting and one standing, or one monk sitting with a group of monks in a circle and inviting one to debate, etc. What ensues are empowered positions ultimately honed to integrally advance one's knowledge of Buddhism, to the accompaniment of claps, passionate speeches and loud gestures!

14.5 Judaism Festivals—Lunisolar Calendar

February/March: *Purim* is a fun-filled festival celebrated on the fourteenth day of the biblical twelfth month (Adar) in Hebrew calendar, typically February–March in Gregorian calendar (in 2021 it fell on February 25). It may be noted that an exception to the above date is made in cities that were walled in the times of the Prophet Joshua, where Purim is celebrated on the fifteenth day (instead of fourteenth). Purim is recounted in the Book of Esther (Tanakh) honoring this queen for delivering the Jewish people from the wicked Haman (Persian) whose name is drowned in boos. The congregation also dresses up to enjoy! Alms donation, exchange of gifts called "shalach manos" or Purim basket, and celebratory feasting are all part of the festival.

April: Passover (Pesach) is the festival of liberation, celebrated on the fifteenth day of the biblical first month (Nisan) in Hebrew calendar, typically March–April in Gregorian calendar (in 2021 it commenced on March 27). It celebrates the Exodus from Egypt (circa thirteenth century BC). God (Yahweh is mentioned) appeared in a burning bush and commanded Moses to take on the Egyptian pharaoh, and also inflicted a series of ten plagues on the Egyptians to demonstrate his power, while "passing over" protected families. It also serves as the date of the harvesting of the first ripe grain. Celebrations go on for seven to eight days while maintaining biblical tradition of abstaining from eating leavened foods. Similar celebrations are there in other religions also, for example, Christianity (Good Friday), Islam (fasting on the tenth day of Ashura in Muharram, the first month of Islamic calendar). Ultimately, celebrations of Passover, Pesach, Pascha and Easter are all synonymous with acts of redeeming ourselves in the worship of the divine.

May: *Shavuot* or Feast of Weeks occurs seven weeks after Passover on the sixth day of the third biblical month (Sivan) in the Hebrew calendar, typically May in the Gregorian calendar (in 2021 it commenced on May 16). Celebrated at the end of the barley harvest and beginning of the wheat harvest, the Bible describes it as the Festival of Weeks when new grain and seven fruits including wheat, barley, grapes, figs, olives, dates and pomegranates were offered to the priests at the temple. It also marks the anniversary of the giving of the Torah at Mount Sinai associated with rabbinical origin of the Ten Commandments. These festivals (including Sukkot, Shavout and Pesach) are complemented with deep religious study (Orthodox) including mass convocation of festive worship at the Western Wall, synonymous with the Pentecost Festival in Christianity.

September: *Rosh Hashanah*[17] marks the beginning of the Jewish new year. The two-day festival falls on days 1 and 2 in the seventh biblical month (Tishrei) in the Hebrew calendar, corresponding to September–October in the Gregorian calendar (in 2021 it commenced on September 6). Synagogue celebrations are accompanied with loud blasts of the shofar (ram's horn) amidst lengthy services. Rosh Hashanah is of absolute biblical nature, although there are rabbinical additions to the holiday, such as eating symbolic foods, including focus on themes of repentance, preparation for Judgement Day, and prayer for a fruitful year. Elaborate meals are also prepared at home to inaugurate the new year. Despite the solemn festival, it is customary to greet fellow congregants after the first evening prayers with a blessing along the lines of "may you be written and signed speedily into the book of good life and peace." And after that first evening, one simply greets with "good year" or "Shana Tovah." Also "Happy Holidays" or "gut yom tov" in Yiddish!

Yom Kippur follows eight days after Rosh Hashanah (that is, on the tenth day of Tishrei) and constitutes repentance, atonement, and praying for divine judgement to enable soul cleansing. It is synonymous with Moses receiving the second set of Ten Commandments and atonement of Jews for the Sin of the Calf. Jews consider this as one of two statutory public "Major Fast" days (note there are also four Minor Fasts, and Special and Private Fasts) and the only fast ordained in the Pentateuch, with lengthy, multiple devotional services including a twenty-five hour fast observed. It is regarded as the most solemn festival in all Judaism.

September–October: *Sukkot* (Feast of Tabernacles) is a seven-day celebration starting five days after Yom Kippur on the fifteenth day of Tishrei. It commemorates the Exodus of the Jews from Egypt, and more specifically gives thanks to God for protecting the Jews (as they traversed the desert from Egypt to the land of Israel) by providing them a continuous shield from the elements. The festival gives thanks for a plentiful harvest festival, including gathering of the second grain crop and autumn fruit, and marks the start of agricultural year heralded by the first rains. A *Sukkah* or temporary hut covered by branches is used (built all over the country) to reflect the temporary abodes during the real

---

[17] Leviticus 23:23–25.

Exodus along with four types of plants—palm frond, citron, myrtle sprigs and willow branches to augment prayers.

Hoshana Rabbah is the seventh and last day of Sukkot and the twenty-first day of Tishrei. It is marked as the final day when judgement on the fate of the Jewish people for the next year rendered (on Rosh Hashanah) and sealed (on Yom Kippur) was finally delivered. It is hence customary to provide good wishes to friends by the expression "Piska tava" or "a good note." Seven circuits are made around the synagogue in honor of prophets and patriarchs such as Abraham and Moses while holding four plants (mentioned in the Torah) including etrog (citron), lulav (closed frond of date palm tree), hadass (myrtle tree) and aravah (willow tree). Parallels can be drawn with tearing down the wall between Jews and God. Recall the tearing down of the walls of Jericho as per Book of Joshua.[18] After the recital of *Piyyutim* or religious poems during multiple services, it is customary to beat five willow branches on the ground to symbolize our plea to send down blessing from the heavens to earth. This is followed by another day of celebration called *Shemini Atzeret* known as the eighth day of Assembly, and the *Simchat Torah* marking completion of annual cycle of Torah reading. It may be noted that in the diaspora, Shemini Atzeret is on the eighth day whereas Simchat Torah is celebrated on the ninth day.

November–December: *Hanukkah* (Chanukah) or Festival of Lights is celebrated on the twenty-fifth day of the ninth biblical month (Kislev), typically late November–December in the Gregorian calendar (in 2021 it commenced on November 28). It commemorates a miraculous victory of the Jews over religious persecution in the Holy Land, also rededicates the Second Temple of Jerusalem and the miracle of burning of oil (to keep the Menorah lit daily, which is a biblical commandment) post-liberation given that it lasted for eight days despite the oil being just enough to burn for one day only. Hanukkah is celebrated for a period of eight days including playing Hanukkah songs, accompanied by burning of candles in a multi-pronged menorah (ancient seven-lamp Hebrew lampstand).

---

[18] Joshua 6:1–27.

Miscellaneous: *Tu B'Shevat* or the New Year for Trees is celebrated on the fifteenth day of the eleventh biblical month (Shevat), typically January–February in the Gregorian calendar. It marks the arrival of spring and our duty to protect nature by planting trees.

This explanation concurs with the concept of "Tikun Olam" (repair, rectification for benefit of all God's creation), interpreted by some that trees are compared by sages to a human, and Tu Be'Shvat marks the day in the agricultural cycle that the net flow of water and nutrients from the ground flows upwards, symbolizing that from this day on humans are encouraged to channel all of the spiritual "nutrition" they amassed over the winter and bring it out of the house and into the lives of other people as well. The celebration is also called *Rosh HaShanah La'Ilanot*. The three-week period between the *Fast of the Tammuz and Tishah B'Av* held between the seventeenth day of the fourth biblical month (Tammuz) and the ninth day of the fifth biblical month (Av), cumulatively corresponding to June–August in the Gregorian calendar, solemnly venerates the destruction of the ancient First and Second Temples and other events such as Moses smashing the Tablets associated with the lost vision of Zion.

Shabbat is the weekly day of rest on Saturday, and is spent with family and friends. Public transport in Israel is suspended, businesses are closed, essential services are at skeleton-staff strength. Family feasts and services in synagogues are meant to be enjoyed, while desisting from travel, refraining from working or using electrical appliances. As per Jewish law Halakha, there are thirty-nine "melakhah" or prohibited activities. *Pesach, Shavout* and *Sukkot* are the names coined for the three pilgrimage festivals celebrating the seasonal harvests of spring, summer and fall. *Yom Tov* refers to a holiday, meaning the high holidays (Rosh Hashanah and Yom Kippur) and the three pilgrimage festivals—in total five holidays. In the days of the First and Second Temples, people would flock to Jerusalem on these festivals with offerings of crops and gifts to the Temple. Note also that all Jewish observances commence at sundown of the preceding evening (same goes for Islamic festivals, timing varies depending on interpretations of the lunar calendar).

Bar Mitzvah and *Bat Mitzvah*—coming of age (12–13 years) ritual for boys and girls—are performed for declaring them capable of bearing their own responsibility for Jewish ritual law, tradition and ethics. These also enable them to participate in all areas of Jewish community life. Mentioned in the Mishnah and the Talmud, these celebrations include religious oration by the boy or girl including blessings from the rabbi to the accompaniment of "seudat mitzvah" or suggested festive meal. These ceremonies are like the thread ceremony in Hinduism, heralding knowledge influx into the life of a child or young adult.

15. Titbits on the Five Religions

15.1 Hinduism: Titbits

Prayer Beads: Yes, called *Japa Mala* used for counting repetitive practices including prayers, chants, mantras and meditation, varying between 103 and 111 beads. Number of beads vary across religions, often with a religious or spiritual significance, and may represent a deity or special quality by each bead. These are also worn on the hands, around the neck or waist.

Protective: Amulets and talismans with mantras and pictures of deities are very popular. So also is the use of red or yellow thread (kalava) on the wrist, as well as black, saffron or other threads worn on different parts of the body to ward off evil and for promoting good fortune, healing and health. Holy ash (Vibhuti) is applied on the body and on the forehead along with other marks (tilak) to attract and conserve good energy, particularly from the emanation (energy loss) point between eyebrows.

Incense: Yes, aromatic incense sticks (Agarbatti) are used for daily prayers in homes and temples and for special religious functions to promote an equanimous devotional environment; also held in hands and rotated clockwise three times in front of the subject deity.

Circumambulation: This is integral to Hinduism, called *Pradakshina* or *Parikrama* including prostration around the statue of worship or a sacred fire; also post-prayer in clockwise direction keeping the deity always on the right side. It symbolizes our spiritual journey towards God as central point externally and within our being. Temples organize circular paths towards the shrine. Number of pradakshinas performed varies upon the deity of worship. Circumambulation is also common during last rites in many religions including Christianity, some sects of Judaism and others. Anticlockwise circumambulation is performed in Hinduism to liberate the remnant subtle life pranic energy.

Daily Prayer: Performed two to three times a day with folded hands. Note the iconic Namaste (greeting), and Shukriya (Shukran in Arabic) as thanks with folded hands. Namaste signifies reverential bowing, is associated with the añjali mudrā (posture enhancing energy flow), and is widely prevalent in Indian and Eastern religions in Asia and beyond.

Charity: Involuntary generosity, both material and otherwise, towards the needy without expecting anything in return is the common practice. Charity (Dana) peaks during religious festivals. Giving food to those who cannot afford it is highly prevalent.

Clergy Clothing: White, yellow and saffron are quintessential colors used. The traditional dhoti is a type of sarong or long waist wrap which is very common. Other priestly clothing includes robes and separate upper and lower garments, although the latter has a light upper wrap in southern India (since it has warmer clime). A sacred thread typically with triple wrap signifying control over mind, body and speech is loosely worn diagonally across the upper body with shifting positions depending upon type of rites being performed. Religious marks (ash, tilak) worn on forehead determine priestly status. Note that many sages and priests shave their heads with a lock of hair, shikha, positioned at the back of the head, which is supposed to promote spiritual well-being and control of desires, gaining knowledge, being associated with the seventh chakra energy center. Note that woman clergy wear clothing and colors synonymous with fundamental traditions followed by their male counterparts in the multiple religions. Footwear is not allowed in the vicinity of religious ceremonies. Headgear is not mandatory.

15.2 Christianity: Titbits

Prayer Beads: Yes, these are used for counting recitation of prayers, chants, meditating upon mystery of the rosary (joyful, sorrowful, luminous, etc.), including rosary beads (with crucifix), prayer rope (in Eastern Christianity), etc. Number of beads vary, for example, fifty-nine for Catholics, ten to 150 knots for Eastern, eighteen beads for Lutheran. Thirty-three beads are popular denoting the life of Christ on earth.

Protective: Amulets and talismans ranging from blessed objects such as the crucifix, holy water, blessed candles and ashes, crystals (gemstones), necklaces, rosaries, blessed salt to devotional clothing are used as sacramentals to protect against evil and to bring good luck. Designs of these aids place great emphasis (across religions) on the natural rhythms of the universe to amplify healings.

Incense: Use of incense is customary in religious church and solemn services, the resultant smoke symbolizing transcendent prayer towards the heavens. A thurible or metal senser suspended by a chain containing embers is gently directed towards the object of prayer during cleansing or devotional practices.

Circumambulation: Yes, it is seen in Catholic, Eastern and Protestant churches, in a clockwise direction, often three times around the object of worship as a reference to the Trinity. Circumambulation is occasionally performed by priests around the altar while gently swinging the thurible. Church design accommodates walking inside in areas such as the ambulatory. An example of service includes visiting the fourteen Stations of the Cross depicting the crucifixion of Jesus. Often walks are performed outside the churches.

Daily Prayer: Up to seven times a day as per ancient church traditions, with folded hands. Making the sign of the Cross with the hands to bless oneself and others is common, including revering the Holy Trinity.

Charity: Acts of generosity are integrally linked with perfection of the soul, reflecting God's glory, extending to equal love for others as for self. Christianity is one of the foremost religions promoting global charitable practices. Such acts are however common to all religions discussed here.

Clergy Clothing: Highly diverse, multi-tier clothing is typical for regular and liturgical wear, including for custom wear (religious habit) by religious orders/ institutes leading frugal, segregated lives as per specific beliefs. Typical regular clergy wear entails the use (which varies) of a cassock (long tunic), often both inner and outer, clerical shirt, cape, veil, clerical collar, hats and other ancillary items. Clothing often determines denomination. Liturgical wear includes vestments determined by regulations (rubrics), again varying across Catholic, Protestant, Eastern and others including the use of cassock-alb, chasuble (long robe), stole, surplice/rochet, gowns, hoods synonymous with academic wear, etc. Reciting special vesting prayers are also common while putting on such clothing. Note also that they are intended to invite focused attention on the Lord and his representation by the priest wearing them (and not on the priest himself). Vestments with colors varying by calendar seasons are worn by religious leaders including a "sticharion" or long inner robe (often white) epitomizing purity, an "epitrachelion" or long stole around the neck symbolizing divine power associated with Christ, a "zoni" or cloth belt associated with God's strength, an "epigonation" or cloth-covered board at the side of the body below the waist signifying Christ's humility, and a "felonion" or outer robe synonymous with judgement of Christ and crucifixion. Greek Orthodox utilize cuffs around wrists, synonymous with the bonds tying the hands of Christ, reminding us that God created everything with his hands thereby reinforcing complete faith in Him. In religious orders including monks and nuns, one hears familiar names of clothing such as tunic, cassock, the iconic scapular, cincture, tassel, coif, hood, veil, mantle, cowl, etc.

Hats are highly prevalent including the biretta, kalimavkion, mitre, skufia, etc. Black-and-white wear is highly common, other colors vary by season— white during Christmas (joyous), purple during Lent, red during feasts of martyrs and apostles symbolizing their blood shed for Christ, etc.

15.3 Islam: Titbits

Prayer Beads: Yes, these are called *Misbaḥa* and typically contain thirty-three, ninety-nine, 100 or 200 beads. Note that the first one is cycled three times for the ninety-nine names of Allah. These are prominently used for short remembrance prayers (Dhikr, Tasbih).

Protective: Views on amulets and talismans vary. Those who believe use it for protection (hafiz) against the evil eye (Nazar), promoting health, positive energies, divine presence and warding off danger. Quranic text, the ninety-nine names of Allah and prophets are popularly inscribed, worn as necklaces, rings, coins, clothing, small pouches, etc. In general, amulets are typically made of gemstones and metals. Talismans expand into clothing, paper, other materials and forms.

Incense: Incense is used for special ceremonies such as purification of the Kaaba (Mecca), for aromatic home environment but not for expelling evil spirits.

Circumambulation: Yes, counterclockwise motion is performed in synchronicity with rotation of natural elements (earth, moon, etc.). Circumambulation seven times around the Kabba (Mecca) is called *Ṭawāf*, and is performed as a fast walk three times, then slowly for the remainder. It signifies oneness and harmonious worship towards Allah. Several forms of Ṭawāf can be performed. It entails worshipping at pre-designated points around the Kaaba, the four corners coinciding with the points of the compass. Similar practices are followed around other shrines also.

Daily Prayer: Praying five times a day is obligatory, one of the five pillars of Islam. Position of hands vary during prayer. For example, raising them to the ear lobes while saying Allaahu Akbar (God is most great), or with palms placed on the knees while bowing.

Charity: In Islam, charity is twofold. *Zakat* is obligatory—donating a percentage (averaging 2.5 percent) of income is one of five pillars of Islam, whereas *Sadaqah* is voluntary and includes non-fiscal benevolent behavior.

Clergy Clothing: The word "unassuming" is wonderfully demonstrated; white features prominently given its purity, although other colors are used depending upon sect. Additionally, teachers (imams) personify unity with their congregation through such simplicity. The fit is loose precluding the possibility of others to see the outline of one's body. An ankle-length garment called a "thobe" with long sleeves and loose pants (izaar) are worn, sometimes with a robe over the thobe. Turbans and head caps typically made of cloth in white or green are worn. Many colors including red, black and blue are used on the fez or Tarboosh. Synonymous names for caps include *kufi, qalansuwa* and *peci*. Gold and silk wear are forbidden (haram). Footwear is also not allowed during prayer. Miscellaneous items of mention include (a) the two-piece white wear as part of achieving pure state of Ihram during Hajj, (b) the *Khirqah* or initiatory cloak of transcendent knowledge between Sufi teacher and student, and (c) the marvelous wear of the Sufi whirling dervishes including tall hat (sikke), the *tennûre* or pleated white robe with a *destegül* or short jacket over it, with the Khirqah over the said clothes. The spiritual whirling dance causes radiance of the white symbolizing purity permeating over the forces of evil.

15.4 Buddhism: Titbits

Prayer Beads: Yes, these are called *Malas* and include counting and thought beads for prayers, meditation, prostration. Numbers vary, for example, twenty-seven, fifty-four, 108 and 216 beads. Note that the number 108 is considered sacred (also in Hinduism). Other beads are multiples of this. Malas may also have a larger mother bead, for example, the 109th bead representing deities such as a Buddha or a bodhisattva. Additional beads may also be included to offset for counting errors.

Protective: Amulets and talisman are highly popular to ward off evils and occult practices, promoting health and fortunes, averting disasters and for energy enhancement. Note the famous Thai *Phra Somdej* amulets with featureless Buddha on multiple-tier throne to match Buddhist cosmology, part of the *Pra Krueang* umbrella of votive tablets including images and sacred text. Others include Guru Monk coin amulets, *Krueang Rang* shamanistic amulets, the bell and the *Dorje/Vajra* (symbolic pronged weapon), together signifying penetrating compassion and sunyata/primordial emptiness.

Incense: Prevalent use is of sticks on censers or thick coiled incense on special stands, or even suspended from above. Worshippers group sticks in bundles while waving in front of the object of devotion. It purifies and creates pristine conditions for meditation and worship of Buddhas, gods, bodhisattvas, etc.

Circumambulation: Yes, walking meditation is integral to Buddhism. Practices are synonymous with Hinduism, including Parikrama, Pradakshina around sacred locales such as temples, holy rivers, mountains such as Mount Kailash (China). Prostrating is very common in Buddhism, adding to length of journeys. Ancient monasteries had walkways built around structures such as stupas and chaityas. Movement is clockwise.

Daily Prayer: Praying three to four times a day with folded hands (held at center of the chest at the heart chakra, similar to Hinduism) is the common practice. The eight fingers represent the "lotus of the heart" or "white lotus" associated with the eight petals of the lotus flower, whereas the thumbs represent the father and mother or reality and wisdom.

Charity: This is one of the six perfections (Paramitas) of enlightened beings. Acts of charity must be selfless as means to relieving suffering, gaining spiritual perfection and enlightenment. And charity towards monks is associated with the act of giving, and is not seen as a means of inequality between the giver and the receiver.

Clergy Clothing: Ancient ways promote purity and non-materialism. Monks or Bhikkus and Bhikkunis (female) have minimal possessions; their sparse appearance is topped off with shaved heads (representing renunciation, shedding of ego). Multi-garment clothing is common with emphasis on purity. Ancient cleaning habits using spices such as saffron, turmeric, etc., led to the color of robes which became popular. The Theravada three-part robe "tricivara" or "kasaya" include (a) "uttarasanga" for wrapping around shoulders (typically over left shoulder), (b) "antaravāsaka" around the waist and knees akin to a sarong, and (c) "sanghati" or further robe for warmth for upper body. Tibetan robes include (a) "dhonka" or shirt with cap sleeves, (b) "shemdap" or skirt with patched cloth and pleats, and (c) "chogyu" or upper body wrap with variations including "zhen" and "namjar." Colors vary by branch and region: saffron/orange for Theravada, maroon and yellow for Tibetan, grey, brown and black in Korea and Japan for Mahayana. White is popular in syncretic sects. Ancillary capes, sashes, stoles and hats (examples red and yellow hats for different sects) are also highly prevalent. Footwear is not allowed at religious ceremonies out of respect.

15.5 Judaism: Titbits

Prayer Beads: Not used. However, knotted fringes (tassel) called *Tzitzit* are attached to the four corners of special prayer shawls and fringed garments called *Tallit* and *Tallit Katan* respectively. And while there is no direct link between Tzitzit and prayer beads, it is suggested that God asked us to wear them to remember the 613 commandments.

Protective: Use of amulets and talismans is common for protection, healing and good fortune. These are of both textual and other designs, the latter including the ancient Seal of Solomon and Star of David, synonymous with the symbol of Judaism in a hexagram, with triumph of God over evil. Symbols such as the *Chai* (meaning alive in front of God) and the palm-shaped *Hamsa* (protection) are popularly worn around the neck. Engraved names of gods and sacred text are also used.

Incense: Incense burning for religious church services was prevalent in ancient times (First and Second Temples) as mentioned in holy scriptures. Special resins, herbs and sweet spices were used. Use was limited after destruction of the Second Temple, and restricted to special occasions only in the synagogue, since concocting the same mixture of spices and burning outside resulted in a biblical prohibition. In modern times snuff boxes are sometimes passed around in synagogues to allow congregants to perform the blessing of smelling natural fragrances. Special *Mabkhara* pots are in use in Samaritan synagogues.

Circumambulation: Yes, *Hakafot* (to circle) is prevalent in festivals such as Sukkot, Hoshanah Rabbah and Simchat Torah. During Hoshanah Rabbah seven circuits are made around the synagogue in honor of prophets. The act is symbolic with tearing down the wall between the Jews and God. During Sukkot and Simchat Torah (reading the Torah scrolls), the practice entails circling the platform (Bimah) to the accompaniment of joyous clapping, singing and dancing, signifying unity in worship and strength. Movement is quintessentially clockwise, symbolic with compassion. Counter-clockwise is occasionally seen (symbolic with true justice), however this is generally minimized given the large focus is on compassion.

Daily Prayer: Prayer is obligatory three times a day: morning (Shacharit), afternoon (Mincha) and evening (Arvit). Hands are folded during prayer. Includes *Shema* and *Amidah* as integral prayers.

Charity: Religious obligatory practice, *Tzedakah*, is integrally linked with righteousness. A designated amount (up to 10 percent of income) is given to the needy. Charity is more prevalent during religious festivals, marriages, etc.

Clergy Clothing: Typical clothing includes (a) *Tallit* or prayer shawl with attached *Tzitzit* or knotted fringes, (b) a *Kippah* or *Yarmulke* or brimless skull cap, (c) a *Kittel* or white cotton robe up to the knees, and (d) a *Tefillin* or small black leather box with Torah text, typically wrapped around the arm with black straps, or on the head. Note that different practices with respect to wear exist amongst the different sects depending upon the type of service and beliefs. Black and white colors are prevalent (in Orthodox circles); other colors include blue, silver and gold. Additionally, frock coat types such as *Bekische* and *Rekel* are popular in Hasidic, including the use of hats and belts (gartel). Ancient clothing used by the high priest (chief religious official) until the destruction of the Second Temple included the priestly robe (robe of the ephod), but there exists a prohibition to create and use articles of such sacred clothing in modern religious practices.

In Jewish tradition, there is a custom during the high holidays for everyone to wear white, to symbolize our yearning to become pure like the angels.

16. The Fundamental Man

16.1 Hinduism: The Fundamental Man

Hinduism states that man constitutes a gross body with multiple subtle layers in increasing order of purity as follows: physical, subtle and causal, with the "pure Self" at our core. Alternatively, man is classified into five sheaths: physical, air, mental, intellectual and the highly pure bliss sheath; again with the pure Self/Atman at our core. And this latter, realized state is in perfect tune with the highest levels of divinity in the cosmos.

The three bodies—physical, subtle and causal—constitute about thirty-five elements of which nineteen are subtle elements (e.g., ego, intellect, mind), while the gross physical body has sixteen chemical elements (note pie diagram in "Overall System of Spirituality" under Table C). These three states are experienced daily by humans and are synonymous with the planes of existence. For example, deep dreamless sleep (best) is akin to causal (near purest); sleep with dreams where almost any experience is possible is subtle related; and the waking state we all know so well.

Ancient sages and rishis organized four stages of life to give us the best chance to transcend by living holistic lives, while focusing on the highest principles of excellence and morality to overcome our confusion and selfish attachments. Note that the rate of spiritual ascent is dependent upon our free will and individual Karma. These life stages are defined in ancient Hindu scriptures (Smritis) as a) student (Brahmacharya), b) married life (Garhasthya) including profession, c) retired (Vanaprastha) and d) renunciation (Sanyasa). Note that analogous classifications exist in myriad cultures and religions based upon development of man commencing from birth.

Profession in ancient Hindu society was also intelligently woven into a working-class system based upon skill sets, again fourfold: priesthood (Brahmins), defenders (Kshatriyas), business traders (Vaishyas), and laborers (Sudras). You will note that this working system has been passed on through the ages and is visible today in some shape or form. An interesting side note of great confusion is the subject of Kamasutra, seen as ancient practices of eroticism including depictions in ancient statues and paintings. Kamasutra was written by a sage, but not as a part of the original Hindu scriptures Vedas. Sex was not considered taboo in ancient times. Temples were centers of higher learning including teaching, and also lessons to balance the instinctive desires of a person based on his current spiritual level. Sanctified desire was promoted with a sense of duty to effect beauty in holy matrimony and reproduction, bringing awaiting souls (jivas) into this world to continue their Karmic journey. Note that once desires are exhausted, there is no need for sex. Similar allegorical references are seen in Song of Songs (Song of Solomon) in the Bible in the last section of the Tanakh (Ketuvim of the Old Testament) symbolizing a transcendental and intimate relationship between scriptures and man, and also in the reference to the seventy-two Virgins (Houris) in heaven in Islam. And while this is debated, Leviticus 15:1–18 in the Bible makes specific references to bodily discharge and related acts of cleansing. Note that the subject of sex is part of a larger umbrella of tantric/esoteric practices and morality teachings across many religions as a means to understand and transcend the desires of the mind, including potentially addictive acts of sexual immorality.

16.2 Christianity: The Fundamental Man

"Yahweh God formed man from the dust of the ground, and breathed into his nostrils the breath of life; and man became a living soul."[19]

The integrated nature of soul and body created in God's image as part of this universe constitutes biblical knowledge. Note how Adam was created from the dust of the ground, while Eve was built from one of his ribs while he slept. It is our duty to treat both soul and body as a temple in which we carry divinity by cleansing the Original Sin, following the teachings of Jesus Christ through the Bible, leading virtuous lives by professing faith and following religious rites (sacraments) under the auspices of the Church as a means to achieving God's grace. Note that while there are wide interpretations on receiving grace ranging from undeserved spontaneous help to practicing aforementioned faith rituals to predestination, it is unequivocally agreed that without the said grace it is not possible to achieve salvation.

Furthermore, "Or don't you know that your body is a temple of the Holy Spirit who is in you, whom you have from God? You are not your own."[20]

This points out that man should rise above his confusion of duality between the physical body and soul, in that the sins of the body intimately affect the soul, ultimately impacting the future of our spiritual body in eternity to come.

16.3 Islam: The Fundamental Man

Man must be an exemplary human being, superior and exalted. Taking inner faith (Iman) and showing it in both deeds and action—social responsibility borne from religious convictions. God says: "In it are men who love to clean and to purify themselves." Following this concept means practicing and promoting Islamic faith by way of truth, sacrifice, generosity, courage, and loyalty.

The totality of life in Islam is body (Jism), mind (Nafs), and spirit (Ruh). Nafs equals the mind, psyche, soul, its center is the brain (decision making). It bridges the body (Jism) and the spirit (Ruh). Both are dependent on Nafs which acts as a processor and connectivity software. There are three main types of Nafs: (a) Tranquil-Self on peace (Nafs-e-Mutma'innah) or one who does not

---

[19] Genesis 2:7.
[20] 1 Corinthians 6:19.

like the materialistic things in life and is satisfied with Allah's will, (b) Self-Aware (Nafs-e-Luwwamah) which has an awareness of both good and bad, analyzes the emotionally attached actions of the heart, repents and aspires for perfection, and (c) Inciting-Self (Nafs-e-Ammarah), one who allows to do evil actions, hence the lowest type whose principles include greed, materialism, primal attachments and fighting with other Nafs. Note that there are additional levels of Nafs culminating in pure Self (Nafs aṣ-ṣāfiyyah) or perfect Muslim who is a person who follows divine guidance and has attained beautification, excellence or perfection in Islam.

Here are some additional notes on the spirit (Ruh) whose center is the chest and which brings life to the physical body. Before birth, Ruh is neither bad nor good. Choices of the Nafs determine the character of Ruh and final destination. According to religious belief, the Ruh of all existing things was created at the time of first creation and stayed in a different world awaiting arrival in this world. After death, Ruh carries one's deeds (Aamaal/Karma) to the final destination. Note that the word Ruh is also associated with denoting both angels (mentioned four times in the Quran) and wandering departed spirits.

16.4 Buddhism: The Fundamental Man

Buddhism defines the fundamental man as five aggregates (Skandhas) constituting physical and mental factors including form (Rupa), derivative sensations (Vedanā), perceptions gained (Saṃjñā), resultant mental conditioning (Saṃskāra) and consciousness (Vijñāna, Manas, Citta). Note the earlier reference to Citta or mind, heart and emotional nature as journeying to achieve realization, nirvana, through the multiple planes of existence which are borne of a chain of impermanence or dependent origination (interdependence).

The Skandhas cumulatively define our being. The physical body created with basic elements (water, air, fire, etc.), along with the ability to cognize via sense organs (ears, eyes, etc.), register sensations (like, dislike), form mental impressions leading to Karmic actions on the path of transcendence to merge with highest consciousness.

Also as mentioned earlier, multiple techniques are utilized for the Citta to experience the divine meditative state of luminous essence, sunyata, or emptiness or pure knowledge while leveraging on the teachings of divine Buddha nature and primordial, detached empty awareness devoid of suffering—synonymous with belief in the non-self (Anattā).

16.5 Judaism: The Fundamental Man

As per esoteric philosophy, man has five levels of soul with higher levels progressively emerging and governing as one grows spiritually. Note that the multiple levels of the soul also directly correlate to the spiritual levels of (a) energetic Sefirot emanations (Item 2.5 above), (b) light energies "Ohr" and the spiritual vessel "Kli" (Item 6.5) which in turn are in perfect tune with the level of the Sefirah plane they are journeying through, and (c) the progressive levels of partzufims in the spiritual centers (Item 8.5) in the human body. In effect, the Ohr and Kli represent the characteristics of the soul with respect to its current spiritual state, earning reward or punishment outlined in the Karmic cycle associated with free will and consequent destiny.

The "Nefesh" is the basic level of the soul (from birth) immersed in action, with "Ru'ach" (emotional) and "Neshamah" (higher discriminative faculty), leading into higher consciousness (Chayah) and the "Yechida" which relates to the highest unmanifest divine Sefirah "Keter." Note that each level of the soul has a guiding Sefirah, for example, "Malchut" Sefirah governs basic soul level "Nefesh," whereas "Binah" Sefirah or understanding guides the third level of soul "Neshamat" and so forth. An analogous explanation of the hierarchy of knowledge extends up to fifty gates (fiftieth being the ultimate, divine). Moses achieved the forty-ninth level which is the highest a mortal man can reach.

The goal is continuing to transcend in the interplay between "Ruchniut" or divinity, spirituality, metaphysical versus the "Gashmiut" or physical, material desires. Note that "Gashmiut" is also linked to anything to do with physical matter. It is a person's lifelong struggle to strive for more Ruchniut and to tame the drive for Gashmiut, while also elevating the Gashmiut and infusing it with Ruchniut.

Note also that Judaism defines the spiritual life cycle of man including coming of age, reading the commandments at age thirteen, pursuing goals at twenty, counseling at fifty, leading to special spiritual strength at age eighty and so forth.

TABLE C

Overall System of Spirituality

Introduction to Table C: Overall System of Spirituality

We now take up the concept of the recurrent life cycle model as depicted in Table C below as a logical sequence to all that we have discussed so far. Starting from initial mental housecleaning (Table A) and involution/evolution of life per Hinduism (Table B-1), we expand on realization achieved on the earth plane into the ascending subtle planes while drawing from common principles of the five-religion analysis (Table B-2) and other beliefs. The result is a composite model with a simple universal message for holistic improvement. This information is not new, but an integrated look at the journey of the soul/seeker through the multiple planes of existence segregated by levels of purity achieved through mastery of energy via developed intuition. And as mentioned earlier, I did contemplate putting together the alternate single life cycle model, but it would have delayed this book by more than a year, perhaps to be completed as a future endeavor.

It is all about understanding that creation, the cosmos/universe as we know it, constitutes electromagnetic vibrational energies complete with a set of limiting factors which we struggle to transcend, thanks to the confusion of our ego. As one commences this marvelous journey via multiple means and methods, one progressively comes to realize that creation is based around variations of light energy in increasing order of divinity. Note the reverence to light across the religions; with all other factors such as time, gravity, opposing influences (e.g., heat and cold, pleasure and pain) being impermanent. It is indeed our ego that precludes us from breaking through this impermanence, binds us to the veiling power of confusion or cosmic delusion. Our strategic vision is to

TABLE C

Overall System of "Pure Undifferentiated Consciousness," "Brahman," "God"

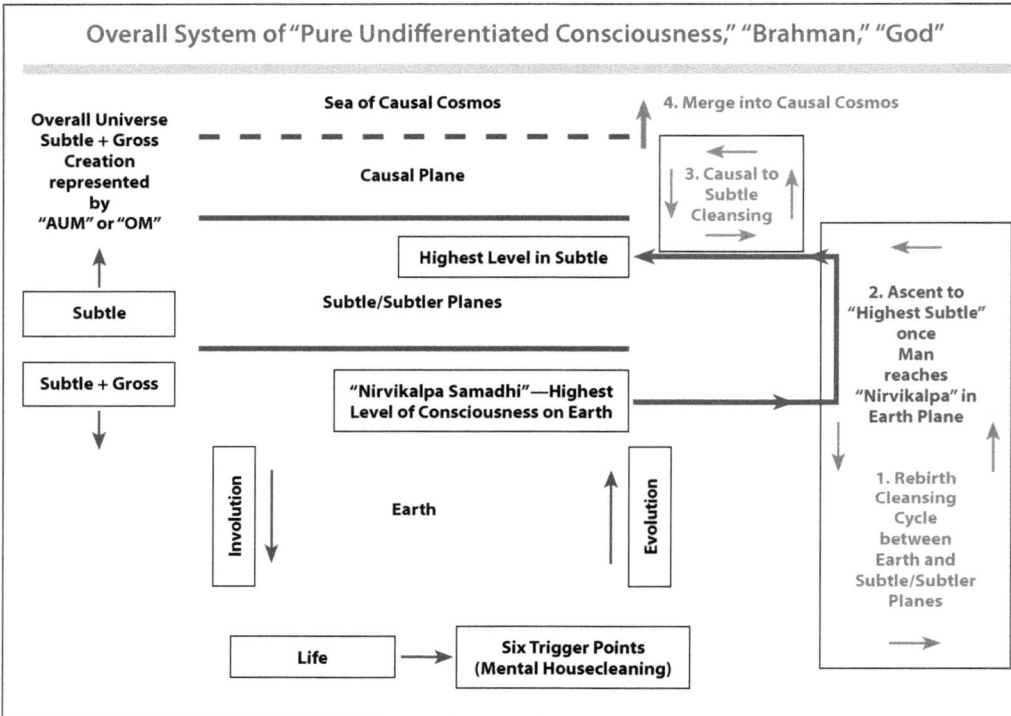

Overall Universe Subtle + Gross Creation represented by "AUM" or "OM"

Sea of Causal Cosmos

4. Merge into Causal Cosmos

Causal Plane

3. Causal to Subtle Cleansing

Subtle

Subtle/Subtler Planes

Highest Level in Subtle

2. Ascent to "Highest Subtle" once Man reaches "Nirvikalpa" in Earth Plane

Subtle + Gross

"Nirvikalpa Samadhi"—Highest Level of Consciousness on Earth

Involution

Earth

Evolution

1. Rebirth Cleansing Cycle between Earth and Subtle/Subtler Planes

Life → **Six Trigger Points (Mental Housecleaning)**

transcend by perfecting spiritual instinct to get to God or the highest possible realms within the universe via progressive emotional detachment and concerted meditative practices.

Let us commence by defining what constitutes the basic man, the pure Self (Atman) which is the essence of pure consciousness or Brahman in Hinduism, with multiple layers encasing it, culminating in the gross physical body. Note that while beliefs vary across multiple religions (Table B-2, Item 16), the common factor is the acknowledgment of gross and subtle layers constituting the fundamental man.

While we looked at different schools, traditional Vedanta (one of the six schools of Hindu philosophy) defines man as the pure Self covered by three bodies—physical, subtle and causal. Also categorized as five sheaths: food, vital air, mental, intellectual and bliss in increasing order of purity, as shown in the following Pie Diagram:

GROSS Physical Body

Food Sheath

SUBTLE Body: 17 non-Gross Elements
enabling Experience via:
• Mind, Intellect
• 5 Sense Organs: Ears, Skin, Eyes, Tongue, Nose
• 5 Action Organs: Speech, Hands, Legs, Anus, Genitals
• 5 Pranas: They maintain Life, energize both Gross and
  Subtle Bodies: breathing, blood circulation, digestion,
  toxic elimination, rebalancing systems

Vital Air Sheath

Mental Sheath

Intellectual Sheath

CAUSAL Body
• Seat of Hidden Ignorance, yet senses Bliss
• Causes the Gross and Subtle Bodies
• Has great power, pervades the other two bodies

Bliss Sheath

The Pure SELF/ATMAN
• Exists as Highest Witness
• Experiences Bliss, Pure
  Consciousness

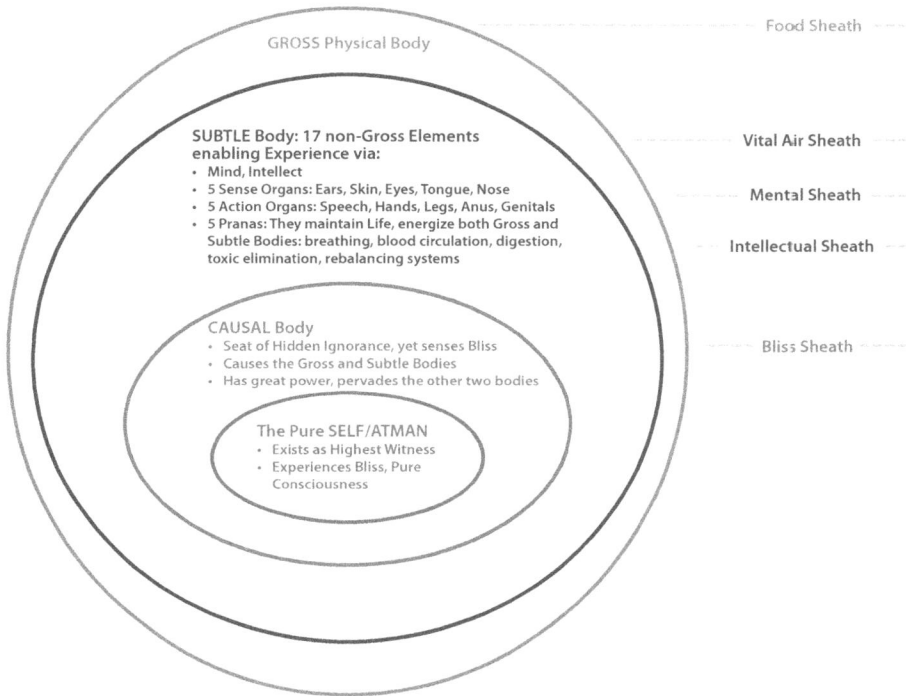

It is important to note (above) that the pure SELF/ATMAN (essence of pure consciousness) pervades the Casual, Subtle and Physical bodies. The Causal body in turn pervades the Subtle and Gross bodies, and so on. Readers are also advised to note four points before going into the detailed Table C discussion:

• The sense organs, action organs, etc., in the subtle body refer to the sense perception or resultant experience gleaned from the related physical organ residing in the gross body. For example, ears allow for cognition of hearing, eyes enable viewing.

• Readers may come across the expression "astral body" in equivalent literature. Note that this is synonymous with the subtle body in the diagram above. And each of these "bodies" (example subtle body, causal body) is synonymous with the planes of existence in Table C above.

• The subtle body houses the ego, home to our desires. People with a strong subtle body are capable of thriving in a materialistic world; alternatively, the ego may be a significant hindrance to true spiritual growth.

- The five pranas perform the critical functions to keep us alive while guiding our Karmic evolution from birth. These are the energy transferred from the soul (ego) to the body via the psychic energetic system (chakras, etc.) to execute and sustain us through all our activities. Recall also the explanation on universal cosmic energy translated to individual prana as discussed under Table B-1.

General Discussion on Table C and the Journey of the Soul through Multiple Planes of Existence

Let us now discuss the features of Table C in brief. In the left-hand side of the table, Aum represents overall universe creation (both subtle and gross planes). It is the cosmic vibratory power behind all atomic energies including creation, sustenance and dissolution. In fact, the sound of Aum, both audible and inaudible, represents all creation (recall Trigger 4 explanation in Table A).

People, places, languages, music, mountains, planets are all resultant examples of this driving force. Chanting or meditating on Aum via appropriate practices gets us into rhythms with the subtle laws of creation, leading progressively to synchronicity of actions and higher levels of consciousness.

The central part (of Table C) represents Tables A and B-1 at a summary level commencing with the overall system of pure undifferentiated consciousness (Brahman, God) at the top, and the six trigger points at the bottom as the initial steps to purity. There are three main vibrational planes of existence in increasing order of purity: gross/subtle (earth), multiple subtle/subtler, and the causal plane. Note that all three aspects of our being (see pie diagram) exist on the earth plane, with only our subtle bodies (upon each death) traveling into the said subtle planes.

The right-hand side of Table C summarizes the steps (1–4) for the soul to transcend through successive cycles of purity, rebirth, and evolution into the causal plane. The realized soul (the Self) ultimately loses any vestige of individuality and merges into this vast sea of causal cosmos which is the highest achievable level. To provide further context, the cycle of life and death (as we know it) first commences between the earthly and subtle/subtler planes based upon our actions (Karma). The first true rung of achievement is when the soul attains the realized state of Nirvikalpa Samadhi (see Step 7 in Table B-1), having cycled to the highest level of the subtle planes. At this point, our physical body is no longer required, and return to earth becomes a purely voluntary act (as humans, other life forms, or in subtle form only) to help others. The process then continues between the highest subtle and causal planes until one merges into the sea of causal cosmos representing the purest form of divine light energies within manifested (differentiated) Brahman, as explained later in this analysis.

There are different interpretations of this. Some schools believe that the sea of causal cosmos constitutes the highest levels pre-God; others believe it merges with the creator. With overall timing exceeding a million years encompassing normal life cycles of birth and rebirth. And a related explanation on the life cycle of the creator Brahma follows later.

Now the specific process of cleansing is through developed instinct, also known as the sixth sense or the third-eye intuition. This is defined as involved rational analysis, reasoning or experience that has become subconscious over time; and is the mechanism to progressively control energy to ultimately reach the lotus feet of the Lord. It is said that during deep meditation the spiritual eye becomes visible centrally on the forehead thereby permeating and seeing all. And man's exit upwards is through the chakras lining up within the body pursuant to concerted meditative, religious, and other spiritual practices.

Detailed Discussion on All Tables (A, B-1, B-2 and C)

With this introduction to Table C, let us now have a detailed discussion covering all the four tables together. The process of involution commences at the macro level pursuant to the interaction of the spiritual and material energies of God, and progressively makes its way down to life via a combination of these subtle and gross elements. This is expanded in the left-hand side of Table B-1 which (as mentioned above) constitutes a central part of Table C. Note that the twenty-four elements ranging from the cosmic-to-individual ego, the organs of perception and action, the subtle and gross elements all combine to ultimately create life as we understand it.

And synonymous with the three planes of existence (Table C), the essence of our divinity, the pure Self/Atman is central to the three bodies (see pie diagram) as follows: the causal body which is purest (of the three bodies), the subtle body where man's mental and emotional nature reside, and the gross physical body. The subtle body constitutes those senses which are not physically materialized, and enables our experiences via seventeen elements including the intellect, mind, five sense organs, five action organs and five pranas (subtle life force). Note that the fivefold specific prana is what keeps us alive by supplying energy to both the physical and the subtle body.

The physical body constitutes sixteen physical elements (flesh, bones, etc.) including its nine orifices such as mouth, ears and others. Table B-1 explains the combination of vibratory forces, first subtle and then gross resulting in creating man's subtle body followed by gross physical form. With our fears and attachments gluing it all together, these forces preclude the possibility of our transcendence into the higher realms.

We daily experience these three states of the human condition. Deep dreamless sleep (best) is related to the causal which is the purest of the three bodies; sleep with dreams where almost any experience is possible is related to our subtle body; and the waking state which we all know so well. To explain this further, the soul (jiva) in the waking state gets tired of dealing with sense objects, disassociates with the body and sense organs and goes to sleep. Note that during disturbed sleep, we experience dreams borne of our desires and sense attachments from the waking state. When the mind itself gets tired of dealing with sense desires, it becomes inactive; the soul now disassociates even with the mind and enters into the purest state of intuitive consciousness in deep sleep. It may be noted that the illuminating light in the dream is not from external sources or of the mind, since the mind itself is an object being observed—we enjoy deep blissful sleep in the absence of the mind and our sense organs, with such absence being clearly observed. Hence, the light illuminating the dream has to come from our intrinsic nature or the highest witness (Self) within.

And it is our non-physical being (subtle, causal, etc.) that survives an earthy death, till which time we display consciousness in the gross body.

So, commencing from the bottom of Table C, we examine the following:

Cycle of Purification

It is our mission to develop that spiritual instinct leading to intuition to transcend the mind (ego) which is the root cause of all pain, given we are always caught in situations where our attachment to earthly desires are greater than the urge to transcend. When the mind pines, anger prevails because of the fear of losing the object of desire. The mind is a deluded projection of our true Self, the highest witness unaffected by time and space; whose nature is pure bliss existing as the essence of pure consciousness and supreme knowledge. Our conscious decisions based on the laws of action and reaction (Table B-2, Item 1.1) gradually readjusts our Karmic balance and future lives through to eventual redemption. A human being may transmigrate down to lower forms (like animals, birds, insects, etc.) but this is to rebalance out prior Karma only; and it is not decision-based influencing of the future life path given the inability of animals to express full divinity. Each species operates within their limiting conditions, for example, we as humans laugh the same way; similarly, dogs express happiness by wagging their tails, most animals hug us when expressing emotion. Put another way, every being or object is in a cycle of evolution limited by their instinct and condition, with humans having the potential to master their instincts to achieve progressive realization.

As for the Karma from previous lives which are coming to fruition in our current existence including those to come, these are beyond our control and we should accept these with temperance. Add to this mix the recurrent patterns of the ego. Pending a step change or significant reform effort, our mind creates patterns of thought and action leading to predictability repeating the same mistakes endlessly. These include tendencies of the mind such as ignorance and the attachment to sense objects—the sense of the ego being a separate entity—the desire to cling to life hence continuing the Karmic cycle and experiences of pleasure and pain. Once we destroy this ignorance, we break the vicious cycle.

Specific Process of Cleansing: Start as a Warrior-Monk and End Up as the Monk

We are continually bound by ignorance, desire and activity. Commence with mental housecleaning primarily through dedicated focus on selfless activities (Table A, Six Trigger Points). Take for example a champion boxer, a NASA shuttle commander, a master chef, an army general, a painter, golfer, professor, guitarist, actor, heart specialist, artist, industry CEO, singer, police officer or any other professional. If you closely watch the best, you will note (for the most part) a relaxed, casual, almost lazy indifference in these top professionals. Examples may be cited of Roger Federer, Sunil Gavaskar, Steve Irwin, Muhammad Ali, Bruce Lee, Kishore Kumar, Michael Jackson, Fred Astaire, Pelé, Julio Iglesias. Note their perfect timing borne of great perseverance, that millisecond slower action with perfect synchronicity of energy deliverance. The hallmark of a music maestro is that we ascertain immediately, through his vision and craft so perfectly compressed in individual moments of time, that we are indeed dealing with something special. I once saw a master sushi chef who had perfected speed, stance and distance by being perfectly positioned between his tools and guests to prepare dishes and serve seamlessly. His technique was perfected from martial arts, with strength and subtlety so beautifully and marvelously intertwined.

Have you ever heard of someone having an aura or electric presence about them? It is organized energy with a higher vibrational frequency of the subtle body, which is developed instinct borne of years of dedicated effort. The same principle extends to group occasions like religious gatherings, sports events, etc., where the collective energy is palpable. As an interesting side note, mention may be made of energy healers who use related principles for localized (hands-on) and distance healing including reiki. They work to generate energies of higher frequency to raise positive vibrations in the mind and body. Such practices additionally work on the principles of energy interconnectedness. Hence achieving the power of distance healing is all about expertise, not the challenges of mileage. Coming back to effort, imagine the sheer bliss of continued extraordinary performance akin to meditation, borne of our sheer focus and dedicated action. At such moments the ego is transcended, and we reach into our highest Self, the essence of our pure divinity within. Genius activity commences, for example the masterpiece paintings produced by artists or the wonderful timing of a tennis stroke by a top professional. Indeed artists have referred to this effect as channeling. At such times, one may involuntarily sense this highest witness within, with the extraordinary ability of not only being fully focused on single-point dedication but also being completely aware of their surroundings and myriad activities. Taking Muhammad Ali again, many opponents said his aura so deeply permeated the ring that you felt he could take you out at will. Dedication to his craft, talent, psyche and strategic vision—all coming together timely. Similar comments were made about Bruce Lee's focus and speed. Or how about Michael Holding, the West Indian fast bowler? Batsmen and observers alike noted that he always bowled "within himself," capable indeed of much more menacing pace bowling!

And if you delve deeper into the lives of these people, you will note extreme sacrifices, tenacity, dedication, and courage to get there. And the best are often displeased with the result! Many have gone on to instinctively sense and transcend the boundaries of their profession to serve (and not dominate) humanity. They reached up to give it their all, which is all about transcending inner fears and living in the moment regardless of outcome. In essence, connecting with one's higher being (the Self) by recognizing that one's ultimate fight is with facing the truth. The point is to pick out your top skill sets and run with it, have the courage to see it through while having a backup strategy. An individual may have many talents, and yet he may fail. To be hugely successful takes great sacrifice, and these people are prime movers of that principle.

So now let us imagine possessing (naturally or through endeavor) this level of dedicated focus directionally pointed towards religious and spiritual study, combined with the holistic approach as laid out in Tables A, B-1, B-2 and C. Mental housecleaning is followed by concentration through to the multiple stages of meditation. We admire physical prowess in martial arts; what about the perseverance and austerity of monks who sit silently for years meditating. The point is that for the majority of us all these steps are preparatory cleansing acts towards the next levels of ascent, and unless that dedicated focus is translated into spiritual intuition, the cycle of life and death will go on. I must state in the same breath that while it is certainly possible to transcend or become a realized soul, given one's expertise in a craft is a meditation in its own right, the resultant purity must also permeate into all aspects of one's life translating into transcendent spirituality. We see so many examples of great talent ultimately failing because while one excels in what one's chosen profession is, one falls by the wayside in other areas. One needs concerted, non-attached, holistic action to transcend from initial cleansing to concentration and meditation.

And those who are fortunate have a true guru capable of eliminating their fears, desires and spiritual ignorance. The acts of such leaders or gurus have reformed millions globally through the ages. Disciples see a guru as the representation of a living God, hence their unconditional love. Gurus lead you unto yourself and not to them! One needs a guru to make those wonderfully insignificant fine-tuned adjustments to effect a step jump in spiritual growth, just like one needs a master professional to teach golf, martial arts, etc. Think about the expertise developed in the latter. A ninja leaves no smell, remains mysterious and makes everybody wonder how on earth he did leave his mark! A direct disciple of Swami Chinmayananda mentioned that her guru considered golf to be a form of meditation—indeed note the serenity of golfers! And how about this one—I was once watching the concentration involved (of professionals) in studying and deoxygenating wine, indeed a sight to behold!

Comments on Yoga and Meditation Techniques

These words—yoga and meditation—are used in a broad sense, but fundamentally yoga is integrated, skilled action utilizing multiple paths to cleanse, and it includes meditation also. Meditation ranges from the quiet fellow focusing on withdrawing from all his impermanent desires of mind and body to the one utilizing accelerated practices such as the ancient science of Kriya Yoga and similar techniques known to many saints, sages and yogis globally. Yoga methods have taken hold with people of all ages, derived substantially from the Yoga Sutras, one of the six ancient philosophies of Hinduism. We looked at Sage Patanjali's (second century BC) eight limbs of yoga which include: 1) refraining from evil thoughts and acts (yama), 2) multiple observances to promote purity (niyama), 3) appropriate body posture (asana) to enable proper focus and meditation, 4) control of our subtle life energy prana via pranayama and specific yogic breathing techniques to control subtle life currents, 5) withdrawal from sense objects (pratyahara), 6) concentration (dharana), 7) meditation (dhyana) and 8) transcendental experience (samadhi) to ultimately achieve impersonal union with pure consciousness. These concepts are substantially discussed earlier under Tables A, B-1 and B-2.

But what really happens in the process of meditation? Let us examine it a bit more. But before that readers are requested to revisit Tables B-1 and B-2 (Item 8), particularly the discussion on prana and the seven chakras to reinforce their understanding before delving into the critical explanation below.

In the initial steps of refraining from evil thoughts and observances, multiple techniques are available, namely the paths of devotion (Bhakti Yoga), dedicated action (Karma Yoga), introspection (Jnana Yoga), or a combination (Raja Yoga) thereof. To transcend, one initially needs conscious choice to subdue our deep vices (vasanas), and integral to this effort is minimizing the irritants thereby cleansing and calming the mind. Examples include eliminating non-sattwic food and drink including meats, alcohol, even garlic, and such others. Just as a clean office indicates your state of mind, maintaining the body as a temple of resident purity permeates into our subtle body energies.

In the advanced stages of reaching the highest levels of consciousness (Table B-1, Steps 6 and 7), we progressively end up operating involuntarily in a breathless state. The implication is staggering, that our rishis (sages and yogis) figured out that breathing is not required for survival, and at the same time came up with concerted mechanisms to transcend on an accelerated basis!

There are two sources of our subtle life energy prana: (a) universal cosmic energy Aum directly received into the sixth chakra (medullary, Ajna) at the back of the neck which is linked to the third eye at midpoint between the eyebrows, and (b) that received through breathing whereby the oxygen intake not only gets utilized by our fivefold pranic energies (see pie diagram) for various bodily functions to sustain us but also gets converted to pranic energy to reinforce our chakras for our spiritual growth.

In the advanced stage of meditation, the secret lies in substantially controlling and redirecting these resident, intelligent fivefold pranic energies towards higher activity by minimizing bodily needs, and thus creating a surplus bank of subtle energies converted from unused oxygen to further reinforce the chakras. Furthermore, meditation also increases our intake of universal cosmic energies [see (a) in previous paragraph] as the medulla naturally opens up further.

So how is this physically achieved? Let us present some statistics, some theory, and then have a discussion on the multi-pronged strategy to achieve this marvelous feat.

First, 20% of oxygen intake is utilized by the brain which constitutes only about 3% of body weight. Note that the all-important third eye (where the sixth chakra is), and the seventh chakra (Crown, Sahasrara) which stores our reservoir of pranic energy reside here! Second, the heart pumps about 100,000 times, about 2,000 gallons of blood daily, to keep us clean, i.e., rid the body of impurities (carbon dioxide) through this heart pumping action. Now consider the needless pumping of the heart when breathing, since oxygen intake in human beings is at best shallow—averaging fifteen breaths per minute under normal conditions, thirty to forty per minute when agitated and slowing down to around twelve per minute when asleep. We yawn when we are tired—this in fact is to intake more oxygen to offset shallow breathing, given our body operating conditions have changed (more inefficient due to tiredness).

The natural inference is that tremendous power resides within us awaiting good use, offset by significant waste. The more agitated we are, the more impurities have to be pumped out and the shallower is our breathing. The reverse takes place when we are sleeping—our tensions of the day have gone, the heart slows down and has to pump out fewer impurities; we also have longer, regulated breathing and hence better oxygen intake. The chakra system gets better recharged which in turn positively affects our mind and body, and we awaken refreshed! In fact, we are slow meditators in sleep.

So how can the body survive without breathing? The answer is simply enthralling. Some theory, Involution and Evolution (Table B-1) contemplates coming together of the spiritual and material arms of the creator to produce vibrations leading to universe creation cumulatively represented by Aum. The continued interaction of these two opposing yet complementary primal forces ultimately equates to two main energetic channels in our bodies called prana (uplifting, positive), and *apana* (downward, trapping)—ultimately translated

to the inhalation and exhalation of breath. Note that prana has multiple definitions (please refer to the first few pages of Involution and Evolution in Table
B-1 until the end of Steps 1–3). These two channels operate to and from the
point between the eyebrows and the coccyx, and are aligned with our chakra
system. In the normal person, inhalation (breathing in) reinforces and further
recharges our body and our psychic energy system (sushumna and the ida,
pingala, chakras) with cosmic energies while exhalation (breathing out) sheds
off impurities. Note that the average human life cycle is typically of 100 years,
but each life has a predetermined number of breaths limited by one's Karmic
evolution. Dogs breathe much faster and have a limited life cycle, seven years
on an average. Continuing on, let us consider a man's specific life cycle, say
eighty-two years. The normal cumulative processes (mental, physical, psychic)
of our Karmic life evolution driven by our pranic energy (which is intelligent,
has memory) ultimately leads to the downward apana current prevailing over
uplifting prana leading to demise timed perfectly (to eighty-two years), with
the positive replenishing energies being overcome by the forces of decay.

Physically, positive cleansing in the normal person is done via the heart
pumping out impurities from our blood system supported by breathing.
Ancient sages and yogis discovered this key link—that breathing and deterio-
ration are interlinked. And if one radically increases oxygen intake via concerted
practices whilst stopping decay, heart pumping and breathing progressively slow
down to the point where it is no longer required. The tremendous energy
expended in simply maintaining our body (e.g., pumping 2,000 gallons of blood
daily) can be converted into additional pranic energies to place every cell in the
body into a spiritually magnetized condition resplendent with wonderful light
energies, while aligning the chakras for transcendence.

And hence the birth of specific, multiple techniques coined under the
umbrella of yoga, thanks to detailed knowledge of the psychic energetic channels or the chakra system. A man's life constitutes a constant struggle of where
his consciousness prevails at any given time with these opposing forces in play.
Prana uplifts, apana keeps us bound to our desires. Specialized techniques such
as the ancient Kriya Yoga accelerate the recharging of the body while minimizing its needs to a rate much faster than that achieved during sleep. A fourfold

process cumulatively takes place: (a) much increased oxygen intake through yogic practices gets converted to pranic energy; (b) focusing on mantras (such as Aum) increases direct intake of cosmic energies through the sixth chakra (medulla opens up), both cumulatively recharging the chakras with subtle energies; (c) decay in body decreases to the point that action of heart to pump out waste is not required and it ceases involuntarily; and (d) the five-fold subtle pranic energies (pranayama equals control of the five pranas) expended in bodily functions withdraws along with our now highly evolved soul from the external senses and organs to unite with the subtle currents in the spine towards transcendence. And in the realized condition the sage perceives his entire being including the universe as a combination of these marvelous pranic and light energies (see Table B-2, Item 9) in increasing levels of purity commencing from subatomic levels.

Thus, we progressively accelerate and align our psychic energy system to awaken the chakras and release our kundalini energy though the central sushumna channel which rises upwards striking the five body chakras through increasing levels of enlightenment reaching the sixth and seventh chakras, our centers of intuition and divine consciousness, respectively.

Once the basic principle is understood, the rest boils down to techniques centered around pranayama, mantras and concentration (meditation) practiced the world over to balance inhaling and exhaling breaths thereby controlling decay (apana) while gaining control of prana for higher use. Sages through their wonderful powers of concentration achieve this by fixing the gaze on the mid-spot between the eyebrows (third eye) which is the confluence of both energy channels ida and pingala, and the sushumna. Kriya yoga similarly accelerates spiritual evolution by channeling the significantly increased reserve of pranic energy withdrawn from the body (now in magnetized condition) up and down the first six chakra centers. And this is most interesting, you may be subliminally aware of your life patterns (mental and physical situations) materially changing in cycles (of about twelve years for well-balanced people), thanks to cumulative impacts of our inner being and variations in energies imposed by the natural laws of the universe (for example, solar, lunar cycles). These cycles are of a lesser time period for the more agitated people. Understanding these cycles and riding along can lead to a much greater chance of success in our lives. Our first six chakras (with double polarity) revolving around our soul are directly aligned with the twelvefold astrological system/signs of the cosmic man (see Table B-1, Step 2) and the sun; and one year of the earth's revolution around the sun provides the same, slow spiritual evolution of our pranic energy revolving around our soul in the normal person. But in the highly evolved, the aforementioned techniques accelerate our evolution, it is said that a half minute of Kriya is equivalent to one year of our natural spiritual evolution!

A word of caution: while we all want to rush into the said techniques, in fact it takes intense physical and mental cleansing, specific training, leading lives brimming with purity, to prepare mind and body under strict tutelage from masters armed with a vision to achieve the highest levels of divinity. Note that involuntary stoppage of breathing progressively occurs, from seconds or minutes in concentration to several hours in the multiple states of samadhi, to ultimately being controlled at will in Nirvikalpa Samadhi. We can also easily infer that experimenting with this great resident power without expert guidance can directly lead to incredibly adverse impacts on both mind and body. Note that the power to withstand the increased levels of this cosmic energy is directly proportional to levels of transcendence (samadhi), and a normal person would not be able to withstand such energies. Yoga teachers do show beginners simple breathing techniques to calm the mind to prepare for concentration; there is no danger of injury in these initial techniques given that breath is not withheld for extended periods or that too much oxygen is rushed into the brain. An interesting analogy of a non-meditative, involuntary breathing habit to calm the nerves is to let out a huge sigh of relief after achieving a task or when a problem beyond our control goes away!

At the superconscious state of Nirvikalpa Samadhi, the yogi completely controls his mind, intellect, suspended desires and fears at will and switches on/off his five senses (sound, sight and others) to head into the first true realm of infinite consciousness (the seventh chakra, Sahasrara or the thousand-petaled lotus) as a boundless source of light or life energy guided by divine intelligence. Our desires, fears and delusions, mind and ego are hence all overcome enabling direct receipt of cosmic life-sustaining energies synonymous with Aum, the resident driving force behind the entire pulsating universe. A swami once told me that he could hear this vibrational energy or cosmic sound by simply covering his ears. And in Nirvikalpa Samadhi, the body is maintained in an energized condition; we no longer need sleep to recharge, we minimize food intake and work fundamentally off these cosmic energies. At this level of spirituality, the yogi can easily convert all his cells into energy, his atoms are etherealized and become light as a feather, and he possesses the power to materialize/dematerialize his body at will. Indeed, levitation of many sages and saints has also been reported in many religions globally through the ages. Sages have also used certain techniques whereby focusing on the fifth chakra (Vishuddha) controls ether existing at our minutest cell levels, thereby enabling yogis to live off its energy. Ether (also called space) is the first of the gross elements to materialize in creation and the most subtle, all the other elements having been derived from it and then afforded space to fill within it. The qualities (or lack thereof) of ether are interesting. It is light, cold, motionless; yet it is all-pervading, formless, limitless and occupies every aspect of creation utilized by pranic energies to drive Karmic evolution.

Herein lies the secret of ascending and the first major step of disassociating with our physical bodies into the non-gross state at will into the highest subtle and causal planes in Table C. Note there is no breathing in these higher states. Consequently our body needs minimal maintenance, being supported by these sublime energies. And when life leaves the human body, in the realized it leaves through the top of the head, for the balance through the lower bodily openings into onward journey.

Whew, that was quite a mouthful! Have a pause to imagine the resident power within ourselves to control our life force at will. And all due to the mastery of breathing via multiple, concerted practices. Know that if we try with dedicated focus, grit and purity while minimizing body needs, we are able to accelerate our natural evolution (Karmic cycle). We effectively accumulate and convert our energies into subtle life force by reinforcing spinal currents to awaken the chakras (and consequently the kundalini force) to spiritualize our subtle and gross bodies into the next level of ascent beckoned by the universe.

This kundalini energy is known by different names depending upon beliefs, for example "chi," "taiji pole" in Chinese philosophy. Ancient martial arts/ holistic practices such as qigong, tai chi and silat are all derivatives of these fundamental energies; even acupuncture is applied pursuant to deep study of the same. Advanced Buddhist practices (including tantra) such as tummo and dzogchen are synonymous examples cumulatively focusing on the resident divine power within our being as a means to transcendence. Amongst other benefits, tummo or inner fire meditation creates yogic heat based upon meditative visualization (e.g., nature, purity). Note the examples of monks seated in perfect posture stoically unimpacted by cold climes. Dzogchen meditation (Nyingma, Bon traditions, etc.) focuses on the divine luminous essence, primordial purity of the undifferentiated universe. Associated keywords include emptiness "sunyata," the primordial state ("the ground") demonstrating pure knowledge "*rigpa*" over delusion "*ma-rigpa*." Integral elements include naturalness, spontaneity and simplicity, perfected postures (lotus) aided by inflow of the essence of pure nature. Techniques also incorporate preparation of life transition (death) into possible purgatory (bardo) by achieving a higher non-material state or rainbow body of light as a precursor to attaining the higher echelons of heaven (pure lands) frequented by the Bodhisattvas and Buddhas.

An example of the chakras is seen during the horrors of war. I was reading about comments made by veterans of World War II operating under extreme circumstances. For example, how one soldier described that in combat one ends up losing all sense of morality, indeed one feels and reacts like an animal in survival mode; or how one felt a sense of psychosis and wanted to kill after seeing his best friend killed in action. And while they were forced to substantially operate from the Root (Muladhara) representing survival, all of them had shown brotherhood, love and selfless acts through all this horror thanks to the inherent goodness within us, all combined with the intense training and discipline afforded to the troops at military academies the world over. How many times have we heard "It is all about the guy next to you" or "I would die for my brothers"?

As a minimum, one must always attempt one's best to work to the highest ideals notwithstanding whether one coins himself as religious, spiritual, agnostic, atheist or other. The selfless duty of a soldier being the defense of his country, which means he must shoot when the need calls for it, the near impossible question is how to do it detachedly. An interesting side note, it may be cited that at the great ancient battle of Mahabharata described in Hinduism's Holy Geeta (Bhagvadgita), a realized onlooker saw only Lord Krishna fighting on both sides in the battlefield! And how about a cricketer, a baseball or a soccer player fervently doing their duty for something larger than themselves, i.e., their country. Or contemplate the divine duty of a husband–wife team to bring waiting souls (jivas) into this world to enable their continued journey of learning and action (Karma). Contemplate also on the love between a mother and her baby, considered to be one of the purest forms of duty known to all humanity.

This highest form of selfless duty is known as *dharma,* appropriateness of action based upon individual circumstances. It can only be based on intuition or experience borne of higher wisdom. Recall Bruce Lee's quote: "Be water, my friend!"[1] While dharma has many interpretations including being considered a natural universal law promoting behavior towards maintaining cosmic balance and order precluding or offsetting chaos, at the individual level dharma stands for how one copes with one's current circumstances to work one's way out of the problems faced. Simply put, try best to accept what comes as a gift (as a minimum an opportunity), understand that what may be considered right action under one circumstance may be erroneous under another; practice every act as an inner meditation for yourself and you will see amazing step changes commence within yourself.

Let us soldier on. Ancient languages such as Sanskrit (a mother language to many) were vibratory derivatives of Aum leading to the creation of holy mantras. Any word spoken with concentration on its meaning results in spiritual effects leading to *samyama* (recall Table B-1, Powers and Self-Restraint) and on to higher state of consciousness. As discussed above, chanting and meditating through advanced techniques help us progressively get into synchronicity and being supported by the laws of creation. And there exists a direct synergy between the chakras and the ascension cycle starting from Tables A to C. The purer (sattwic) we become, the higher meditative plane we transcend to; awakening of these

---

[1] Permission granted by the Bruce Lee Family Company. All rights reserved. BLE, LLC.

chakras (light lotuses) is the sacred goal of the sage to exit out to achieve the ultimate levels of consciousness via separation from the physical body.

And as our consciousness transcends with our progress through the stages of concentration and meditation, the mind gets focused from cleansing, and by-products such as occult or *siddhi* powers may develop. Examples of these are telepathy, clairvoyance, healing powers, etc. Intuition is experienced spiritual guidance to our being, and our willpower turns our focus into energy. A relaxed, focused mind reinforced by strength of will (emotional power concentrated on the heart) enables projection from the midpoint between the eyebrows to both send and receive messages through the ethereal realm, even receiving messages from bodies of the departed. Note that these acts are not necessarily spiritual in themselves but are a sign of growing spirituality. It is strongly emphasized not to get caught up with these powers given they can result in negative effects; we have heard of many fallen souls resulting from misuse of the same. Many sages seldom mention these subtle skills while unobtrusively operating them at will. Interestingly, those indulging in substance abuse may temporarily sense these powers. One hears about how they talk about the oneness of nature; but the downside and after-effects are well known to all.

Now let us examine some additional Aum links. Let us look at nature, music, holistic medicine and astrology.

Nature

Aum represents overall universe creation, and nature is a manifestation of Aum. See the list of gross elements such as ether, air, fire, water and earth in Table B-1, left-hand side (Step 2). Our evolution from nature brings out the instinctive draw or attraction to these elements without us realizing it. Why are we so attracted to mountains, volcanoes, lakes? Ancient sages also discovered the integral sound allegiance between man and nature (discussed under the next heading), thereby learning to obtain control over such creation through the use of certain mantras or chants.

Additionally, our collective, universal roots (nature, Aum) breed involuntary respect for both the animate and the inanimate. I watched a program on Gordon Buchanan travels where humans given certain boundary conditions are able to peacefully interact and coexist with animals—lions in the Kalahari, anacondas in eastern Ecuador or crocodiles in Papua New Guinea. And how about the 1,300 years of man–cormorant relationship in southern China to achieve successful fishing! Even ancient martial arts are derived from the study of such links into nature.

Music

As we are an expression of Aum, sound has an immediate effect on us causing a temporary awakening of one of the chakras, reminding us instinctively of our divine origin and thereby providing that instantaneous, timeless joy. Music comes in all forms, from devotional songs to the modern. Look at how instinctive it is at all stages, note the unbridled joy of young children, and even animals swaying to music! Inuit, San Bushmen and shamans, who believe that the land is imbued with magical properties aiding communication with nature and the spirit world, use a combination of dance and chanting to shake loose their healing energies, focus and go into trance to affect their art. Read about "n/um energy" used by San Bushmen and the enhanced state of "!kia" achieved to enable healing for the needy, considered synonymous with the enhanced states when kundalini energy aforementioned is released.

Let us take the drum. This marvelous instrument unites us all at an instinctive level. It interacts with the heart and our sense of space and time, making us want to dance. Dancing, like music, is considered a form of meditation in its own right. Have you ever seen John Birks "Dizzy" Gillespie or Gurdas Maan performing on stage? You can see traces of these cumulative principles—note their intense concentration, almost keeling over, given that trance-like focus on their amazing expertise and overall craft.

Note that Aum is initially practiced vocally—to preclude any other thought entering the mind—and later in silence to feel the awareness and all-encompassing vibration (considered a higher practice).

Holistic Medicine

The following is a brief excerpt from an ancient Sanskrit Ayurveda text called *Charaka Samhita, Sushruta Samhita* and *Ashtanga Hridaya Samhita* provided by a distinguished practitioner, Dr. Bheema Bhat from New Delhi, India, who holds the distinction of also being a fully licensed MD (general practitioner) and is also a gold medalist recognized by the Government of India for his contributions.

> *Ayurveda is the ancient Indian holistic medical science which deals with mind, body and soul. It aims at maintenance and promotion of health, prevention and cure of diseases. It is based on Panchamahabhuta (Space, air, fire, water, earth) and Tridosha (Vata, Pitta, Kalpha) theory. Tridosha or biological humors, in their equilibrium condition maintain normal health and in their imbalanced state cause diseases. Perfect physical, psychological, social and spiritual well-being is called health. . . . Ayurveda groups all human beings into 7 different types of constitution (Prakriti) according to the predominance of biological humors (Dosha) and similarly groups them into three psychological constitution according to the predominance of psychological qualities (Sattwa, Rajas, Tamas). . . . Panchakarma therapy is one of the great specialties of Ayurveda, which is also known as detoxification or purification therapy. It includes different types of oil massages . . .*

I happened to come across this article posted on a wall outside Dr. Bhat's clinic, and was amazed to see the links back to the roots of our involution (Table B-1). Note the familiar words. As mentioned earlier, Ayurveda states that our individual physical constitution comprises variant proportions of three fundamental bio-energies or doshas called Vata, Pitta and Kapha which have evolved from the fivefold gross elements of ether, fire, water, etc. They influence all aspects of our being, including but not limited to the shape of our bodies, our sleep and digestion patterns, skin tone, emotions and thought patterns, intellect, etc. Within each of these doshas are five sub-doshas that govern specific parts of the body and their functioning as under: (a) *prana*—keywords (characteristics) are inward, inhalation, receptive, propulsive, magnetic, attractive, providing life-giving energy; (b) *apana*—downward, outward, exhalation, elimination, reproduction; (c) *udana*—transformative, propelling both quantitative (body evolution) and qualitative (consciousness) growth, positive enabling speech, standing, willpower, buoyancy; (d) *samana*—inward towards center, balancing, reinforcing digestion and absorption of food, oxygen in the body, sensory and emotional experiences; (e) *vyana*—outward from center, promoting, circulating, driving both circulation of nutrients and oxygen in the body, and mental thoughts to provide vitality, strength and preservation.

These sub-doshas of Ayurveda are in fact none other than the five specific pranas referred to under Table B-1 and the Table C pie diagram, as a subset of the critical, driving universal prana force (synonymous with Aum) in spirituality! Also, these five specific prana drive our Karmic development from the embryo stage to adult, commencing from progressive creation of the psychic nervous system which in turn creates and energizes our gross bodies. For example, prana (assisted by udana) governs creation of the openings and multiple channels in the head and brain down to the heart. Of particular mention is the mouth (and vocal cords) given this is considered as not only the main body opening with the physical body as its extension but also as the means of sustaining and expressing ourselves. Note that our face represents our inner being, and is the primary means to size up others when we first meet! Apana creates the genital and excretion systems, samana the midsection including digestive system and openings, and vyana the peripheral channels going into the arms and legs including veins, arteries, muscles and bones.

Note that the reverse is also true, i.e., there is a systematic process of death or exit of the soul from the body as these specific pranas withdraw from the body leaving the latter to merge back into the gross earth. Known examples are that bodies feel heavy to lift (udana or buoyancy has left), bodies are known to twitch even after death, given related sensory activity is still going on for limited period as bodies cool down. It may also be noted that many have cited near-death experiences, including but not limited to hovering of the soul, experiencing light energies, interactions with angels, etc. Immediate actions are taken post-death, for example, in Hinduism: (a) to tie the big toes of feet to preclude re-entry of the soul that has lost its discriminatory bearings but hovers around, trying to re-enter; (b) to fast-track funeral activities (within one and a half to four hours) to preclude any chance of revival through esoteric/tantric practices; (c) to continue sequential prayers for up to fourteen days to ensure that the preservative nature of vyana has fully departed; and (d) to ultimately enable timely departure of the soul and permanent conclusion for both the departed and loved ones.

In summary, these three doshas parallel our basic nature comprising the three gunas outlined earlier: sattwa (purity), rajas (passion) and tamas (dullness). The combination of our physical and spiritual elements represents the sum total of our Karmic evolution to date, and imbalance of these fundamental energies is what causes disease which Ayurveda aims to eliminate via purification of mind, body and soul to reinstate the natural balance within the body. Similar extension of these fundamental principles entail natural medicinal healing practices by shamans, curanderos and sages in religions and cultures the world over. I was most fascinated at what training these Ayurveda doctors must be undergoing to be able to read our vital signs utilizing a three-finger pulse technique, one for each of the doshas!

Astrology

Astrology studies the impacts and man's reactions to the detached, energetic influence of celestial stimuli (planets, stars, moon, sun) borne of our past Karma, whereas a horoscope represents an astrological chart of the positions of these celestial objects at the time of our birth suggesting a probable future. Cumulatively, they provide an iterative, evolving complex snapshot capturing man's Karmic action/reaction cycle to the power of these elements of nature (detached positive, negative radiations), our ego and the power to change—all harmoniously captured reflecting one's past and extrapolated future outcomes. Horoscopes (*kundali*) are popularly also used in matchmaking in some parts of the globe!

Akashic records (keyword *Akash* or Ether) on the other hand are the energetic records of all creation stored in a dimension beyond space and time. As mentioned, ether (space) is the first of the five gross elements to materialize in creation and the most subtle. All the other elements are derived from it and then afforded space to fill in. Consequently, these ethereal records include as a minimum our Karmic past (including prior incarnations) and binding relationships, present and potential future, akin to a huge database capturing every thought, act, intent, words, etc.

Indeed, all vibrations and evolutionary memory encompassing each galaxy, planet, stone, object, plant, animal have their own akashic records.

Even a cursory glance at the definition reveals the source of akashic records pointing to a derivative or subset out of the unmanifest condition of Brahman comprising pure knowledge. Note that the manifest universe appears out of the former as vibrational creation represented by Aum. Astrology, past life regressions, hypnosis, numerology, tarot card readings, palmistry, reading tea or coffee leaves, extrasensory perception are all examples of the ability of people to connect into these records.

And yet again, how about the interconnectedness of it all. As I continued to research, I was amazed to learn that the vision of tarot cards was to connect with one's higher Self, that minor arcana cards are associated with practical daily ups and downs in life whereas the major arcana cards represent the dominant longer-term energetical events. Furthermore, it helps a person to develop his intuitive abilities via related selection(s) of these cards, and that tarot cards are inherently linked to the gross elements of creation (nature). For example, ether fire, air, water, earth—which in turn (per the chakras in Table B-1) link into astrological categories.

And how about palmistry? We already know that the human body is an expression of the mind. Consequently, impressions of the latter are stamped and manifest in different ways in the body. Take our hands, the pads and mounts in the fingers and palms that store physical nerves (in turn linked into psychic nerves/chakras) are named after planets. Energies stored herein are directly linked to planets through their astrological impacts on the mind. These pads and mounts coupled with the lines serve as a cumulative photographic snapshot including permutations and combinations representing our personalities and potential future life path. And about numerology, it is generally understood as an interpretation of the universe translated into basic numbers, and that a numerical representation (horoscope) of one's life is charted out similar to an astrological natal chart. I was again amazed to find that numerology had its origins (to some degree) in the mathematical revelations of Pythagoras! And while mathematics, calculus and other sciences constitute study of quantity, structure, space, logic, rates of change with emphasis on repeatability and predictable rigor, the point being made herein about numerology (and other divine sciences) is not so much about accuracy which is much debated (also dependent upon expertise) but ultimately about the interconnectedness of all. Engineering and divine sciences are together attempting interpretations of how energy works at varying levels in the universe represented by Aum.

The point to note of course is that man possesses hidden spiritual strength which, if appropriately used, will progressively transcend planetary and other influences. And in addition to the meditative practices mentioned, sages discovered the use of aids such as amulets and bangles containing materials such as quartz, certain metals, and even plants such as the holy basil, etc. These aids countermand the negative effects of planets and other electrical and magnetic radiations to accelerate our growth.

Coming back to the cycle of purification, this is an energy bubble. As you adjust (based on free choice), *so does the energy around you.* The purer (sattwic) you get, your actions progressively get into synchronicity as energies change, attract new patterns of organized energy via positive Karma. And as you work through into meditation, you progressively come to control energies (by way of siddhi powers). The aforementioned represents a higher example of the theory of synchronicity put forward by the eminent Swiss psychiatrist Dr. Karl Gustav Jung as meaningful coincidences beyond the realm of probability. Note that many examples of synchronicity are mentioned in this book, and we all note examples from time to time in our lives if we are alert enough. A disciple of Swami Chinmayananda mentioned that every moment of this sage's life was a siddhi! The point is that a realized soul in the gross plane can pretty much craft his own destiny henceforth. Take the immense opportunity offered to you by creation to utilize your enquiring mind to enable learning and growth to effect necessary Karma (choice-based) while also bearing the effects of actions from past lives. We are a soul with a body (not the reverse); know that the latter represents the grossest aspect of our overall existence in the universe.

And for those yet to become realized, the ego drops away post-death and departs for the subtle plane (see further details below). Actions are reviewed (akashic records) and depending upon our cumulative Karma, a new ego is given to the soul to commence new learning with an appropriate veil of illusion in place. Point to note here is never to look down on someone else. An alcoholic may be on a faster learning curve than you, may simply be rebalancing past Karmic actions while contemplating his free-will choices. And as Karmic balance takes place and one transcends, we get progressively placed into higher spiritual platforms to work from.

And on the subject of our past lives, I once asked Swami Chidrupananda from the Chinmaya mission, "Swamiji, can we not remember our past lives?" And Swamiji replied with his inimitable humor, "Well, Deepak, I'll make it simple. Suppose you go shopping, and lo and behold, you run into your wife from a past life. You recognize her, but she doesn't. You joyfully go up to her in the busy marketplace and hug her. Can you imagine the racket you will create, all the more so if her in-laws have tagged along?"

Comment on Death

Why do we fear death so much? Attachment to life is inherent in both the ignorant and the realized—albeit to a minimal degree in the latter—because we all retain impressions of death from previous life cycles. Ancient Hindu scriptures state that there exists a subtle body state in between lives where one is exposed to the review of one's past actions and the resultant Karmic effects for future lives. This must be agonizing ("Did I really do this?"), given that we are forced to review the pain we have caused to ourselves and others, thanks to the delusions of our ego. Consequently, the intuitive fear of death and the interim state is deeply rooted in most of us who have yet to cross many transcendental planes to the point of minimizing fear.

Notwithstanding all this, neither death nor rebirth interrupts the cycle of Karma, and reincarnation reinforces impartial justice as a means towards progressive enlightenment. The process of passing away takes one out of sense attachments back into a higher meditative state, hence breaking this critical, delusory chain of attachment to life and fear of death. One ultimately understands this instinctively and goes with great dignity at the time of passing away. And it is said that the last thoughts are an involuntary product of cumulative, concerted Karma up to that moment which leads into one's next life platform (higher or lower). We determine our next cycle in such a manner, with factors such as DNA and genetics repositioning us for future efforts. A Swami mentioned that trying to gauge every single action/reaction in our lives equating to a future life cycle would be tedious, and there has to be a relative balance established as a means to equitable justice provided.

Desires and Feelings

Ultimately, the more advanced we become, the less attached we are to desires. We learn through our journey, both imposing and experiencing—laughter, tears, pain, joy, relationships, betrayals, successes, perceived failures, travels, food, nature! Note that experiments have been conducted to study and confirm that many of these feelings are experienced by plants and animals alike signifying commonality at a basic level. And at some point, we come to realize that while we face challenges daily which are largely beyond our control, stress is primarily self-imposed given the choices we make in dealing with these situations due to our Karmic signature of the action/reaction cycle including destiny, our current spiritual level and free will. For example, a high meditation practitioner would know how to deal with and divert the wall of negative (tamasic) energies coming at him thanks to his concerted spiritual practice to preclude self-harm (mental and physical). Birth, sustenance and dissolution are all taking place at once, the question is how we deal with it to grow.

Subtle and Causal Planes

Having briefly discussed the ascension cycle in the earth plane, let us discuss the subtle/subtler and causal planes. Two clarifications: first, you will note that earth or the gross universe is referred to as a hybrid gross/subtle plane in Table C, given that aspects of both are clearly present. Second, many names are quoted the world over for the higher non-gross planes including astral, mental, buddhic, spiritual, divine, etc. For convenience and discussion, these are cumulatively defined herein as "subtle/subtler" and causal (also referred to as the sea of causal cosmos) planes in Table C.

Once the highest level of consciousness, Nirvikalpa Samadhi, is achieved on the earth plane where the yogi has worked out his material Karma, he still retains subtle and causal Karma (emotional, feelings, ideas) to work out, and progressively takes abode or cycles between the highest subtle/subtler and causal planes. For the rest of us who have yet to attain realization on earth, the cyclical process of birth-death-rebirth continues between the material universe and the lower subtle planes. There is also a defined hell (multi-tiered) in the lower subtle plane for lower spirits to resolve their Karma before rejoining others in higher vibrational zones. Above hell we see great beauty constituting subtle variations of light leading progressively into the multi-tiered heavens. Overall, the subtle and causal planes are significantly larger than our universe with a parallel, subtle network of cosmic systems. Souls in this subtle region work with their consciousness and feelings with a subtle body of pranic life energies complete with brain, heart and the chakras to effect Karma through will, intuition and cosmic energies. Subtle beings also possess powers to change (through will, mantras) something already existing in these zones (note similar analogy in our dreams). Desires are fulfilled through intuitively sensing the sights and sounds as expressions of light energy variations. Life cycle is typically longer than on earth, timing is determined by the extent of their physical Karma drawing one back to the earth plane for continued rebalancing efforts. Death in these subtle planes consists of dissolution of the aforementioned subtle form, unlike the physical suffering on earth.

And given that our subtle body retains our individual psychic/karmic signature from our progressive, prior earthly experiences, we are easily recognized by others from our past interactions with them. Know that we make "contracts" here to help each other in the next life cycle(s) in our great school of learning called the universe. Ever get that strange feeling that you have met someone before but cannot put a finger on it? Well, here is your answer! And it sure can get confusing when you run into multitudes of past life relationships. This naturally leads into a deeper understanding that impartial love is the way to go, given the interconnectedness of it all. And as mentioned in Table B-2 (Item 3), it is from the highest subtle plane and above that the integrated network of guides, angels, master guides, devatas and deities perform their activities to help out problems of souls in the gross universe and lower subtle planes. And highly evolved souls on earth and young children connect into our subtle and causal support system of guides. Note that young children sometimes achieve this, given their minds are pure, with their ego yet to solidify.

As for the next level, the causal plane, once the highly transcended souls (nearly free) reach this plane through progressive cyclical cleansing, they now rise far above their prior physical and subtle experiences in the lower planes. Their aspirations and dreams are fulfilled by their remarkable powers of perception and thought. While we at the earth level experience life looking up as a pulsating universe in all our joys and sufferings, for a causal body looking down the gross material and subtle/subtler planes it is akin to a mirage; even their life cycle of birth and death in the causal plane is via thought process. And imagine the feat—the divine powers of concentration of these transcended souls to cross over into this causal world—to visualize that the physical and subtle/subtler planes in all their complexity and duality exist now in ideas only. They are now very close to the realization that all created beings and objects are forms of integrated consciousness. Here they realize that it is not about the physical cosmos being primarily constructed of electromagnetic energy, or that the subtle/subtler planes are composed of subtle pranic life energies, but that the power of cosmic delusion and duality (opposites) creates divisions precluding realization. Life in the causal plane constitutes thousands of earth years. And through further realization, the freed soul then sheds its last vestige of causal individuality to merge into this combined bliss of the sea of causal cosmos.

Summary of Karmic Cycles of Birth

Now that we have covered so much ground, let us summarize all the Karmic cycles of birth through the multiple planes of existence in Table C (right-hand side). The human soul has to overcome three veils of ignorance—gross, subtle and causal bodies—to reach his highest Self to merge into the highest realms. This is done in the following four steps:

- To preclude the rebirth cycle between earth and subtle/subtler planes, the desires of man must be worked through to elimination; and any ascension into the causal plane is precluded at this stage. This rebirth cycle can go on for countless life cycles. Note also that an underachieved soul may not get to enjoy the beauty of the subtle worlds despite undergoing the cycle.

- Once earthly Karma is worked out and the highest level of transcendental experience on the earth plane, Nirvikalpa Samadhi, is achieved, these souls get into the highest level of the subtle/subtler plane.

- In this third step, those who have transcended the above have only their subtle and causal Karma to work out. At subtle death which constitutes disintegration of subtle body life energies, they pass into the higher causal world but go through a similar cycle and are brought back to the highest subtle plane to work out their residual Karma borne of minor deviations in their acts from the synchronous, spiritual laws of the cosmos. Permanent stay in the causal plane commences once the being has transcended any karma associated with the subtle plane and cannot be tempted back there.

- The final stage is reached as the soul progressively reaches into the highest Self and breaks through the three aforementioned layers of ignorance and merges into the sea of causal cosmos. Combined bliss is now the way forward in all of its interconnectedness in this sea of infinite love and joy. Realized masters may voluntarily choose to return to the gross universe (earth) or reside on a subtle or causal plane to help others, including but not limited to partially bearing their burdens to accelerate their continued ascension cycle.

And before we go on, take a momentary pause to try and imagine just what level of beings and realization we are dealing with here, and what these wonderful beings have achieved through sheer dedication and perseverance. From their vantage point, they truly understand the universe as pure love in all its trials, tribulations and calculated imbalance while providing an overall balance. It is also said that they possess awe-inspiring capabilities, for example, they can travel amongst the stars, have incredible powers of creation from sheer thought, and possess the amazing ability to genuinely help others. The universe is now truly their oyster; can you envisage their bliss?

Delusory Power of Maya

Having understood the process of ascension, let us also consider the root cause precluding it—the much debated cosmic delusory side (power) of maya and its links with science and spirituality. Maya has dual functionality, both veiling and creative; hence the discussion around its definition. On one hand it is linked with universe creation (as discussed under Table B-1, Steps 1-3), while on the other deluding us from our true nature in recognizing ourselves as the essence of the highest achievable levels of pure consciousness.

Simply put, the ego is associated with this delusive power, seeking satisfaction and fulfillment in our world, thereby binding us to all the opposites: good and evil, birth and death, pleasure and pain, action and reaction (Newton's law) including the physical laws of creation. How does it all come together?

Physical Laws of Creation

Amongst several theories is the big bang on universe creation around 13.8 billion years ago, commencing from the first set of high density and temperature conditions originating from a gravitational condition called singularity (infinite gravity, also considered integral to black holes). Expansion and cooling, timely aided by the four fundamental forces of electromagnetism, gravity, weak (decay) and strong forces (binding), led to creation—initially from subatomic particles such as protons, neutrons, etc., all the way to ultimately forming galaxies of stars, planets.

The created earth, around 4.5 billion years ago, cooled enough to form water and elements starting a chain reaction leading to the first metabolic cycle where chemicals were converted into a series of other chemicals, the entire system taking on energy in the process. It is theorized that creation of the first ancestral cells (behaving like living cells) spurred on by metabolic cycles led to progressive adaptation of life, leading into modern-day molecules such as DNA. These constitute self-replicating material present in almost all living organisms and also function as carriers of genetic information. Cumulatively, creation of the inanimate to living cells to plants and animals and ultimately to humans largely captured in Darwin's theories on natural selection.

It is further theorized that any object, plant, animal or human being constitutes an integration of rotating energy vortices, which interact with certain binding energies and give physical structure and density (mass) to the object. This is what constitutes all matter and being, keywords herein being life associated with interconnected, vibrational energy segregated by discrete physical mass. The emphasis here is on the interconnectedness, resulting in universal energy as a common source to creation.

We can now deduce that science and spirituality converge to a certain degree (interpretations vary) on life and interconnected energies once we get past questions on what caused the actual initial conditions kick-starting universe origins, or what precisely caused creation of living cells. Further research has been conducted by renowned scientists on predictability of events, and even on time travel including space–time curvature due to gravity and parallel universes. Examples can be cited of Einstein's theory of relativity, Werner Heisenberg's uncertainty principle of speed versus position of particles (challenged by Laplace transform), Schrodinger's wave equation on quantum mechanics, Max Planck's quantum theory. And while there is a certain level of predictability and multiple theories put forth, there are no definitive conclusions to date on life creation.

Seeking Answers through Spirituality

Let us soldier on and now look at our aforementioned, collective challenges (physical, emotional) explained through spirituality. These combined experiences leave impressions on our mind and create powerful inclinations or samskaras. They control our character and life, giving us ego, thereby precluding us from defeating the cycle of birth, death and rebirth. What is widely acknowledged is that our highest goal is to rise over the delusions created by these opposites via the meditative route and equivalent practices to perceive progressive states of transcendental experience (samadhi in Hinduism). Experienced by very few to date, to transcend this cosmic delusion (maya) is to understand the subtle laws and rhythms of the universe.

Particularly fascinating are the relative analogies offered by both science and spirituality on light energy. Examples are Albert Einstein, Stephen Hawking and Paramahansa Yogananda. Einstein's theory of relativity contemplates light velocity as the only constant in an evolving universe; Stephen Hawking postulated the link between time travel and the speed of light; and Paramahansa Yogananda viewed the universe essentially as being an undifferentiated mass of light. Science to date states that light is a subset of electromagnetic energy, its waves passing freely through the vacuum of space, and that factors such as time, space and gravity are relative, variant and finite. Modern research so far (2023) even offers that the speed of light does not change in extreme conditions such as a black hole, precluded from being visible due to conditions of space–time curvature through extreme gravity.

Paramahansa Yogananda further elucidated that this light energy which is resident within all atomic energies constitutes the essence of all creation guided by a divine intelligence; that only a material body whose mass is infinite could equal the velocity of light. It has been learned timely by sages through the ages the world over that we are dealing with light energy in increasing levels of divinity, and to understand what constitutes matter is to ultimately gain power over it. Masters utilizing their powers of realization can materialize and dematerialize their bodies through control of these pranic energies moving with the velocity of light by transforming their physical appearance.

This is the whole point of evolution as presented in the right-hand side of Table B-1, Steps 4-8. Factors such as time, gravity, laws of opposites (physical or mental)—be it pleasure and pain, heat and cold, joy and sorrow, good and evil, birth and death, day and night—are experienced due to our inability to rise above them. This the great spiritual masters conquered through concerted meditative practices by understanding the divine energies (cosmic essence) of light, commencing from mental housecleaning followed by concentration through the multiple levels of meditation until one gets to the highest levels of transcendental experience, i.e., samadhi. Achieving Nirvikalpa Samadhi is the first step at which a soul can attain substantial freedom from the cosmic delusive side (powers) of maya. The realized sage possesses the ability to transfer his transformed body of light with ease through the created universe, both gross and subtle. Coming in and out at will, he serves humanity including rebalancing energies by sending out holy vibrations into the universe. Given his concerted control over the minutest energies plus his willpower, he can make the seemingly impossible possible. I had posed a question about Covid to Swami Chidrupananda, "Sir, since these are all lower (tamasic) vibrational energies, how come a group of realized souls have not come together to sort this out?" The Swami's answer was twofold. First, he said that action/reaction of individual and collective Karma is playing out, coupled with the impact of cosmic governance cycles (see "Timeline of the Universe" below) for us to deal with. Second, he asked how I knew that such work was not being performed?

An interesting point to note is that a byproduct of growing spirituality is the development of different forms of powers (siddhi), common examples being telepathy, clairvoyance, healing, etc. The astonishing commonality of this is noted in the accomplishments of some of the great renowned sages and monks of different religions in different parts of the world. Examples include San Martin de Porres (Peru), Shyama Charan Lahiri Mahasaya (India), the Yamabushi Monks (Japan) and so on. Seek and you will find the list goes on and on. During a visit to Peru, I had been to churches in downtown Lima and was amazed to hear how San Martin was known to have teleported himself, seen in different places at the same time, a theme well known with Lahiri Mahasaya in India! On this latter point, recall the experiments in quantum physics and the behavior of photons and also the theories of existence in parallel universes. Spirituality offers that be it one, parallel or multiple universes, the purpose of man is to transcend these by understanding his power over such created cosmic delusion.

I was relating some of these points to a highly respected swami and his comment was that ultimately heaven has its own cosmic divine light, of which these variations of light energies in increasing levels of purity (gross to subtle to causal) constituted its essence. He also mentioned that what is also very significant is the reference to light across multiple world religions and beliefs (see Table B-2, Item 9) as a means to salvation: "Let there be light" in Christianity, "Ner Tamid" or eternal flame/light in Judaism and so on.

Ultimately, Aum represents all universe creation, sustenance and dissolution comprising variations of light energy guided by divine intelligence as the essence of pure consciousness or Brahman. And before we get into the inevitable question of whether our very existence is a dream state or illusion (indeed a subject of much debate), let us examine one additional major point—the life cycle of Brahma (the creator) in context of the cosmos (depicted in Table C). The explanation given here is modeled on the recurring cyclical patterns of the universe (also discussed earlier in Table B-2, Item 12.1).

Timeline of the Universe

According to Hindu scriptures, the life span of the creator Brahma, also considered a higher soul/jiva is 100 years (cosmic time), translated into human years as follows:

> One day (12 hours) or one night (12 hours) of Brahma = 4,320,000,000 human years each, in other words 8,640,000,000 human years constitutes a full day for Brahma. Consequently, the life span of Brahma the creator in human terms is 8,640,000,000 x 360 x 100 human years, i.e., 311.04 trillion years. Within the said time period there are recurring cycles of cosmic governance (yugas) defining overall guiding energies we have to contend with or grow from.

Four such yugas are the following:

1. Kali Yuga, the first 432,000 human years, is defined as a period of difficulty where spirituality degenerates, where greed, anger and excesses, animosity, detraction from moral duty (dharma) are common.
2. Dvapar Yuga, the next 2x 432,000 years, is defined as a period of compassion and truthfulness with some challenges. Larger collective divinity is reduced, leading to deceit; people are plagued by ailments, diseases and desires. Penance and realization inevitably follow post-suffering, including worship and offerings to enhance spiritual growth.
3. Treta Yuga, the next 3x 432,000 years, is defined as a period where the overall power of humans marginally diminishes. People grow more materialistic and less inclined towards spirituality. Collective disturbances including wars, unrest and negative climate changes are frequent, translating into a better understanding of nature, the subtle laws of the universe and societal reformation practices.
4. Krita or Satya Yuga, the next 4x 432,000 years, is the golden age. Humanity prevails, every manifestation or work is close to the purest ideal and intrinsic goodness shines through. Knowledge, meditation and penance hold special importance; people engage only in good, sublime deeds.

Cumulatively these four periods or yugas are called a mahayuga constituting 4,320,000 years (4.32 million). Thus each of these periods determines a limited cosmic future/cycle.

One day of the Creator is 1000 times of this mahayuga or 4,320,000,000 human years, and the same holds for one night. Thus, Brahma's full day constitutes 8.64 billion human years as mentioned earlier.

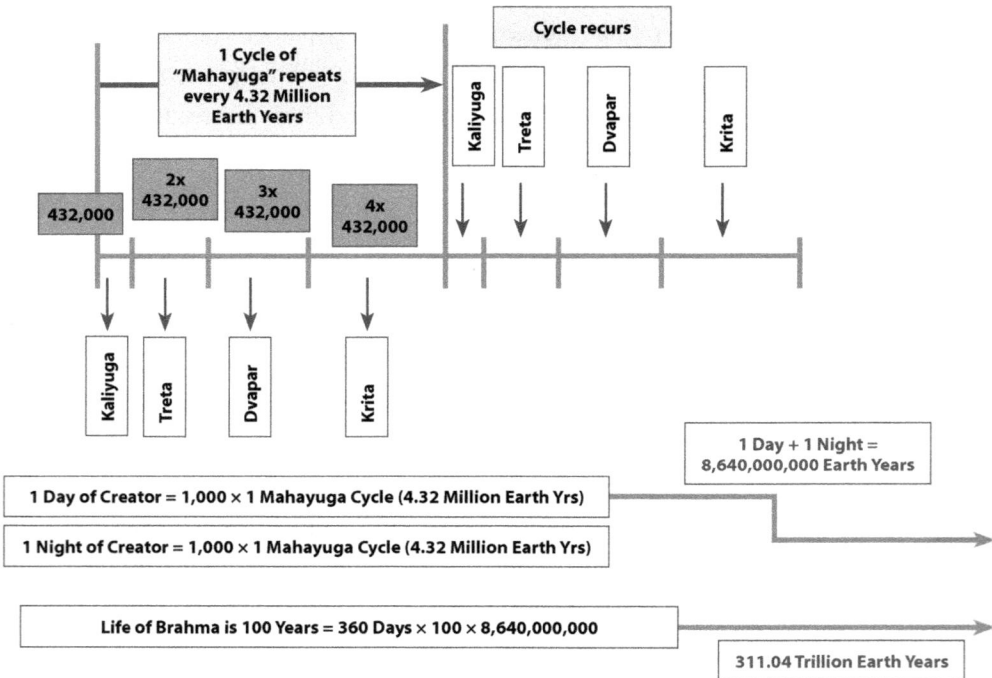

The scriptures further state that the day of Brahma promotes projection or manifestation of the universe, night of Brahma the reverse. At night, the condition of the universe is akin to the latent form of a tree in a seed during this period, the entire cosmos merges back into the unmanifest Brahman as per defined time periods. And given that all the knowledge of this creation is retained within Brahman, the universe then periodically re-emerges as per the cycles aforementioned utilizing the said knowledge. At present, we are in the fifty-first year of Brahma, and the cycle repeats itself after 100 years with a new creator (Brahma) in place.

It is said that a realized master who has reached the highest levels has transcended this cycle of day and night. For the rest of us, the cycle of Karma continues where it left off just before the previous day cycle ended, or when the next 100-year life cycle of the new Brahma commences. And unlike these cyclical universes, Brahman or pure consciousness itself is not destroyed. Unlike waves which rise and subside, the ocean itself is always present; so all the worlds come in and out of Brahman.

And as outlined earlier, interesting analogies exist in science, where initial creation commencing from a single point (singularity) of origin ultimately results in millions of galaxies, stars, planets, including expansion or moving away from each other. There are also theories about the pulsating universe with both expansion and contraction, which is analogous to this predetermined spiritual theory of creation.

Concluding Remarks on Table C

So what does all this mean? If one reverses the view, i.e., sees it from top-down (origins of involution), the cosmos exists in thought; realized masters can cross this barrier to come and help those who cannot transcend due to ego and consequent barriers. Think of viewing a sphere (earth, universe) from a distance which is veiled by a sheath of cosmic delusion that we are stuck in thanks to our ego. Conversely, from the bottom-up position, those within the sphere cannot break past this murky surface and are thus subject to all its trials and tribulations, and pairs of opposites including physical and mental, time, gravity and others. One must slog, work hard, concentrate, then meditate with expertise in order to transcend. You may have also heard how a realized master sees things differently like images on a movie screen devoid of factors such as time and gravity, utilizing light energy as the only medium of existence. But for the majority of us, we are indeed subject to a pulsating universe of reality with aforementioned opposites governing.

Let us now move on to the much debated question of why this is all happening? Why the merger of soul and body—this question has been asked the world over. The answer is that this is "the will of God," or "*Bhagwan's lila*" in Hinduism. Some mysteries are best kept being studied through eternity.

Notwithstanding this, our duty is to rise above our limitations to get as close as possible to God via progressive transcendence over sense attachments.

And there it is, the total picture—our journey as warrior-monks in our world of interconnected energies. From something as trivial as a person having a relationship with his car (some people can sense its energy) to breaking boards with the power of the mind using ancient advanced martial art techniques, to achieving Nirvikalpa (highest) Samadhi on the earthly plane into the subtle beyond. We continue to chart our own destiny in our marvelous journey borne of engineered, spiritual evolution. Ultimately, it is not the evolution of the body but that of our soul, courtesy of a growing consciousness leading to a gradual dropping of our gross bodies and their attachments, taking us back to our highest Self as the essence of pure undifferentiated consciousness.

And this journey commences by holistic living "in the moment" as a first step as summarized in the representative mental housecleaning (Table A), with the six trigger points as a visual, universal, strategic, highly subliminal aid to drive our journey. These represent the first spiritual steps critical to advancing us in life lessons, be it choosing a dedicated path of being religious, agnostic, atheist or any other. I was most impressed by the teachings of a lady priest to the effect that we were indeed so fortunate to have taken birth as humans with free will to make the best choices. Be the best person you can be, devote your life to a higher cause, live outside your comfort zone to progress. Pick your instinctive best skill sets, question intensely, dare to dream via strategic vision and go to make your life extraordinary.

Spiritual Travelogue: Global Perspectives

In this section, I shall proceed to discuss some of my select experiences with nature, places, and extraordinary people gained during my global travels to comprehend the integrated nature of divinity. Cumulatively, these in some manner or form reflect the spiritual traits mentioned herein. Note how far some of these people progressed with the tools they were given or developed through great efforts. Their examples shone the best of humanity, and the comments included bring out the divinity seen in each experience. We all exhibit these traits to a certain degree (some more than others) but it is for each one of us, through scientific techniques laid out in all our great religious and spiritual writings, to find our own *unique swing in life.*

1. With His Holiness, Tenzin Gyatso, the Fourteenth Dalai Lama of Tibet

Try to imagine what it is like to have this command view of His Holiness, Tenzin Gyatso, the fourteenth Dalai Lama, for eleven hours, which is precisely what I had on a Delhi–Tokyo flight the first time I met His Holiness in 2009. And it was such a moving sight to see the air hostesses kneel past him at the end of the flight while taking his blessings. They then all ran back into the galley and cried together. He had earlier beamed at me with that lovely moon-face of his, and kind of encouraged me over! As I took his blessings (he clasped my hands in his), I mentioned to him that I knew the reason for this meeting taking place was that I had just commenced reading the Bhagvadgita. He gave me an enquiring look and cheerfully exclaimed, "the Gita!" And as our 747-400 jumbo came

in for landing over Tokyo and we first saw land (there was low cloud cover), he raised his hands holding his rosary and started praying. I recall saying to myself *"Deepak . . . it does not get any better than this in life . . . cherish this moment for all times."*

And then came my second opportunity ten years later, this time at his official residence in Dharamshala in Himachal Pradesh, north India. This time, I sensed his all-enveloping aura of peace flooding over me as he emerged some 60 feet away; obviously my awareness had grown. This lovely town perched in the lower Himalayas features possibly in my list of top five places to visit globally due to its vibrational overtones of peace, thanks to the marvelous confluence of the spiritual Tibetan and Indian communities, reinforced in no small measure by the breathtaking backdrop. Just look at the sunrise they collectively awaken to.

This second meeting included about fifty Tibetan refugees and at most ten people from other countries. Amongst the latter were Valerie DeVille and Charlie Corry (see picture), a psychotherapist and a Vietnam veteran, respectively, who had faithfully carried the ashes of their son Andar from Florida, USA, for his blessings. Valerie later related just how His Holiness captured it all with an

Author's note: My sincere thanks to the Office of His Holiness for enabling use of the pictures for the book.

all-encompassing "*Ohhhhhhhhh*" as he heard of the task before him. Indeed, Charlie also said how he was having such a hard time letting go of his hand. As an aside I may mention that Charlie later opened up about his intense personal struggles post-war (he was in the artillery), and how he was struggling with an invitation he had received to visit Vietnam again. I mentioned I had heard the story of a US veteran who was fearful even after so many years to go back to Vietnam to meet the daughter of a North Vietnamese army solider he had killed in combat, with intent to return a picture (of the soldier and his daughter) that he had taken from the soldier's body, and how much the meeting had helped all to relieve the intense, pent-up pain. And I prayed that the law of dharma, the highest wisdom applicable to individual circumstances, would prevail for Charlie to take the best possible decision to overcome his long-standing grief.

Coming back to this visit, what a backdrop to create lifelong friendships. Valerie later said that she had seen a program on these Tibetan monks, how they were recounting the aggressive days of their struggles; and how one monk said that his greatest fear (whilst in great physical pain) was the possibility of developing animosity towards his captors. Try and understand the level of development here, it is stunning, expressed as it is through the divinity of the monks around His Holiness, truly something to behold. We also had the chance to have a lengthy discussion with one of the security guards. I instinctively noted that this man, through sheer association with this marvelous institution, had acquired a sense of divinity far above mine!

And let us look at a minuscule portion of the teachings of His Holiness. My takeaways: every living entity has an innate desire for happiness, even our bodies need peace. A proper mental attitude and equanimity will go a long way to overcoming unfriendly environments. The reverse equally applies in a happy situation! Genuine compassion is a product of mutual respect (not pity) and understanding that others have an equal right to be happy, that their lives are just as important to them as yours to you. Once you grasp this, it innately leads to an unbiased affection and concern for others (friends and foes alike) with a genuine smile of compassion shining through. It teaches us to be equanimous, while developing an involuntary sense of caring responsibility and inner strength enabling us to communicate with all—even animals and plants sense it. Society comprises individuals who in turn lead movements—for example, religious, sporting, community, national—to create marvelous collective rhythmic magic; hence we must be brave to individually lead.

Train your mind to view situations from different angles (often the viewpoint of others) to preclude adverse situations. If we are honest enough, we will realize that we may be equally responsible for creating that circumstance. Take a similar approach with problems—viewing from a wider angle diminishes its scale and impact. I have been told that it is easier to get to know five different continents better than to understand the complexity of the human mind, and that a closed mind stocks up on fear. Non-violence precludes further exacerbation and resentment, and is truly full of compassion in action. Positive dialogue is key to effecting equitable compromise, no one ever fully wins or loses. True tolerance is where we have the ability or options to act, and we pick the most humane. And as much as we are all saddened by negative situations, with it come positives. Take for example the sacrifices of those brave Filipinos trying to help prisoners of war during the Bataan Death March, or those nameless heroes globally trying to help the Jews during the Holocaust. The world ultimately works on in harmony and perfect balance—look at the examples set during the Covid-19 outbreak. As painful and full of suffering as it has been for us all, fear dealt positively created defensive solutions. Out of this negative shone a progressive step change in holistic practices, healthier eating styles, better social hygiene and customs, reinforcement of family relationships, an emergence of higher-efficiency business standards including videoconferencing, reduced travel, etc.

His Holiness truly reflected what the commentary on the Geeta by Swami Chinmayananda[1] talks about.

The brilliance of his intellect, the twinkling joy in his eyes, the thrilling fragrance of peace around, the serene poise in his activities, the dalliance of his love for all, the light of joy that ever shines forth from the innermost depths of his being—these constitute the irresistible attraction of the personality of the sage, who, with abundant energy, serves all and discovers for himself a fulfillment in that service.

In fact, Swami Chinmayananda and the Dalai Lama were friends! I could venture to guess that the Swami had him in mind when he wrote the lines quoted above. And look at the life and sacrifices His Holiness has made for the world, all the while with a brilliant glow and cheerful serenity. Indeed every minute of his life, mind, body, soul have been dedicated in the service of humanity. And as for the interconnectedness of it all, try this. I didn't know that these two great sages were friends, based in the same town, when I commenced my initial research on Swami Chinmayananda's *Commentary* on the Holy Geeta at around the same time I first met His Holiness on the Tokyo flight in 2009.

And I have cogitated much about the following statement. We all approach life from different angles, perfecting our intuition through varied experiences

---

[1] *The Holy Geeta: Commentary by Swami Chinmayananda*, Central Chinmaya Mission Trust, Mumbai.

including professional, social, travel, relationships, etc. We may be street-smart, kind, grizzled, egoistic, may possess unique skills, be rich or poor, be the best at what we do; but there is something indeed about the divinity of such sages and saints with their childlike humility that makes us instinctively bow before them thanks to their marvelous energies in play. Given each one of us is trying in our own ways to improve, it begs the natural conclusion that we each instinctively realize what they have achieved is ultimately our true goal in life.

2. ISKCON Hare Krishna Mission and the Saints Cyril and Methodius Cathedral, Prague (Czech Republic)

With Narakriti and Rasabehari, ISKCON Mission, Prague

These Czechs are a shining example for all given their devotion (bhakti). They routinely start their day at 4 a.m. with prayer. When I first met them in 2010 and casually enquired about the extent of their Geeta reading, Rasabehari calmly told me she had read it fifteen times, cover to cover. Incidentally, she is also trained in the Indian dance form Bharatnatyam, in fact gave a performance for the prime minister of the Czech Republic. I was so struck at the first meeting by their uplifting pure energy, as you can clearly see from the picture above. I was also tremendously impressed when I realized just how far and wide their research on Hinduism extended, culminating in a laser-like focus on Bhakti Yoga via Krishna consciousness.

My son and I also took the opportunity to visit the Saints Cyril and Methodious Cathedral in Resslova Street, Prague, to pay respects to those brave Czech commandos—Jan Kubis, Jozef Gabčík and others—who perished at the said cathedral after being rooted out by the Gestapo for assassinating Reinhard Heydrich in June 1942. I was amazed to see just how much these Karma Yogis working to higher ideals, with love for their country had influenced people from all walks of life. The place was indeed multicultural and packed to the full. Particularly moving was when a group of visiting students asked for the lights of the crypt to be turned off to feel just what these soldiers experienced for several weeks in pitch-black darkness awaiting a safe passage that never materialized. Their venture culminated in a final brave fight out of the skylight while trying to tunnel their way out (note the broken wall behind me). And a childhood dream was truly fulfilled when I was alone in the crypt for just a couple of minutes to say my quiet prayers for these great souls.

My sincere thanks to the Military History Institute and the Saints Cyril and Methodius Cathedral in Prague for the use of the two pictures commemorating these two great souls.

3. With Dr. Franklin Story Musgrave, NASA Shuttle Program

Dr. Franklin Story Musgrave was a key member of the mission to repair the Hubble Space Telescope. What an honor for me to have met him not once but twice! He symbolized sheer "Work into Worship" power and recognition of "Cosmic Power within Self" (recall Table A, Triggers 2 and 4). NASA astronauts are amongst the most highly trained professionals you will perhaps meet in your lifetime. I read his resume on the Internet and it made me feel remarkably like an ant. A mathematician, a United States marine, physician, astronaut, public speaker, author, the list is near endless. I got the distinct impression he worked through problems progressively, armed with that natural curiosity and intense situational awareness. For example, when I met him the second time, I was asking him a question while standing at the podium, and he came up to take a look at the document I was reading from! I also asked him questions about NASA quality control—he later thanked me for asking about it. Incidentally, we also saw the booster rockets on the launch pad of the fateful Columbia February 2003 mission.

Author's Note: My thanks to Dr. Musgrave for use of his quotes for the book:

I come from the heart and soul because I am a deeply spiritual person. I am driven by the spirit; it is who I am; I find it in all things in the earth and the cosmos and I worship and pray in all sacred places.

My message is always metaphorically transcendent: acknowledging and referring to a higher principle and a divine being beyond ourselves.

There are so many wonderful quotes by this great soul on the Internet. My favorites include his relationship with animals and children, and how it taught him to view things differently; how his affinity to nature helped him overcome difficult childhood experiences; how living beyond one's comfort zone is the path to exploration; and about facing the physical challenges of the shuttle launch to get to the serenity of zero gravity!

Talk about the courage of these leaders in space aviation dealing with such high risk/high rewards to continue pushing the boundaries of existence in search of knowledge for the advancement of global humanity. Here are some shuttle statistics: did you know that at the time of launch there are no other humans within a 3-mile radius? Utilizing thirty-seven million horsepower the shuttle attains a speed of 3,000 miles per hour in two minutes; traveling ultimately at twenty-five times the speed of sound to sustain an orbit around earth at thirteen times the speed of Concorde, seven times faster than a bullet. And what about the millions of pounds of explosive fuel used? The dual rocket boosters utilize 11,000 pounds of fuel per second, or two million times the fuel rate of an automobile. Ultimately, the shuttle flew 135 missions with 355 astronauts from the US and sixty other countries. How about that for global connectivity? And coming back to the point made in Table A, Trigger 4, about being born for a certain profession, could you envisage yourself as a shuttle pilot dealing with the stress of the launch given such statistics? Watch the movie *First Man* where Neil Armstrong is involved in one of the pre-Apollo 11 launches, and you will get a whiff of the risks they dealt with. The visualization of the launch, the vibrations and the odds he endured and overcame by living in the moment are nothing short of mind boggling. As for Apollo 13, notice the interconnected nature of humans when they came together for this larger cause to save the three astronauts. A series of miracles happen when many get involved and are willing to act timely. I have witnessed the same in so many other humanitarian efforts globally.

4. With Dr. A.P.J. Abdul Kalam, President of India

Affectionately called the People's President, Dr. A.P.J. Abdul Kalam was the recipient of seven honorary doctorates and innumerable awards including India's highest civilian award, the Bharat Ratna. He wore many hats as an aerospace scientist, technology developer (civilian space program, missile and launch vehicle, tablet computers, medical devices), politician, visiting professor, musician, poet and spiritual writer. Dr. Kalam also persevered on his goal to timely meet 100,000 students to richly embolden their lives to seek excellence in all their future efforts.

A prime example of exhibiting traits of Dynamic Quietude and the Eye of Wisdom (see Table A, Triggers 3 and 5), he was sheer humility, knowledge and brilliance all rolled into one. He insisted several times that I sit with him, which I politely declined *out of sheer respect*, kneeling before him instead. What an

JFK to Delhi - April 20th, 2010

Dear Isham & Sheila,

Greetings,

A.P.J. Abdul Kalam
20/4/2010

experience to take his blessings! As one of the officials of the Indian embassy in Washington DC accompanying him remarked, "*Dr. Kalam is a very young eighty-year-old getting younger by the day!*"

Well versed in both the Koran and the Geeta, Dr. Kalam was also equally learned in Sanskrit, indeed a rare feat these days. He maintained a simple life, was a vegetarian and had few personal possessions. Revered for his multiple contributions, he was admired as an outstanding statesman by millions all over the world for his integrity, and for promoting global cooperation and religious tolerance. He maintained a stolid work regimen and seldom took a holiday. He enjoyed a near-perfect self-sustaining energy system borne of his deep pursuit of spirituality.

The outpouring of grief following Dr. Kalam's demise was global. President Barack Obama noted his achievements as a scientist and statesman—in particular his role in strengthening Indo-US relations and increasing space cooperation between the two nations. Other leaders cumulatively spoke about his outstanding material contribution to the social, economic, scientific and technical progress India made, also ensuring its national security while cementing cooperation between countries.

The world has much to thank those selectors who rejected his application as a young man to become a fighter pilot. As per the law of dharma (the natural universal law promoting cosmic balance), what appears seemingly as a rejection under one set of circumstances is in fact an opportunity under another—this time for the extraordinary benefit of humanity.

5. Mr. Friar: Our Resident Wild Chipmunk

The oneness of all mentioned in Trigger 4 of Table A. Mr. Friar was my friend for seven years. For animals that are so wary, lightning-fast and self-protective (given the elements), look at the trust. I was amazed to see they have memory! He first surfaced in our yard in 2012, eventually coming close for raw peanuts. When he surfaced after the first winter, he made a beeline for me. What a character, once he sat atop my son's car and refused to get off until fed, despite much pleading. Probably he holds the distinction as the only chipmunk globally of having the horse sense of staying inside the car bonnet for four hours when accidentally taken to a school soccer match. Some kids spotted him as

he came out to take a look at where he was! Most remarkable was when he once came and sat with me for ten minutes; I was basking in the sun having a non-alcoholic beer, and we just chilled out together. What a pleasure to deal with this friendly, beautiful little guy (and others—they are all unique characters). They collectively provided daily stress relief and much joy to us all. He liked my son, was wary of my daughter (she had once yelled at him), and loved my wife who would always scream when he came close! I also made friends with another that played peekaboo with me over a period of six months!

I'm sure Steve Irwin is laughing down at me with his inimitable, enthusiastic smile, saying "Criiiikey . . . well done, mate!" What an inspirational man, what a spellbinding action-packed life. Note that marvelous innate connection to nature which he pursued with passion, grit, integrity, humility and cheerful dynamism to drive his strategic vision of conservation of animals and the environment. While we all marveled at his reflexes and handling of dangerous animals while perhaps musing if he was a tad too close for comfort, in fact he was a true scientist and a vibrant educator besides possessing an incredible sixth sense. Whether he was reaching for crocodiles or out to his TV viewers, it always felt like a direct one-to-one experience. Among the treasure trove he left us with, I'll mention three: (a) Leaping into a pen cheerfully wishing a large crocodile called Douglas a hale and hearty good morning! Steve was easily within striking range as he turned to the camera, yet the sheer inaction of the crocodile spoke volumes. Someone later commented that animals were just as comfortable around him as he was with them. (b) I was marveling at how he was once embraced by a wild orangutan holding her baby, a sight to behold. (c) His intense concentration (gone was the laughter) as he was overseeing wife Terri's safety while she was handling a poisonous snake.

Last but not the least, how does one forget the day this great soul passed! I was comforted only in the sure knowledge that millions of people globally, irrespective of age, collectively mourned his passing from relatively "mundane" circumstances. Steve taught us that life was fragile, so we must lead it to the fullest, employing all the tools we have in our power for a larger cause. A big Namaste to you, Mr. Irwin!

6. The Divinity of Movie Making

So how do energy and divinity relate to movie making? Now there is an exercise for an engineer to unravel.

I have had the honor of meeting several top artists globally through both planned and chance encounters, including a former Miss Universe and a Miss World, much to the envious love of many friends! Jokes aside, the brilliance of these individuals never ceases to amaze me.

Timed and placed precisely by cosmic laws to serve the global community, these creative souls possess wonderful traits including unrelenting dynamic energy, an abundance of inner radiance, undivided focus, physical prowess, adaptability, a sensitive nature, love for the language of music, the grit to face their fears, the courage to sustain the highs and lows of public life, and a vibrant love for their fans. And yes, they do appear smaller in person!

Let us examine together my meetings with two legends of cinema.

I met the first in 1996 in Washington D.C. and have visited him several times since. What struck me instantly was his situational awareness and his ability to engage everyone with ease. A warrior with an aura of dynamic energy and aggressive restraint, he is an all-round genius exhibiting prime traits of Work into Worship, Dynamic Quietude and Progressive Fearlessness (see Table A). I once saw him practicing a ten second movie scene take for six hours—the dedication and focus were life lessons. His mass marketing and brand extension strategies are prime teachings for schools and companies globally. He revolutionized entertainment by becoming an artist and entrepreneur, thus setting the bar so high with this dual strategy. A seeker of knowledge and a man of few words, I have learnt so much from his dynamic silence. We met him and his wife at their home, it became clear that they see hospitality as a sacred duty, much akin to the perspective he shared about his profound bond with his billions of fans worldwide.

As for the other, I must relate the humor amidst the lessons learned. After running into him on an India business trip, I met this lady once I got back home to New York, and she professed her ardent admiration for him. I had surfaced in my 17-year-old rusted green Chrysler, fondly referred to as a car in which you can run but cannot hide. I was a tad ragged, and unshaven with dark glasses. Incidentally, personal cleanliness is advocated the world over for spiritual growth. And when I related about meeting the actor, she looked at me quizzically and asked, *"He was traveling coach (economy) class?"*

It was all I could do to prevent driving off the road, laughing all the way home. And upon relating this to my inimitable wife, I received a withering look plus the inevitable admonition, *"Hmmmff . . . Bakwaaaaas (nonsense) . . . it's a sign . . . time you cleaned up your act, mister!"* Incidentally, a perceptive person can sense that organized vibrational energy (Subtle Body) in this man, an almost physical dynamic tension that many others have also noted.

And the concept of energy can be expanded universally. I noted how the cities of Mumbai and New York, some 7,900 miles apart, have a similar feel—you can sense that electric, vibrant energy of these places and the people, which motivates you to get up and do things!

And let us take a crack beyond the obvious—that we all love to be entertained. Fascination with movies is universal, so how does this dynamic and competitive industry relate to divinity? Let us commence with the confluence of collective energies, the expertise of multiple craft and technology. For example, scriptwriters, editors, cinematographers, animators, lighting experts, make-up artists, agents, actors, musicians, choreographers, producers. All experts of their craft (Karma Yogis)—with the best movies brought to life by the unique style, simplicity and single-mindedness of each director. Watch the differing styles of Francis Ford Coppola, Clint Eastwood, and Steven Spielberg to name a few. Spielberg created forty-five minutes of D-Day action for *Saving Private Ryan* from around twelve photographs of the actual WWII Normandy landings. Clint Eastwood subliminally sets us up for what is to come in the next shot (see *Unforgiven* or *Letters from Iwo Jima*). The genius of *The Godfather* and *The Godfather 2* by Coppola lies in the fact that every scene ties into another, with resultant permutations and combinations teaching you something new each time you watch these movies. Truly masters of their craft with originality as the key, try and imagine what perspective on life these directors must possess.

Reinforced by technological and support functions, they cumulatively portray that perfect marriage of an actor to the essence of the character brought out by perfect casting—indeed something *unique* about the selected actor that hooks right into the character on script. This unique aspect or instinct may be both developed and natural, the latter being sometimes labeled as that "x" factor which many directors state is God-given. Note the star power of leading men like Sean Connery or Jean-Paul Belmondo, dripping their magnetic charm (see explanation on prana, the magnetic subtle body energy under Table C) in addition to that all-encompassing, innate self-confidence powering through any situation; or the natural inner radiance and iconic sophistication of Audrey Hepburn (see *Roman Holiday*) combined with her honesty. It is no small an achievement indeed that she was loved by millions. In the 1973 *The Day of the Jackal*, Edward Fox (who plays the assassin) used his resident ebullient nature within his *first few scenes* to set the vision early for the viewers that the Jackal was the classy, complete professional, and in fact, really quite likeable! Here was a guy with whom one could have a good chat, a good game of chess, and perhaps a great game of golf?

These are indeed all flashes of the pure Self, resident within us all splashing onto the silver screen! And the greatest actors have unique perspectives. Robert De Niro once advised that acting was all about *not doing anything*, allowing the audience to read into it as opposed to telling them what they should feel. Al Pacino, when asked what turned him on, said "everything!" Sir Anthony Hopkins practiced every line 250 times! The camera lacks emotion and is hence surgical, picking up every aspect of an actor's reactions—both involuntary as well as what they are trying to bring to the role through the varying combination of the three traits (see Table A, Trigger 1—purity, passion and dullness) in perfect synchronicity with the script and images to create that masterful illusion on the screen.

I could not help musing, while taking into account our admiration for perfection of their collective craft (which excites our sense of professionalism and curiosity) to address a range of social, ethical and moral issues including bringing people and history back to life. Is our fascination in some subliminal way due to the extraordinary ability of these top professionals to temporarily transcend themselves (their ego) on screen, indeed our spiritual goal in life.

Last but not the least, I was most impressed by a Jeff Bezos (Amazon) comment that critical viewer feedback constitutes divine discontent. What a marvelous acknowledgment that producers of global entertainment at the top echelons have worked out a feedback loop to continuously improve upon their collective craft while keeping up with evolving consumer tastes.

7. Visiting Istanbul (Constantinople), Turkey

Pure Cosmic Power (see Trigger 4, Table A) and beauty in action. Istanbul—old time Constantinople—Asia to the East, Europe to the West is the only city in the world spread over two continents, with magnificent cultural perspectives. Amazing how the color of the sky changed within a span of thirty minutes. And the Blue Mosque on the right (European side) was the venue for the Sean Connery film *From Russia with Love* (1963). The Turkish (like the British) are some

of the finest street-smart, commercial negotiators I have come across globally. Turkey is truly the confluence of the East and the West in terms of culture, having taken the best of both.

And incidentally, the single greatest party I attended was in Taksim Square (Beyoğlu district in downtown Istanbul) at one of the restaurants hosting live music. It is said that the best parties are the spontaneous ones; note this underlying principle behind flash mob dances in varied public venues (I loved the middle eastern "dabke" performed at Beirut airport in 2011 which I saw on YouTube) although they are a product of superbly choreographed, combined rhythmic energies in play. Coming back to Istanbul, I was on a business tour with a dozen or so colleagues, we were at dinner when the wife of the Turkish restaurant owner came out on the small cozy dance floor and started to perform the traditional Turkish "Oryantal" belly dance complete with weaving hand movements. It was then only a question of time before I got on the floor to commence the traditional "Bhangra" dance of north India executed by way of vigorous kicks and leaps, squats, and rhythmic arm/shoulder thrusts. The ensuing result—this wonderful lady sped up while I slowed down—to reach an equitable medium; and the restaurant came alive. All the guests and staff joined in, and a dozen cultures collectively danced for three hours!

8. Filming Mount Everest (Nepal) and Mount Fuji (Japan)

It was once again pure Cosmic Power (Trigger 4, Table A), organized energy, courtesy of Mother Nature (hence our fascination). One can only preserve these sublime moments in memory for all time to come. As we were flying past Mount Everest, I will never forget how excited my fellow passengers were, including the Japanese air hostesses. We were all like little children in a candy store!

I would suggest for all to take some time to read about Rob Hall (head guide originally hailing from New Zealand) who perished on the Everest south summit during the 1996 descent. Here was a man who steadfastly refused to leave an ailing climber (and friend) above the death zone; and whose final words to his pregnant wife (base camp patched a call through) were reportedly "not to worry about him too much." Talk about integrity being the ultimate currency, what a spiritual man indeed, one to be cheered from the rooftops for all time.

There are equivalent stories of heroism, for example, Gerard McDonnell and others on K2, albeit not confirmed to this extent.

9. Giza Pyramids (Egypt), Chichén Itzá (Mexico) and Analysis on Origins of Religions

What an opportunity to walk through history and witness the brilliance shone through human endeavors. Little did I know there were over a hundred pyramids in Egypt until I visited; I always thought there were three! And pursuant to visiting the temple of Kukulcán at Chichén Itzá Complex Yucatan, Mexico, I simply had to research further to understand that while these two ancient pyramids looked somewhat similar, they served different purposes.

Source: iStock.com/Lindrik

All you can do is look and marvel: "How on earth did they . . . ?"

Source: iStock.com/JoseIgnacioSoto

Source: iStock.com/uchar

Egyptian pyramids were built primarily as tombs for the ancient rulers called Pharaohs, with belief in the integrated nature of the body ($\underline{h}t$) and soul ($k^{\jmath}/b^{\jmath}$) with efficient preservation of body complete with memoirs signifying achievements to effect proper judgement and hope for a blissful, eternal afterlife. Mayan works on the other hand served both burial and religious purposes with a place of worship. Mayan pyramids are characterized by steps leading to flat tops. Mayans (like many cultures) were also expert astronomers with their pyramids positioned to note important points in the calendar (solstice, equinox, etc.), time being symbolized (cycle of the sun) for beckoning agricultural and religious activities. Egyptian pyramids are also believed to represent descending rays of the sun complete with polished white limestone to reflect the light.

This inevitably led me to further research on the underlying religious and spiritual principles of some ancient civilizations including Egyptian, Greek, Mesopotamian, Zoroastrian (Indo-Iranian), Indian to Mesoamerican and Andean, ranging from 3500 BC onward. I came away marveling at the astonishing patterns and interconnectedness notwithstanding vast geographical separations, and the links into modern day practices. Cumulatively, these beliefs include but are not limited to acknowledgment of the divinity of nature, from single to a hierarchy of gods and deities to anthropomorphic representations, messianism, universe creation energies constituting manifest and unmanifest combinations, relative order of the universe including opposites (cosmic delusion), belief in astrology, the integrated nature of soul and body together with free will and afterlife, the threefold path to happiness, prevalence of formal religious practices (both group and individual) involving varied sacrifices.

I am deliberately mixing and matching herein some examples of the above to reinforce the interconnectedness. While I recall (with a groan) the days of my misspent youth sweating through history, geography and English school classes about the aforementioned including poetry, prose, Shakespeare, Latin and so on, here I was, some thirty-odd years later, standing in front of these mesmerizing creations of humanity—researching, marveling at their underlying principles and patterns of relative commonality. Examples of divinity of nature include from Ra the Egyptian sun god to Lord Zeus of the Greeks presiding over the sky, lightning and law and order, to Lord Indra, god of heavens, rain, lightning in Hinduism, to the unmanifest and manifest nature of the universe. Egyptian pyramids are thought to be shape representative of the primordial mound to and from the waters of the Nun (Nu), creating the cosmos from its unmanifest (source) condition, and the concept of duality emanating from Maat (goddess) providing order in the universe offset by her counterpart Isfet. Similar beliefs exist in Hinduism about Purusha (spiritual) and Prakriti (material) forces emanating from unmanifest conditions (Brahman) to create the manifested universe, with cosmic delusion (opposites) governing as the limiting factor to enlightenment. Note Zoroastrianism also has similar beliefs in dual cosmology of good and evil.

Land topography was used to revere the elements, deities and ancestors, animal characteristics, historical and mythological events. For example, Mayans assigned mountains, wells and caves to honor their gods, Mesopotamians assigned specific states such as Sumer, Assyria, Babylonia to the multiple deities worshipped. In fact, the ancient Peruvian Nazca, Chavin and Paracas cultures produced the Nazca Lines consisting of very large geoglyphs (over half a mile long in some cases) with representative designs of animals and plants interpreted by some historians as having religious intent. One hypothesis is that the highly visual nature of the Nazca was intended to be seen from above by deities. There are innumerable examples of belief in a single creator to multiple gods and hierarchies of deities—from Ahura Mazda the creator of the universe in Zoroastrianism to Hinduism's holy trinity (Brahma, Vishnu, Shiva) and the thirty-three deities, to the twelve major Olympian gods and goddesses in Greek religion including Zeus, Poseidon, Athena, Aphrodite, Hermes to gods such as Achilles and Menelaus who took part in the Trojan War, to the nearly 2,100 deities in ancient Mesopotamian religion (primarily considered anthropomorphic). As for the afterlife, many civilizations (like the Greeks and Persians and others) believed in this. Greeks differentiated it as Elysium (heaven) and Hades or Tartarus (hell). Such beliefs were laid out in ancient texts of Homer's *Iliad* and *Odyssey* and Hesiod's "Theogony" and "Works and Days."

If one compares the aforementioned to some of the principles outlined in the five-religion analysis (Table B-2), one will easily note the early links and influence of these ancient beliefs into modern formalized religious and spiritual systems including the most recent such as New Age and the Bahai faith. For example, I was most fascinated by Zoroastrian faith promoting messianism, free will and judgement after death, the threefold path of Asha (truth, cosmic governance) via good thoughts, words and deeds or Humata, Huxta and Huvarshta, respectively. Also note the familiar tone used later in Buddhism and other religions. This should hardly be surprising as history has shown that the early human beings, irrespective of timing, have been facing many of the same fundamental problems of life, with the consequent search for solutions to preclude suffering to achieve lasting happiness. Beautifully summarized by the Dalai Lama that if we could hypothetically reach out to those ancient humans we would be able to communicate because we are fundamentally all the same notwithstanding evolution of cultures and expression. I would encourage everyone, irrespective of age, to visit a museum of natural history at least once in their lifetime, where you will find some of the most amazing links into our ancestors and our collective evolution.

Last but not the least, this commentary would indeed be incomplete without mentioning the super-friendly nature of Egyptians (some of the most welcoming in all my travels); or the marvelous, resourceful and driven nature of Mexicans!

10. Visiting the Rock of Gibraltar, UK

Looking South towards the Northern Coastline of Morocco (Africa)

Atop one of the southern forts of Gibraltar, possibly the greatest picture taken by me to date (hence the inclusion) celebrating nature and technology in perfect contrast, depth and details. The faint specks in the middle that look like dirt spots are in fact buoys, including a soaring eagle! One gets the feeling one is in the UK except for keeping to the right while driving and the fascinating accent of the locals—a form of "Spanglish," indeed a combination of British and Spanish accents and more. The British had taken over Gibraltar during the War of

the Spanish Succession in 1704. This was contested by Spain but the promontory was ultimately ceded to Britain in 1713. With a small population (approximately 34,000 in 2021), Gibraltar's economy comprises tourism, financial services and ship-

ping. Gibraltar served as an important Allied base during WWII. Of particular fascination is Winston Churchill Avenue crossing the airport runway, the main road comprising the only access to and from this British Overseas territory—indeed one of the most interesting destinations in all my travels.

11. The Northern Lights (Aurora Borealis), Yellowknife, Northern Canada (62nd Parallel)

It was −42° Celsius/−43.6° Fahrenheit, and my son later told me that he was yelling in both pain and amazement. He further commented calmly, "Dad, you were the center of action yelling the loudest at the raw beauty of the aurora, with all others yelling along with you!"

It is hard to match this experience. Scintillating astral beauty courtesy of the solar winds interacting with the earth's magnetosphere to create a spectacular show of myriad lights (typically green, red, blue, pink) in varying intensity some 50–100 miles above the earth. Depending upon the strength of the solar winds (flares due to sunspots, corona) and the vantage point where one looks at it, auroras typically range from large coronas to rays/arcs curving across the sky, patches that resemble clouds or mild glows in the horizon. The aurora borealis along with its southern counterpart, the aurora australis occur in higher latitudes near the magnetic poles of the earth. Look out for key related terms such as "auroral zone," "aurora oval" used by scientists and aurora enthusiasts alike.

As you might have guessed, the lights derive their name from ancient Greece. Indeed Aurora is the Roman goddess of dawn; borealis is derived from Latin, means "northern." This is backed by legends such as magnificent celestial chariots carrying heavenly guests for divine weddings, to the spirits of the animals hunted, to nimble foxes with their tails causing sparks across the snows, to representing the departed spirits of loved ones reaching back out to us, to celestial battles of good and evil dragons breathing fire, to the lights seen as forebearers of good news and fortune. No wonder young couples the world over come out to these remote nature locales to get engaged or married in front of these divine spectacles.

It is also said that the beauty of the subtle planes (see Table C) is akin to that of the borealis, and that the very essence of creation is light in levels of ascending purity. Perhaps we all understand this subconsciously while viewing these awe-inspiring spectacles, that pure consciousness/Brahman and divinity lie here in one of its purest visible forms available to man, and unify people globally (our group had a dozen cultures), viewing it to sense that instinctive, collective joy?

And note the ability of those who live close to nature to see life in perfect clarity. I once saw an Anthony Bourdain program where they were discussing how the Inuit (an indigenous people for northern Canada, Alaska and Greenland) and Bedouins (from the desert regions) live on the edge of human tolerance. A common trait in them is their friendly, open nature despite living thousands of miles apart.

We all need to get away to such places and reflect, which we did for three nights along with Joe Bailey ("the Aurora Hunter") of the Dené people on this remarkable 2016 trip at the sixty-second parallel, some 400 kilometers south of the Arctic Circle. Note that the Dené are part of the First Nations, who along with the Inuits and the Métis comprise the indigenous people of Canada (around five percent of the population). Residing mainly in the boreal and Arctic regions, the Dené speak up to thirty-one northern Athabaskan languages alone!

What impressed me most about Joe (see picture) was his incredible connection and respect for nature, and just how ruggedly strong he was thanks to

the same! At times I had that subliminal feeling that he was actually conversing with the elements as we went along chasing the gaps in the clouds, consequently spending time at multiple locations within the icy landscape (including at frozen lakes where the reflection of the aurora is a sublime sight). We also stopped for some time on the Dettah ice road (which is around four miles long) linking Yellowknife to the small community of Dettah; it was a surreal feeling to feel and hear the loud cracking of ice underneath our frozen feet!

I recall Joe mentioning that when good people come together, the aurora comes out to welcome and dance for them—and my word, did his words come true! As mentioned in Table B-1 (Step 2), we all possess the five gross elements of nature (ether, air, fire, water and earth) within our being—and the aurora, as the epitome of nature in all its magnificent beauty, came out to blaze a divine bridge into our higher nature (which comprises the Self or divine light essence at the core). It is no small wonder that people come away finding an instinctive, healing connection within themselves after such a miraculous journey—*into themselves*, thanks to our Mother Nature.

And last but not the least, it was interesting how at the end of the tour we would say that a temperature of –27° Celsius/–16.6° Fahrenheit was *not too bad*.

Above: For scale, note the top of the tree line on bottom right.

Thanks in no small part to a bunch of friendly dogs (my son and I took a day tour early in our six-day Yellowknife visit) who took us ice sledding around a large frozen lake for about an hour. The ice being kicked up froze around my eyes (the only part exposed), I have never been so cold in all my life. I also recall that layering up with clothing (and layering down) was a daily event all by itself, and after engaging in one such outing (daily), we did not have much energy left to do anything else!

12. The Great Storms of Tornado Alley, USA

Above: Note the car (faint speck center right) trying to get out of the way!

Below: The larger tornado was anticyclonic, seen in only 2 percent of twisters produced. Tornadoes cannot ever be taken lightly; the largest (Category F5 on Fujita Scale) produce over 300 miles per hour winds and significant destruction. The Twins (F0) below eventually merged into a three-quarter-mile-wide twister.

How many times in life can a group of friends come off saying they just saw about six to eight tornadoes (we lost count) within a period of an hour and a half. Picture taken just after (see next page); rarely does one go through such philosophical highs to the accompaniment of awe and thrilled silence. And buried into my eternal memory is the mesmeric view of three back-to-back storms, each about a width of two miles. While watching these great storms, a thought arose in my mind about how insignificant we were compared to nature, yet how complex we make our lives. At the same time, I must state that we had the benefit of seeing the best of nature under closely managed conditions, courtesy of a professional storm chase company. Our hearts go out to those who have suffered and lost so much by getting caught in the path of these supercells (great rotating storms capable of spawning tornadoes).

We drove about 3,500 miles (exceeded the breadth of USA!) across six states in eight days, sleeping in different motels each night chasing these storms. And know that it is easier to see the northern lights than it is to see a tornado! It takes a complex sequence of events to create a tornado: SLIM (shear, lift, instability and moisture) plus a host of ancillary ones—research terms like "rear flank downdraft" (RFD), "wall cloud," "anvil-top cloud," "scud cloud," CAPE values, etc. Isolated storms are best, whereas a line of linear storms negate formation of tornadoes.

The storm chase team, as we noted, were intellectual achievers, resourceful, cool under pressure with expert, consistent focus on interactive strategic positioning while maintaining critical focus on safety. With a never-give-up motto laced with humor and above all the highest levels of personal integrity, these are attributes taught globally that would make corporate leaders proud!

Next, the guests: they were eclectic, ranging from nature lovers to adrenaline junkies—in statistical terms, largely based on the extremities of normal distribution curve of society. I noted flashes of extreme purity; each had in some shape or form overcome difficult experiences to figure out the path of purity borne of nature. For example, we had a cancer survivor, a former drug addict, a voluntary fireman, an aura reader, a nurse, a juror, a cardiologist, an animal advocate, a gay rights activist, some Google techies. We even had a lady who used to clip the toenails of lions at a zoo! We also met several other well-known chasers, and what stuck with me was that these were men who led life on their own terms.

And courtesy of this unique travel, you also end up living through experiences marvelously captured in three movies: *City Slickers*, *The Breakfast Club* and *Planes, Trains and Automobiles*! The collective enthusiasm (energy) in the vans ride in waves; we once drove about 500 miles, from Oklahoma to Nebraska to position ourselves for a storm, and then nada! Note the blog below by Mike Worden (one of the guests) written just after, indeed one of the most hilarious I have ever read!

What about the lessons learned? Watching how cool these tour directors are under pressure—it's not what but how to deal with your current predicament or problems in life. Like the Special Air Service Regiment, the secret of

The three most annoying aspects of the past 12 hours, in order:

3. I gave a few head scratches to some guy's dog at the hotel first thing this morning, and my petting hand has smelled of a recently deceased bottle-nosed dolphin ever since.

2. I walked into a giant gnat cloud about 8 hours ago and inhaled approximately six medium-to-large-sized gnats, who proceeded to host an advanced-level four hour Jazzercise class in the back of my throat.

1. We had a morning tornado forecast that sizzled hotter than bacon, but it ended up being that lameass low-calorie turkey bacon that tastes like someone cut the seat out of a 12 year-old city bus.

A very frustrating day out here on the Plains today that started out so promising, yet fizzled out before it even began. One by one we watched our storms collapse, each one more crushing than the last. I'm just a rookie out here and I have to learn to accept that's how it goes more often than not. But man, what a kick in the ass.

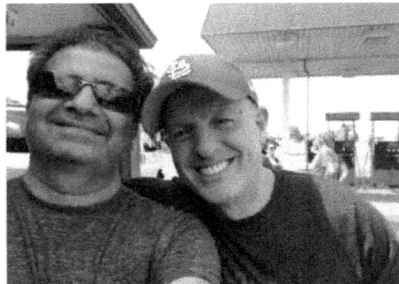

success is understanding your current plight and creatively working your way out of it; fear is about the future precluded by focusing on the present moment. We also may not realize but we come from nature, indeed a certain vestige of this awe-inspiring power is resident deep within us at the purest level. Hence we are intensely drawn to it. And the roaming nature of chasing, each night in a different motel or in a different state in part reinforces the detached, equanimous manner of leading one's life.

Last but not the least, I must comment on the visual, mesmeric nature of watching great storms while listening to the music of Vangelis, Kishore Kumar, Hans Zimmer, A.R. Rahman and others, truly a manifestation of Aum "in the moment" given such combination. Incidentally, may I humbly add that Hans and I went to the same school in England, albeit a few years apart! And tornadoes versus northern lights, which prevails? I humbly offer that the borealis ultimately does, given their beautiful, non-threatening and intensely spiritual visual feel. Tornadoes (and the supercells) on other hand take precedence from the point of view of a surreal feeling given the awe-inspiring power; you stand there wondering "am I watching a television set?"

13. Mario, Champion of Global Humanity, Ecuador, South America

Mario, the unsung champion of global humanity. Mario devotes his free time bringing much cheer to all at a young children's hospital in Guayaquil, Ecuador. I saw he was donating from his earnings, indeed a sacrifice considering the efforts he used to make ends meet. Genuine purity (sattwa) in action, I learned so much from this young man with his heart-warming maturity and generosity. He also mentioned how he had trained to be equanimous in conducting himself amongst these children. We made an instant connection; he was indeed fascinated about the blessings I received from the Dalai Lama given his admiration for this great sage. He also took me to some magnificent churches in downtown Guayaquil where I could feel the marvelous energies!

Mario also took me to one of the cacao farms to see how original chocolate (tastes salty, a tad bitter) is produced, the farm being run by a joint family of thirty. Such interesting people with a life nurtured by Mother Nature. I was greatly surprised and chuckled on hearing that the eighty-four-year-old head of the house was thoroughly annoyed on being advised for a minor surgery. Mario told me that many in the locality lived beyond 100 years given their connection to nature. Similar examples can be cited from other parts of the world too, for example, some villages in Japan. I was musing how long families like these would stay together given the mobility and the increasing wealth of the youth today. Same is the case in present-day India also. The lesson one should learn from this is to maintain one's body as one's temple of heaven. At the very least, minimize indulgence while executing your *vibrant* strategy to vanquish desires; this will lead to a step change in your energies.

Incidentally, I rate people from Ecuador amongst the friendliest in South America. I thoroughly enjoyed witnessing the unbridled joy of reunions at Guayaquil international airport, whose sights and memories will remain etched in my memory forever. And yes, I also enjoyed much the sociable iguanas milling around at the downtown park!

14. Visiting the Golden Temple (India) and the India/Pakistan Border

The uplifting energy of around 10,000 people was palpable, focused on devotion and divine wish to see the holy Sikh scripture, the Guru Granth Sahib, with queues leading to the Golden Temple (Sri Harmandir Sahib) by day and night. Sikhism originated in Punjab and was founded by Guru Nanak (AD 1469–1539), the first of ten gurus. Teachings are centralized around this main scripture written in Gurmukhi script. One of the world's youngest religions, it also incorporates beliefs from Islam and Hinduism. It believes in meditating on a sole creator (Ik Onkar), promoting equality while engaging in selfless service for humanity. Guru Gobind Singh, the tenth guru, ruled out any future gurus by naming the Guru Granth Sahib as his successor and the guiding spiritual principle henceforth. He also created Khalsa (the true Sikh) by establishing a code of five Ks for the initiated Sikhs, including maintaining Kesh (uncut hair), wearing a Kara (steel bracelet), carrying a Kanga (wooden comb) and a Kirpan (dagger), and wearing a Kachera (cotton underwear). Khalsa's birth is celebrated on 13 or 14 April annually as the festival of *Vaisakhi*. This day is also marked by Hindus as a north Indian spring harvest festival, and for heralding in the solar new year. Sikhism believes in the law of Karma and promotes expression of the Guru's word (Gurbani) through hymns (kirtans) while minimizing rituals and derivative gods.

Sikhs are admired as defenders of righteousness and helpers of those in need. The community kitchen (langar) at the Golden Temple feeds up to 100,000 people a day around the clock for free, all volunteer work. The clanging of dishes being cleaned is legendary. Tough and resilient, Sikhs have featured in many battles globally, including serving in foreign armed forces. Read about the defense by twenty-one Sikh soldiers against more than 10,000 Afghan soldiers during the battle of Saragarhi near Gogra (modern day Pakistan) on September 12, 1897, between British and Afghan forces. These valiant Sikhs held off their attackers for more than eight hours, which was a turning point in the larger conflict, and were ultimately martyred after refusing to abandon their fort or surrendering. Their gallant achievements were honored by the Order of Merit, the highest merit at the time for Indian soldiers, and their accomplishments are celebrated each year on Saragarhi Day in many parts of the world. Examples of famous Sikh battle chants associated with action in brotherhood, glory and devotion to God include *"Bole So Nihal... Sat Sri Akal"* and *"Waheguru ji ka Khalsa, Waheguru ji ki Fateh."*

You can see the aggressive, confident manner in which these fine, proud men, women and children conduct themselves on the streets of Amritsar (Punjab). As Swami Chinmayananda[2] wrote:

> . . . *it is a divine call to Man to discard his melancholy dejections in the face of life's challenges and to come forward to play as best as he can "the game of life," with a firm determination to strive and to win.*

I saw very few beggars during all my Punjab travels, a statistic highly representative of these proud and wonderful people. Sikhs constitute roughly 58% (16 million people) of the population of Punjab.

---

[2] *The Holy Geeta: Commentary by Swami Chinmayananda*, Central Chinmaya Mission Trust, Mumbai.

We also visited the India–Pakistan border at Wagah, venue of the highly choreographed, friendly aggression during daily closing of the connecting gate between the two countries. One would marvel at the athleticism while enjoying the sight of a number of these proud soldiers marching on both sides cheered by around 7,000 people!

15. Travels to Uruguay and Chile, South America

Want to spot similarities between people from different regions of the world? A wonderful example, note the interconnected nature of the peoples of India and Uruguay in varying combinations of the three traits (gunas). I was delighted to run into the Uruguayan Carnival. As I milled around the dancers and the spectators, I realized the family nature of such events and formed a completely new point of view that could never be gained from watching TV programs on the subject. I spoke with some of the proud parents who had come to cheer their enthusiastic sons and daughters in this national celebration. And the marvelous rhythm of these Latin Americans was something to behold.

I visited Casapueblo[3], the summer home of Carlos Páez Vilaró, the legendary abstract artist, painter, potter, sculptor, muralist, constructor, writer and composer. We hear about master painters getting lost in their art; even a cursory glance confirms the sheer brilliance of this Karma Yogi. Similar to the constructions in Santorini, Greece, it took nearly thirty-six years to complete, with thirteen floors and tiered terraces enabling the occupier to view the magnificent Atlantic Ocean. I have seen similar views in Viña del Mar and Concón in Chile (see next two pages), even slept to the vibrant music of crashing waves and salty sea breeze permeating through an open window at the hotel!

Casapueblo also pays tribute to his son Carlos Miguel, one of the sixteen Uruguayan survivors of the much publicized Flight 571 crash in the Andes Mountains (October 1972).

At Piria Castle,[4] between the districts of Minas and Piriápolis (see next page), I almost fell over admiring several paintings. Grinning at me was A.C. Bhaktivedanta, founder of ISKCON, the International Society for Krishna Consciousness! It was so interesting to see the spread of Hinduism in one of the remote corners of the planet. And a smiling chef folded his hands and gleefully said "namaste" to me at the Mercado del Puerto (famous market) in downtown Montevideo. Uruguay incidentally had a population of 3.2 million in 2018 but the number of cows it had was a staggering fifteen million!

---

[3] Permission granted by Casapueblo Workshop Museum, Punta Ballena, Maldanado, Uruguay
[4] Permission granted by the Municipality of Piriapolis, Maldanado, Uruguay.

Piria Castle, Uruguay.

I also had the great fortune to visit the Atacama Desert in northern Chile, the driest non-polar desert on earth complete with its immense salt flats, ancient volcanoes, stony terrain, sand and felsic lava. And did I forget to mention the blue water, in some cases no more than a few inches, creating the perfect reflection of the mountains during the daytime and at sunset. Of course Bolivia has a much larger area with the same effect. We went up to about 12,000

I salute to this man fishing in front of the mesmeric view at Viña del Mar!

My travels to Chile took me to the famous coastline resorts of Viña del Mar and Concón, where one can enjoy the haunting beauty of sunsets.

feet to the Los Flamencos National Reserve where the lagoons attract a variety of birds including flamingos. The Atacama is also famous for the Mars Rover testing mission, and venue of multiple space observatories. As I was looking up into the Magellan Clouds of the Milky Way, the rings of Saturn, Jupiter and three of its moons, star clusters, the Ring Nebula and multiple satellites passing over, it reminded me of the saying that only when we come to realize just how small a speck we are in the universe, does nature and life truly divulge its pearls of wisdom. And in that beautiful light of the predawn sky a great thought came to my mind that the ancient sages, through their meditative practices, had

The Atacama Desert in Northern Chile.

accomplished the technique of dematerializing their body at will and teleporting themselves at the speed of light to travel amongst the stars. Now that is a mission for all of us to achieve.

16. Visit to World War II Concentration Camps: Auschwitz-Birkenau (Poland) and Dachau (Germany)

Not only was this an intensely extreme experience by way of the visits, but also the most challenging to describe, given the consequent derivative questions I was forced to confront. My humble suggestion to all readers for whom this subject could be sensitive, is to skip this section if so desired.

Spirituality teaches us there is divinity everywhere. With this in mind I visited the three camps. Auschwitz I and Auschwitz II-Birkenau constituted sheer industrial-grade elimination treated as business ventures, whereas Dachau initially commenced as a labor camp for political prisoners, its goals being primarily (initially) strategic, including training for the larger camp network (over a thousand) in Germany and captured territories. An estimated 41,500 people perished at Dachau whereas 1,100,000 people perished at Auschwitz I and Auschwitz II-Birkenau. It may be noted that all WWII concentration camps were strategically located near transport depots to enable timely movement of prisoners and goods.

It should be stated that no ordinary person can withstand torture, and ill health largely precludes concerted religious or spiritual practices. Then try to imagine just how challenging it must have been at these camps. Observers post-liberation noted the slow, measured, almost premeditated movements of these helpless survivors; their body and mind went into defensive mode in an attempt to survive, conserving every ounce of energy. Let us try and fathom what their concept of time must have been. Spirituality teaches that time is an interval measure between two discrete events. The greater the number of experiences that target and trigger the mind within a certain time window, the greater is our attention. Note how eyes bulge out during intense fear or danger. Hence time appears to extend, and the level of intensity (focus) even leads to people experiencing time reversal. Have you ever heard the expression "life flashed before my eyes?" Note that the reverse is also true—blissful sleep is timeless just like periods of joy; hence time flies with lack of disturbance. So, before we move on, let us cogitate over what three to four years of the Holocaust did to those suffering through it, given that even a few moments of pain are unbearable for the average person.

Dachau Concentration Camp, near Munich, Germany
Author's note: My thanks to the Administration
of the Dachau Memorial Site for use of the picture.

Continuing on, these camps represented the worst of humanity and extreme suffering with survivor accounts similar to those of war veterans that war was hell, and one lived like an animal for a while and could become numb, desensitized against the backdrop of continued fear. So, for all my intense research and time spent in temples, churches and other religious establishments in various parts of the world, I was forced to question as I walked through these places sensing those dreary, depressing energies: Where lay the divinity amongst all this engineered elimination through systematic starvation, extreme work conditions and perfected recycling practices. As an example of the latter, a wall-to-wall exhibit had only human hair used to produce socks and other goods, in fact around 15,000 pounds of it were found at Auschwitz. I for one will never look at hair again in the same manner. Another bone-chilling comment was how one survivor was explaining to someone trying to find a lost relative that this person *"was lucky"* to go early to the gas chambers. And as we slowly shuffled through these chambers, it hit me with full force: What went through the minds of those mothers as they stood there trying to protect their babies?

My humble conclusions on divinity here are threefold. First, the shining sacrifices made by prisoners for others. A survivor said you either became stronger or weaker during the experience. At Auschwitz our guide took us to the underground cell where the Catholic priest Reverend Maximilian Maria Kolbe, venerated posthumously as St. Maximilian Kolbe, died after volunteering to take the place of a Polish prisoner condemned to death by starvation. And he did so while leading others similarly condemned through prayers and hymns. Given that the ego is a deluded projection of the highest Self, it follows that it is a trick of the mind to be afraid, and many in these camps transcended by *"living in the moment,"* facing their fears through extreme sacrifices to help others. Bravery in our everyday lives presents itself in all forms based upon our state of being, for example, some excel on the battlefield, some save lives as medical staff, firemen, etc., some have the courage to take on public speaking, yet others exhibit courage by engaging in extremely dangerous sports/events.

Secondly, we have no choice but to take the larger viewpoint. Religion/spirituality professes that collective Karma can take place to resolve and rebalance one's action/reaction cycle. A priest mentioned plane crashes as an example of this group principle. Collective Karma even takes place at a basic family unit level, various examples ranging from the collective suffering when a son goes out to take part in a war effort (imagine the plight of the parents) to everyone being impacted when an argument takes place between two family members. While it is considered a privilege to be born as humans, given the ability to make conscious choices as opposed to other life forms that work primarily by instinct, not everyone can become collectively realized at the same time. And in these cases the world witnessed great suffering due to extreme combinations of passion and dullness traits (recall our threefold nature), with collective mentality degenerating into sheer brainwashing, dogma and madness. As for torture, only men of a higher state of being such as advanced yogis and realized souls can keep themselves aloof through concerted meditative practices from these effects. Others are operating in survival mode working out of their base chakras (same goes for war). I was most impressed by the unrelated examples of such transcendence by the comments of the Buddhist monk, as related in the first item under this section, that his greatest fear was to possibly develop animosity toward his captors. And what about Louis Zamperini, the long-distance US runner at the 1936 Berlin Olympics (in which Jesse Owens competed) who was captured and tortured for two years in Japan during WWII to later become a Christian evangelist advocating his strong beliefs in forgiveness. These men certainly came to understand the larger perspective.

Thirdly, the positives that ensued. It was heart-warming to hear from our guide at Auschwitz that they see around two million visitors every year from all parts of the globe. Indeed the collective effort is to attempt to understand extremities of the human mind, to preclude such events from ever taking place again. Many great souls went on to become strong advocates for this greater cause. Look at what Benjamin Ferencz achieved for us all by materially influencing the creation of the United Nations International Criminal Court to protect the rights of people through the rule of international law.

And after much cogitation and the greatest of apologies, I asked a Hindu swami and a visiting Christian minister if people in extreme professions (for example, executioners) could become realized, and secondly why such sufferings were imposed on these helpless souls. I received some fascinating responses.

Taking up the second topic on suffering first, the Christian minister responded that some believed that God set up this imperfect world, offered us redemption and everlasting life, but that we were always subject to the "sins" of this imperfect world such as the war and the Holocaust, man being evil. God is perfect, we are not. Others offer that it's all part of God's master plan, that He is in charge, and that this is all part of His plan. And that it all works together for His greater good. And given that His plan is timeless, we cannot measure a six-year event like the war including the Holocaust against His timeline of eternity. The minister went on to explain that his personal faith was far more rooted in the first postulate above, and it was almost impossible for him to believe that a loving God would want people (especially children) killed in the Holocaust as part of His plan. The minister continued to elaborate that He gives us free will that leads to evil, but that the very same free will to choose to follow God is what draws us even closer to Him, especially in times of trial. The swami explained that suffering is substantially due to Karmic rebalancing (action–reaction cycle) from past and current lives leading to these "predesignated" events (individual and collective Karma therein). Furthermore, how the individual best copes (becomes stronger or weaker) while surviving to the extent of their designated number of breaths in this particular lifetime—all cumulatively adjusts one's future life path.

On the issue of people in extreme professions becoming realized, the minister said that one can become "redeemed," for example a murderer asking God for forgiveness through genuine repentance. God will know he means it, and as He loves all of us the same, He will welcome him to His kingdom. The same principle applies to an executioner who kills in the line of duty, again condi-tional upon genuine love for God while confessing one's sins with genuine repentance. Christianity has a system of beliefs for mortal (and venial) sins with methodology for redemption, including further belief in purgatory (in some sects) and a permanent hell if one does not fully repent.

The Swami's response, however, was that it all depended upon where one had reached in one's spiritual transcendence, courtesy of his prior Karma up to that moment. As people in extreme professions both witness extreme suffering and sense the effects of energies associated with lower chakras during such acts, the impacts are extremely challenging to overcome. So while an executioner kills for duty, the question arises as to how he deals with such acts. A detached spiritual soul may become realized, there are also many examples of men in extreme professions suddenly turning to religion and spirituality. Even a mur-derer, who operates from a non-holistic platform out of free will can at some point, given the iterative nature of Karma, end up burning negative energies thereby reaching the same position as a soldier-turned-preacher subject to timely inevitable, genuine repentance.

The minister then came back with a scintillating question: Does being "redeemed," saved by God including eternal life in Christianity, mean the same as becoming a realized soul in Hinduism? Oh, what a great derivative question! My humble take is that be it Hinduism, Christianity or any other religion, the world has recognized great saints and prophets, and their level far transcends that of a normal person being redeemed. Indeed many religions acknowledge multiple layers of heavens with variant levels of beings borne of their resident divinity. And the Hinduism definition of "realized" points to these higher-level beings acknowledged across all religions.

These visits were a life-changing event. I take blessings each morning from these brave departed souls at a small shrine in my home office, which contains a picture of women, children, and old people going to the chambers at Auschwitz. I remind myself daily of their sacrifices made for us in the global community to make the absolute best of our lives, and to stop complaining about minimal stresses and strains. And I try my best to absorb ancient teachings that macro-level judgement rendered is ultimately impartial to escape the bondage of cosmic delusion, with genuine repentance and purity being the keywords to success.

17. Iceland and The Northwest Passages (Canada)

Nestled on the Mid-Atlantic Ridge, this astonishing island nation is a paradise for nature lovers. Iceland welcomes you with fire and waterfalls, fjords and black sand beaches, mountains and glaciers, hot springs and geysers, the northern lights, a special breed of pony-sized horses, whale watching and some "touristy" volcanoes. A tour guide said she even saw rain reversing its course (winds can exceed 100 miles/hour). Did you know that Iceland modernized at the time of WWII, and has a scant population of under 400,000 with some sixty percent based in the vicinity of Reykjavík? And as for their quaint North Germanic, lexical Icelandic—try pronouncing Eyjafjallajökull ("Ei-ya-fyat-la-yer-kitle") for practice!

We visited the Katla Ice Cave and Jökulsárlón Glacier Lagoon; it was sobering to see global warming effects and the receding ice amidst the great beauty.

Be prepared for physical activity and take at least two pairs of shoes, given the shearing power of lava rock. Rejuvenating sulfur fragrant showers are to be relished in this land of geothermal energy, whereas touching moss causes irreparable damage to these ancient plants! Enjoying the Viking myths and esoteric stories, I chuckled when a guide (with a PhD in physics) said he was still befuddled over the existence of elves. Another calmly advised that she observed a rainbow following our bus over a certain distance. I admired the eclectic purity in these people, which shone given their intrinsic links to Mother Nature. As for synchronicity of events, try this. During the historic 2010 Eyjafjallajökull eruption which severely disrupted air travel, my delayed New York–Delhi flight led to a "chance" meeting at JFK with the President of India, Dr. A.P.J. Abdul Kalam (see Travelogue #4). All the guides unequivocally agreed that this event, so indelibly linked to their wondrous land, must be mentioned in my spiritual travels.

And speaking of ice, I simply must include a picture taken from a separate trip, flying west from New York City over the Northwest Passage to Beijing, China. Nothing prepared me for this view. We are at 37,000 feet.

18. The Interconnectedness of It All—
I Meet My Doppelgänger

Hey, who says miracles do not take place! Well, not really, just an extension of the fundamental principle of interconnectedness. Another Deepak Parashar, also with the same birth sign as mine, lives in the UK. My son came across him on the Internet, and we eventually met in 2012. I could see his wife Manjiri was having a field day. While opinions on facial likeness vary, it was his mannerism that was stunning; I realized I was literally looking into a mirror. He has a PhD in mathematics, made up for all my misdoings as a lazy student. Yet a complete stranger, no relationship whatsoever. Incredibly, we had also traversed the same parts of the globe at the same time. For example, they had lived in Swansea, Wales, while I visited there twenty times in twenty months for a project during the same period. We even frequented the same supermarket! I also met his parents in Delhi. His mother burst into tears, came over and gave me a big hug. It was very moving, one of those brilliant moments in life when one can only wonder about the magic of God's creation. His mother said that we were at nine or ten in similarity, on a scale of one to ten. Mothers always know.

19. True Nature—from Cooling to Searing, Niagara to Sahara!

The awe-inspiring amazing power of nature can be compared to our resident energies (three traits/gunas). Acts born out of our resident passion plus purity are analogous to properly directing water resulting in rich rewards. Similarly, negative acts of passion plus dullness lead to the reverse. Our ego is representative of the latter: it precludes appropriate channeling of nature.

Riding the edge of sand dunes is considered a sport, indeed one of the most surreal, endearing experiences in this vast ocean of perfect clarity at a temperature of 120°F (49°C). I watched our expert Pakistani driver taking turns casually holding the wheel with his left hand. He later told me he would come back alone at night, and revel in the enchanting stillness enabling perfect meditation. He considered his relationship with the desert deeply spiritual.

20. The Alps in Switzerland and Germany

"It is all about emotion up here. And please stop by that office to see the greatest view in the world and meet the happiest professional on earth." Thus spoke a distinguished stranger at the Gornergrat Kulm Hotel on my second trip to admire the legendary Matterhorn located at the Swiss/Italian border, and the magnificent panoramic views from a height of 10,285 feet.

Mountains are synonymous with divine energies, the abode of gods, and venues for religious establishments the world over. Examples of mythical mountains include Mount Sinai, Mount Olympus, and Mount Kailash. We have evolved from nature (see Table B-2, Item 10), and hence are instinctively drawn to it. I met people from myriad cultures who all stated that they felt an energetic divinity emanating from this mesmeric creation of nature. I agree!

Incidentally, the Matterhorn (at 14,692 feet) is a magnet for clouds. I fondly recall the collective groans and recommend staying a night in the charming Swiss town of Zermatt to enable early morning views. And I am so proud to state that an old Swiss colleague was a mountain guide and saved lives up there.

And after fifteen visits to this land of punctuality, decorum and great beauty, I can gleefully say that these polite and charming people generally take their time to get to know you. But once accepted, they are fast friends for life!

We also visited the Bavarian Alps in Germany, and Lake Geneva in Switzerland. The panoramic views left us speechless.

21. My Guru at Jalandhar, Punjab, North India

I met him when he was in his early nineties. He gave me a mantra and I use it daily. He barely spoke, and when he did, it was in Sanskrit. It is said that the face reflects the inner state of being, as was evident from his facial expression.

These realized souls (note levels of consciousness in Table B-1) are typically mysterious, and their acts are free from compulsions due to past Karmas, given they have substantially broken that cycle. They are not worried about their next meal, this guru indeed lived in a mud hut with no income and was looked after by the village community. Their looks are deceptive—they may look absent-minded, in a bit of a stupor, perhaps even distracted. But in reality they are deeply focused personifying that marvelous, detached air which only men of this spiritual level can truly achieve. I was attempting to speak to one of these great souls, and I could see he was having to cycle in and out of a trance-like state to respond. And their styles are known to vary. Some remain

Picture taken c. 1945, he was in his mid-sixties then.

quiet and motionless typically in a remote location, others travel, some teach, some perform miracles; but all have one unifying factor. They are all tapped into that deep perception of the divine infinite, personifying supreme bliss through universal love and service. All understand the subtle laws of creation—how energies work thereby enabling degrees of control. A miracle is quite normal for them as it is only a by-product of growing spirituality. They have transcended body identification, may choose to go at will but sometimes stay on to affect/accelerate their future Karma in their path to the highest subtle and causal planes. For example, they may through certain methods transfer the suffering of others (disease) on to themselves, then stoically ignore it or go at will. Material riches are of no consequence, they are completely fulfilled rejoicing in the raw, boundless divine nature of God. A realized master of the higher echelons may not need separate time for meditation as he is already one with the Lord or the highest states of consciousness. And on the path to reaching these highest planes, they may from time to time exhibit minor lapses, also may not be knowledgeable on every single subject (contrary to belief). And their final journey from earth into higher planes is called "Maha Samadhi." They are buried (not cremated) as the act of burial is symbolic of cremation in the flames of knowledge.

And what is the difference between a yogi and a swami? The latter is a pre-ordained monk or designated clergy as opposed to one who practices scientific technique for divine realization. Conversely a yogi may be both married or otherwise, either a man of worldly responsibilities or formal religious ties. There has been much debate on yogis and swamis but ultimately they are all involved in concerted action along differing paths to achieve oneness with God—be it through selfless, detached service to mankind, mastery over desires, intense love for God or concerted practices borne of tremendous focus.

22. My Mother and Mahatma Gandhi

My mother was a woman of higher knowledge in the sense of the Bhagvadgita, possessing great humility. She spoke Sanskrit (a skill rare these days), attended Mahatma Gandhi's prayer session as a child; she also knew Mother Teresa in her later years. Little did I know until after she passed away that she used to go into areas of Mumbai (India) to do charity work even well-established missionaries would avoid. Here was one of the pure (sattwic) souls one could ever perhaps encounter in one's lifetime. Truly she set my goals in life.

And speaking of the Mahatma, he was truly multidimensional, naturally curious and a master strategist. He wrote on many subjects. He was a voracious reader in pursuit of knowledge and spirituality—reading religious scriptures of many faiths, and also writings of naturalists and philosophers like Henry David Thoreau and John Ruskin, to name a few. His practice of silence for a day every week to work on critical letters manifested into spiritual necessity. He maintained sheer simplicity and self-sacrifice to serve community. He was also openly critical about his own faults.

His daily routine included getting up at four in the morning for prayer. He used to observe occasional fasting with emphasis upon less being more, his diet being focused on involuntarily reducing sexual desires! Reportedly childlike in divine quest, a man of much wit, he could apparently detach from his senses at will. Once he went through a minor surgery without anesthesia, happily conversing with others. He was of the view that perfect state of being could be reached only through perfect coordination of mind, body and speech.

Ben Kingsley, the lead actor in the 1983 movie *Gandhi*, once mentioned during an interview how, at the time he was engrossed in reading a book on this great man, he received the call from director Richard Attenborough asking him to play the role. When told about this coincidence, Attenborough's response reportedly was that the Mahatma's life was full of so many sublime coincidences. Synchronicity with the rhythms of nature and creation laws again!

Gandhi spent many years in jail during a lifetime of public service. His concept of nationalism clearly transcended any geographical boundaries. He preached and practiced forgiveness as being the most powerful of tools ultimately leading to lesser violence all around on the path to peace. Read also about Albert Einstein's famous quote about this great soul.

Picture of my Mother taken in 1959.

Mahatma Gandhi with Sir Charlie Chaplin, Kasturba Gandhi, Sarojini Naidu (hand on Kasturba's shoulder) and others (1931). Note the obvious delight in both men.[5]

---

[5] With permission from Publications Division, Ministry of Information and Broadcasting, Government of India.

CONCLUSIONS

Sheer exhilaration epitomizes this twelve-year journey of relentless learning which taught me that no bridge was too far, no challenge was insurmountable if I stayed the course in my spiritual quest. I found everything was a test, it was all about conscious choices. I realized that the purpose of existence in our sublime universe, which operates in perfect synchronicity through concurrent creation, sustenance and dissolution, constitutes achieving the collective divinity of humanity. This revelation was the hidden surprise of my enthralling research as I progressively stumbled into the interconnectedness of it all.

I had decided early on that my strategic vision would be to examine practical examples of divinity in all corners of our beautiful planet, juxtaposed against related theoretical principles. Armed with the blessings of His Holiness the Dalai Lama, an engineer's investigative streak and a determination to unabashedly pursue any question that iteratively dawned in my mind, I had inadvertently stumbled into my calling. For example, while admiring the temple of Kukulcán at the Mayan city of Chichén Itzá (Yucatan, Mexico), I was musing about the flatness at the top, wondering why this was different from the Egyptian pyramids at Giza I had earlier visited? This sole question propelled me into a dozen religions including their origins, thereby opening up a new portal of understanding of ancient, interconnected principles of worship and beliefs, despite these cultures being thousands of miles apart with no apparent connectivity. Similarly, I had stopped to research the expression "pranic energy" (the underlying source for pranayama and equivalent yogic practices) or subtle life currents for about three months as I was struggling to fully comprehend its meaning, again leading into a world of transcendent learning.

It was indeed amazing to find how when one looked at data from different angles with single pointed focus, it brought forth different dimensions. Suddenly, all the linking dots sprang into radar view in the eleventh year of my research. The aforementioned two examples alone opened up a world of connectivity from chakras to palmistry to numerology to astrological signs to holistic medicines to the five gross elements; from n/um energy of the San community in the Kalahari region of Africa to the Kundalini Yoga in India to Dzogchen Meditation in Tibet; from Ra the Egyptian sun god to Lord Zeus of the Greeks to Hinduism's Lord Indra of the heavens. And suddenly, the world became a global village notwithstanding history and the passage of time. The realization dawned on me that people of all religions, caste and creed, the rich and the poor, the powerful and the helpless, accepted that this world was not our permanent home. That there was suffering and bondage here, and the search was on to find solutions for eternal joy devoid of fear—may it be seeking a personal or impersonal God, having a belief in a larger energy system, being an atheist, or simply attempting to be the best possible person one could be through kind acts towards our brethren and other life forms.

So, having successfully established the connectivity of it all, what comes next? The consequent answer naturally points towards helping others, but to achieve that we must first learn to help ourselves! People lose their confidence when they lose control of their environment; indeed we miss the key point that if we do the real work to take control of ourselves, it substantially prepares us to take on life's challenges. The ground reality is that in the larger scheme of things, we control little and once we grasp this, it frees us up enabling us to let go of control, attachment, and hence fear. And as our focus naturally shifts from "I" to "We," we become impartial and selfless, serving the larger community, humanity. To give generously, one must inculcate resident generosity!

Hence, the bottom line is *persevering daily for that divine knowledge—may it be God that we seek within ourselves, a higher cause or the supernatural*, be it through religion, being spiritual, or an atheist, agnostic, or divinity achieved through professional accomplishments by living in the moment. Whatever the path, we must learn to grow and be genuine opinion leaders and role models by exemplifying grit and strategic vision, reinforced by a personalized holistic system that involuntarily spurs excellence. And while we all pine for the highest states of meditation pursued through concerted religious and spiritual methods, just know that a majority of us have to start (starting with self) at the lower rungs of the ladder. Table C is representative of the overall system of the universe, both gross and subtle, and helps each of us gauge exactly where we are in our marvelous journey.

And how about starting by energizing the minds of our young children reinforced by a stable family life, keeping in mind that the age group of six to fourteen is generally considered as the most impressionable. I knew a Jesuit priest from Spain called Father Valero Aleu who was principal at St. Stanislaus School in Mumbai, India, who used to visit the homes of students to see if they had the requisite environment to achieve future excellence. It is rarely that one comes across such dedication to community notwithstanding beliefs and training. Let us learn from Mother Nature, how it protects our young; even babies instinctively know not to hurt their sensitive body parts. Let us help them find their passion and path in life. Fortunate indeed are those who do not have to work even for a day as their unique gifts bloom into professional expertise as a means to natural transcendence. Look at budding tennis players, how they are nurtured with special training from a young age to aim for getting into the top echelons. And for those who do have to work for a living, critical it is to develop your hobbies with fervor and single-pointed focus; not only will it keep you centered, but you also never know what doors it will open up for you later! A CEO friend once said that he keeps an eye over young talent who have the courage to go and experience something different, in that they have a cool story reinforced by oodles of self-confidence which will harness them in their careers to dare to dream strategically!

And conversely, note just how much children teach us through their humility and innocent charm. Note how gurus touch the feet of others in respect! And the guru should not just be a man of theory, he should inspire communities to rise to soaring levels by his own personal example via scientific, rational methods. And gurus lead you into yourself, not to them.

And speaking of Mother Nature, how about envisioning the beauties of the universe, something common to all ages, given it is an integral part of our evolution. Did you know that our Milky Way alone has 100 billion planets, 400 billion stars? Did you go out and see the December 20, 2020 confluence of Jupiter and Saturn (once in 800 years at night), and did you realize that when the slight gap re-emerged between them, you were looking at a distance of 456 million miles? How about the mesmeric picture of the first black hole in the Messier 87 Galaxy? Did you marvel at the brilliance of the human mind to create an integrally coordinated telescope the size of the earth to capture its view? Did you know that algal dust left behind due to the drying up of the world's largest desert lake in Sahara, Africa, ultimately fertilizes the Amazon rainforests—each day in winter the wind picks up 700,000 tons of this mineral-rich dust to sustain the famed Latin American region half a world away? Or that nearly 30,000 gray whales execute a 10,000-mile journey each year from Alaska to Baja California to give birth, and that their females are slightly larger? I was fortunate enough to take part in one such expedition, making that eye-to-eye connection (what a moment!) with a 45-foot, 35-ton whale. What a lifetime experience it was! I met people in Mexico who had actually gone into the southern lagoons where mother whales and calves come up to the boats! Inculcate curiosity early together with a sense of humility and gratefulness, and the universe opens up its wonderous doors of divine knowledge.

And for those who can travel, go out and experience! For those who cannot, know that the answers ultimately commence from within. Realized souls can do the latter at will, given their developed intuition to understand the interconnected nature of the universe and to find divinity in each discrete experience.

While it may not seem so at times, the world ultimately works in harmony and perfect balance, and if you want to do your bit, aim high! The secret lies in the holistic nature of our strategic execution to become that "spiritual billionaire." Note the examples all the world over of so many brilliant people who excelled in their passion but fell by the wayside. Success has many connotations—whatever your interpretation may be, do it selflessly, holistically and with integrity! Make money, don't get tied to it! Whatever we are, whether a flamenco dancer, a soldier, an airline pilot, an R&D engineer, a developer of disruptive innovation, a businessman, we as timeless students must continually remain alert to be able to connect the dots that have woven and propelled our life path.

We must recognize those magnetic, sacred moments that pull us towards higher consciousness to glorious, instinctive joy. One must have an intense goal for liberation, and when one's fear of losing a supposedly valuable asset is overcome by one's desire to grow, one will dramatically ascend, amazing the impact!

Do not get upset about what you cannot influence or control. All you can do is your best and let it go. But you will almost certainly be better off as a person as a result. Sense the tremendous power within, and the consequent realization that one does not have to be a slave to anything. It is a trick of the mind that makes one a coward in life; perceived failure is in fact a great impetus for change. And be that ferocious tiger of self-control. Arrogance and egocentric desires make us carry an agonizing burden; be aware that we all have a basic tendency to revert back to our basic nature and learn to interactively guard against it. Bridging the gap between the "perfect me" and the "real me" is difficult, and has to be dealt with sincerity and resolve. When we stay within the realm of scriptures or a positive environment as a minimum, it is a continuous enabler for self-improvement. I was at a lecture when a swami asked, "You may have gone through the scriptures several times, but have the scriptures gone through you?"

Constant cheerfulness builds energy and dynamism and becomes an immediate sanctuary away from sorrows; the world becomes an indescribably beautiful place. As you change, so will the energy around you in subtle fashion. Fortunate indeed are those who can maintain their sense of humor in tight corners. Laughter and anger are involuntary reactions; if you wake up and start smiling with the birds first thing without knowing exactly why, that is Mother Nature's way of telling you that you are doing something right. Conversely, frequent rage implies you have much work to do, and can develop into a fatal flaw materially impacting the lives of your loved ones in severely adverse ways. Note that even one such flaw can overcome all the resident goodness within yourself, and must be ferociously protected against.

Strive to be the absolute best you can be. A famous boxer once said a champion is one who gets up when he cannot. Laser-focused, divine-dedicated activities by living in the moment without constantly pining for results is the way of the true Karma Yogi; bringing about holistic purification and spiritual awakening while understanding the interconnectedness of it all. Look at Mahatma Gandhi's example of humility, respect for all mankind, or the Dalai Lama's compassion for all beings. I sensed (during my second meeting) just how much His Holiness genuinely loves everyone irrespective of who they are, complete with all their faults! And how about Eric Liddell, the 1924 Olympics British athlete (and missionary) who recognized early that God had made him fast, and that he would feel God's pleasure when he ran for Him—and just how much joy he gave to the world as a result!

Introspect actively, learn from mistakes and watch yourself daily—it's easy to slip, sometimes within a matter of a *few days*. As a minimum, avoiding self-destruction hugely improves your chances of success. With your mind under control, you progressively become a master under the guidance of your evolved intellect leading into intuition or primed spiritual knowledge propelling your being into transcendence. Pursue your duties in life without fear of results while envisioning your goal. Treat life with respect, life will in return respect and revere you. Understand the inevitable power of nature and the universe within ourselves to get in synchronicity. Meditate daily, stay physically energetic and intellectually dynamic, develop repertoire to bring forth your inherent genius streak. Always remember that an exhausted person can never practice devotion or his craft efficiently; hence maintain an efficient system of timely rest. And success without happiness has no meaning.

Know that life will continue to present challenges, do not try to win by being like others—indeed the perfect recipe for failure. Creation, sustenance and dissolution are going on at any given moment—it all depends upon which way you choose to view it from. Setbacks can be leveraged as a future opportunity to grow with. This commentary examines leadership in various scenarios such as in the armed forces, industry, space programs, sports, the arts, etc. The greatest leaders drive with their incredible selflessness (and hence unparalleled honesty and humility), expertise, grit and strategic vision. Combined with intense situational awareness and attention to detail, they continually operate beyond their comfort zone—while leading from the front and living in the moment.

To achieve extraordinarily demands high self-esteem. Know that your life is special, be intimately and intensely aware of your surroundings and have the courage to go and find yourself—and it is in extreme circumstances that we find our true capabilities. And while you may possess many talents, trying to be a master of all may result in falling short of the goals you aspire to achieve. The recommendation is to introspect deeply and pick the path most suited (for example, run with your top two talents) in synchronicity with your individual style to lead within the domains of your strategic vision. Give it your absolute best to avoid harboring regrets, or they will manifest as innate frustrations bubbling up in later life. Take your issues head on and try your best to resolve them, shout when you need help, the latter alone will keep you humble. And sometimes we get numb from witnessing negativity and become immune to the pain of others, so we must defend vigorously against those emotions!

I have indeed been so fortunate to travel over a quarter of the planet, and the brilliance of mankind has never ceased to amaze me. I have additionally observed that people the world over are simply a varying combination of the three traits (gunas) of purity, passion and dullness reacting to their immediate circumstances to cope with and win the best they can on a daily basis. This of course takes into account certain boundary conditions; it is an extreme challenge for the common man to focus on religion and spirituality when in extreme circumstances as during war, torture, ill health, etc.

And I came to understand that when you ask for help out of sincerity and selflessness, your messages travel within the ethereal realm; someone is listening to effect synchronous, timely results. If I had any doubts, they were taken away when I ran into the rabbi and the high Buddhist practitioner (now lifelong friends) on the flight to Santiago, Chile, on the very day I asked God to help me with these two sublime religions, and the resultant great learning during the five-religion structural analysis. Note there has been no flattening of the knowledge curve as I progressively came to see myself as a beginner in terms of the true knowledge of the universe. I did however, after twelve years of research in my infinitely humble way, come to realize just what a master painter does as he progressively drives his vision coupled with concentrated energy at the viewer through sheer dedication to his craft. Note how extraordinary paintings give you a different dimension with each view (classic movies achieve an analogous effect), indeed an example of divinity timelessly synchronized in every second. Juxtaposed against this is the principle of "dharma" in Hinduism or the best efforts taken in any given situation based upon intuition or experience borne of higher wisdom. And given the aforementioned, you will understand that a master painter cannot replicate the same painting.

Keep all channels of your mind open, interactively reason through multiple viewpoints guided by your intuition to take the best possible decision under a particular set of circumstances. Let us take a magnificent example of the Eiffel Tower (Paris). At thirty million visitors per year, more than two billion people (and counting) owe their heartfelt thanks to the German general of WWII, Dietrich von Choltitz, who refused to obey Hitler's order: Paris is not to fall into the hands of the enemy except as a heap of ruins. Think of the pressures on him for taking this decision and his dharma, and the highest possible wisdom he applied to his particular set of circumstances to work his way out of the issues he faced. Hence, know that there is no hard and fast rule, a decision applicable to a given circumstance may not be the best possible one for another scenario; and even the most stringent professional systems allow latitude to embrace lessons learned to enhance their overall mandate. And once you dedicate your work for something larger than yourself (examples God, country, community), you inevitably tap into your dharma, and any debate on whether you are a believer or otherwise—be it dedicating every act in oblation of the Lord, or being an atheist and relying on your grit and self-confidence to get you through difficult situations—becomes irrelevant.

Simply put, try to accept what comes—as a gift or as an opportunity. Practice every act as an inner meditation within the realms of your dharma and you will note material, step changes within your being. Understand dharma, and you also will learn to overcome perceived humiliation!

As for hope, try to understand that there are sages, saints, monks, imams, rabbis, priests and gurus amongst us to whom the universe presents no secrets; that their efforts resulted in that intuitive experience to achieve synchronicity of actions in perfect tune with the subtle laws of the universe. Attained through the path of relentless reasoning, action and other concerted methods, we can all get there by progressive shedding of our outer gross and subtle states into the highest realms of the sea of causal cosmos depicted in Table C.

This commentary initially started out as a set of personal notes with a vision to improve myself on a daily basis; the thought of publishing only came after much encouragement from friends, family and colleagues in multiple countries. Ultimately, I exceeded all my expectations in that not only did the information grow iteratively over a twelve-year period (release extended by another three years for research), but the results far outgrew the original intent of creating the visual, strategic, holistic, daily "Six Trigger Points" outlined in Table A. Many wondrous doors of knowledge and insights opened up on the integrated nature of divinity via consequent, impartial structural analysis of the world's great religions and philosophy, a deep study of nature and energy, blessings received from so many wonderful people from all levels, and derivative lessons learned on leadership, cultures and spirituality. Let me offer my apologies in the event of errors (perceived or otherwise) encountered within this exhaustive twelve-year analysis, but what has undeniably come through is the intercon-nected nature of our global community and the remarkable opportunities afforded to each one of us—in our unique, inimitable ways—to effect timely positive change for the benefit of all existence.

Ultimately, the genesis of Table A, the six daily trigger points constitutes a common thread after researching fifteen religions and spiritual teachings to split the mind into six main actionable quadrants to best affect one's daily out-comes. I best describe it like a highly subliminal box of tools including their myriad permutations and combinations, almost like a baseball player or crick-eter memorizing outfield positions and then hitting into negative spaces to score, only the reverse is true here. Your mind utilizes the appropriate trigger point (including combinations) to succeed to the extent you daily can in each situation. Note that external factors such as stress, abuse, etc., all translate into a host of adverse, palpable energies, all leading into discomfort, both physical and mental including disease and mental disorders. Timely management of the same in holistic fashion is the key!

My humble recommendation is to review them for at least five minutes every morning to help you get centered again. In summary, the six triggers represent an engineered approach of our basic nature split up into quadrants to effect analysis, and a seamless, subliminal holistic improvement as a first step in our continued evolution in synchronicity with the rhythms and the subtle laws of the universe.

ॐ

(AUM)

BIBLIOGRAPHY

Augustini, S. Aurelii, *De Catechizandis Rudibus*, 3rd ed., London, UK: Methuen, 1915.

Baskin, R. Judith, *The Cambridge Guide to Jewish History, Religion, and Culture*, 1st ed., New York: Cambridge University Press, 2010.

Bible, World English, *The Holy Bible*, Independently Published, 2019.

Carroll, Sean, *The Particle at the End of the Universe: How the Hunt for the Higgs Boson Leads Us to the Edge of a New World*, 1st ed., London: Oneworld Publications, 2012.

Chinmayananda, Swami, *The Holy Geeta: Commentary by Swami Chinmayananda*, 2nd ed., Mumbai: Central Chinmaya Mission Trust, 1996.

Chodron, Thubten, *Buddhism for Beginners*, 1st ed., Boston, MA: Snow Lion, an imprint of Shambhala Publications Inc., 2001.

Epstein, Ronald, *Buddhism A to Z*, 1st ed., Burlingame, CA: The Buddhist Text Translation Society, 2003.

Frager, Robert and James Fadiman, *Essential Sufism*, 1st ed., San Francisco: HarperOne, 1997.

Gimbel, Theo, *Healing with Color and Light: Improve Your Mental, Physical and Spiritual Health*, 1st ed., New York: Fireside, 1994.

Hawking, Stephen, *Brief Answers to the Big Questions*, Hardcover ed., New York: Bantam Books, 2018.

Helwa, A., *Secrets of Divine Love: A Spiritual Journey into the Heart of Islam*, 1st ed., Capistrano Beach, CA: Naulit Publishing House, 2020.

His Holiness the Dalai Lama, *The Dalai Lama's Book of Love and Compassion*, 1st ed., London: Thorsons, 2001.

Hodson, Geoffrey, *The Hidden Wisdom in the Holy Bible, Vol. 1*, New Impression, Wheaton, IL: The Theosophical Publishing House, 1967.

Kane, Gordon, *Modern Elementary Particle Physics: Explaining and Extending the Standard Model*, 2nd ed., Cambridge: Cambridge University Press, 2017.

Kloetzli, Randy, *Buddhist Cosmology: From Single World System to Pure Land: Science and Theology in the Images of Motion and Light*, 1st ed., Delhi: Motilal Banarsidass, 1983.

Kozak, Arnie, *The Everything Buddhism Book*, 2nd ed., Avon, MA: Adams Media Corporation, 2011.

Mariner, Rodney, *The Torah*, 1st US ed., New York: Henry Holt and Company, 1997.

Nasr, Seyyed Hossein, *Islam: Religion, History and Civilization*, 1st ed., San Francisco: HarperOne, 2002.

Prabhavananda, Swami, *Patanjali Yoga Sutras*, 1st ed., Chennai: Shri Ramakrishna Math, 2003.

Rahula, Walpola, *What the Buddha Taught*, Revised and Expanded Edition with Texts from *Suttas* and *Dhammapada*, 2nd ed., New York: Grove Press, 1974.

Roman, Sanaya, *Spiritual Growth: Being Your Higher Self*, 1st ed., Tiburon, CA: H.J. Kramer, 1989.

Tejomayananda, Swami, *Vedanta Book of Definitions: Tattvabodha*, Revised ed., Mumbai: Chinmaya Prakashan, 2016.

Van Uffelen, Chris, *Masterpieces: Sacred Architecture + Design: Churches, Synagogues, Mosques*, Multilingual ed., Salenstein: Braun Publishing AG, 2013.

Walker, Dael, *The Crystal Healing Book*, Volume 2 of the Crystal Book Series, 2nd ed., Pacheco, CA: The Crystal Company, 1988.

Wheeler, Brannon, *Prophets in the Quran*, 1st ed., New York: Continuum, 2002.

Yogananda, Paramahansa, *Autobiography of a Yogi*, 13th ed., Los Angeles: Self-Realization Fellowship, 1998.

Yogi, Maharishi Mahesh, *The Science of Being and Art of Living*, 4th ed., London: International SRM Publications, 1967.

www.ingramcontent.com/pod-product-compliance
Lightning Source LLC
Chambersburg PA
CBHW051943090426
42741CB00008B/1255